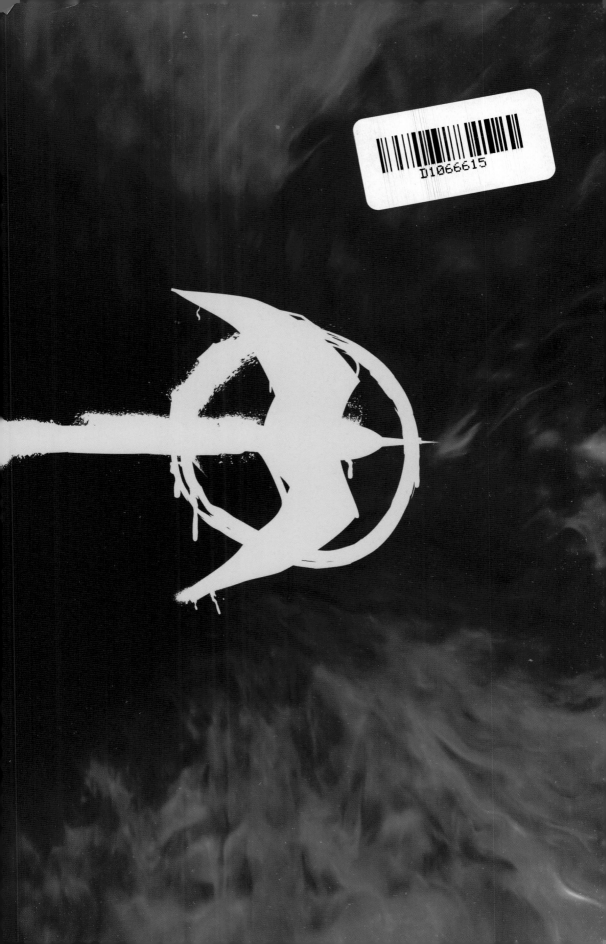

THE HARBINGER

WORDS
COLLIN KELLY
JACKSON LANZING

ART
ROBBI RODRIGUEZ

COLORS
RICO RENZI

LETTERS
HASSAN OTSMANE-
ELHAOU

SERIES COVERS
ROBBI RODRIGUEZ

ASSISTANT EDITOR
AUDREY MEEKER

SENIOR EDITORS
LYSA HAWKINS
HEATHER ANTOS

GALLERY
CLAUDIA IANNICELLO
LEWIS LAROSA
ADAM POLLINA
BRIAN REBER
ROD REIS
RICO RENZI
ROBBI RODRIGUEZ
DAMION SCOTT
NIK VIRELLA

**COLLECTION
COVER ART**
ROBBI RODRIGUEZ

**COLLECTION BACK
COVER ART**
DAMION SCOTT

**COLLECTION
FRONT ART**
CLAUDIA IANNICELLO

**COLLECTION
EDITOR**
IVAN COHEN

**COLLECTION
DESIGNER**
STEVE BLACKWELL

VALIANT

The Harbinger® Book One. Published by Valiant Entertainment LLC. Office of Publication: 239 West 29th Street, New York, NY 10001. Compilation copyright © 2022 Valiant Entertainment LLC. All rights reserved. Contains materials originally published in single magazine form as The Harbinger #1-4. Copyright © 2021 and 2022 Valiant Entertainment LLC. All rights reserved. All characters, their distinctive likeness and related indicia featured in this publication are trademarks of Valiant Entertainment LLC. The stories, characters, and incidents featured in this publication are entirely fictional. Valiant Entertainment does not read or accept unsolicited submissions of ideas, stories, or artwork. Printed in Korea.

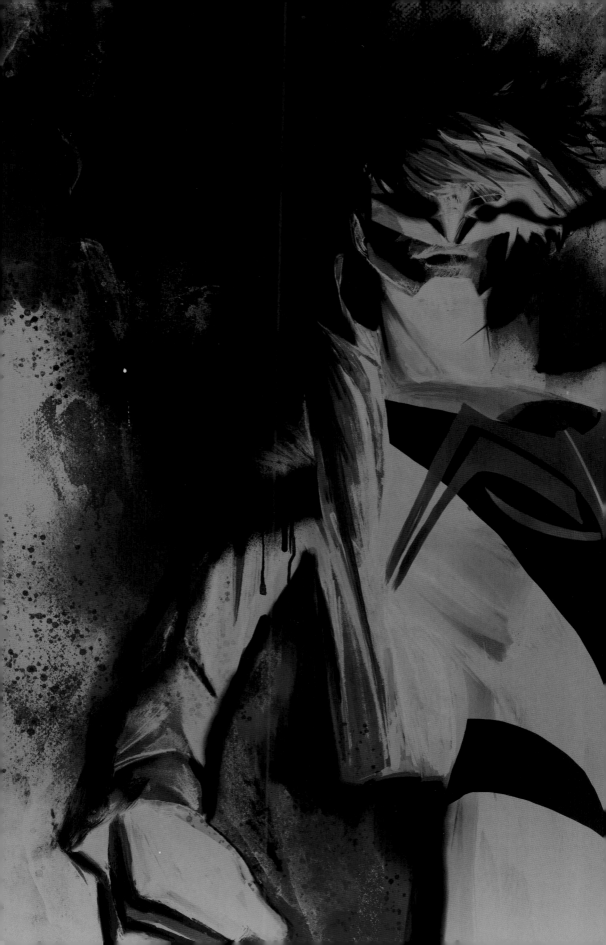

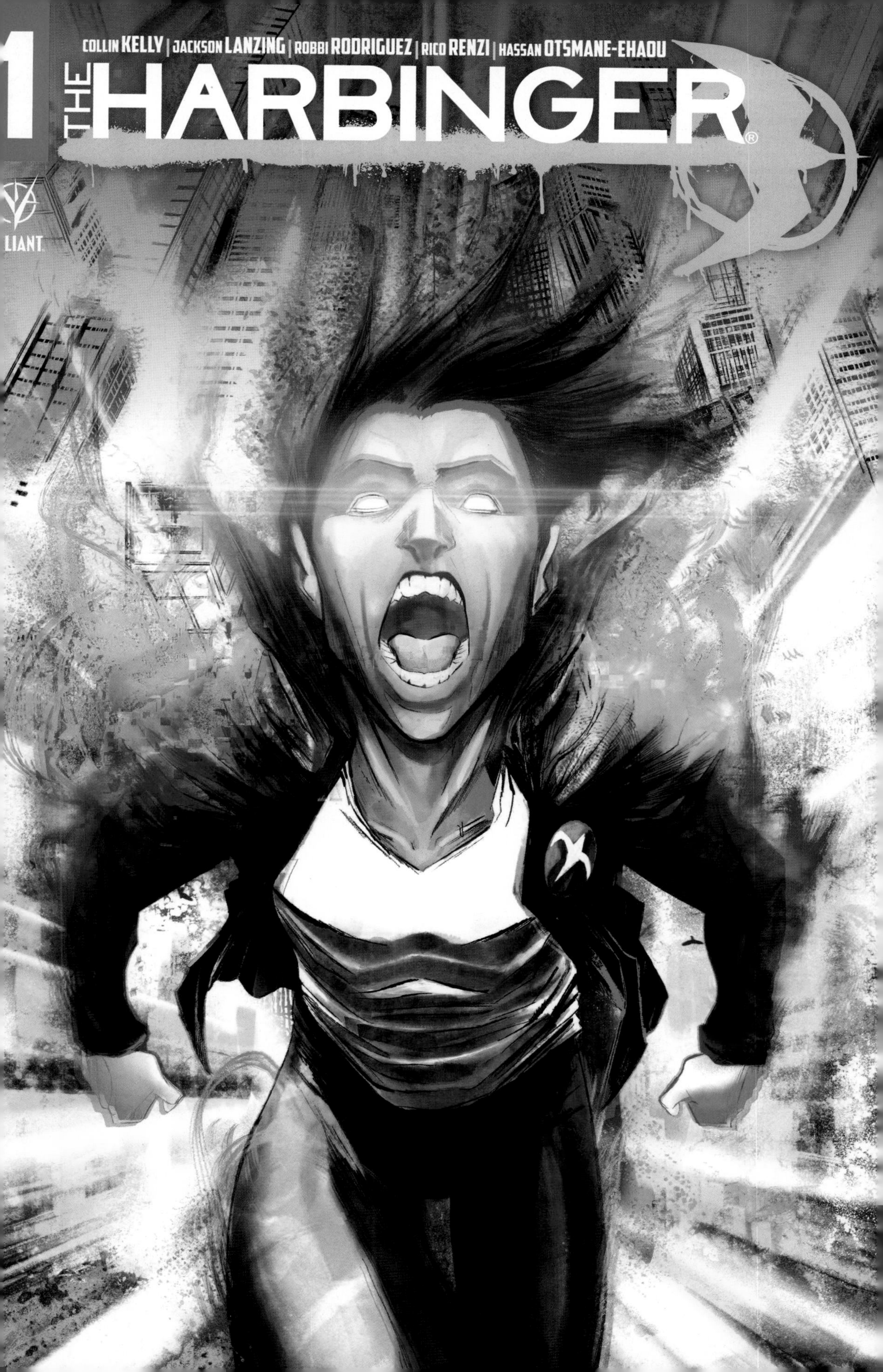

1
COLLIN KELLY | JACKSON LANZING | ROBBI RODRIGUEZ | RICO RENZI | HASSAN OTSMANE-EHAOU
THE HARBINGER®
LIANT

"Be Better: Chapter One"

THE HARBINGER #1

WORDS: Collin Kelly and Jackson Lanzing
ART: Robbi Rodriguez
COLORS: Rico Renzi
LETTERS: Hassan Otsmane-Elhaou
COVER ART: Robbi Rodriguez
ASSISTANT EDITOR: Audrey Meeker
SENIOR EDITORS: Heather Antos and Lysa Hawkins

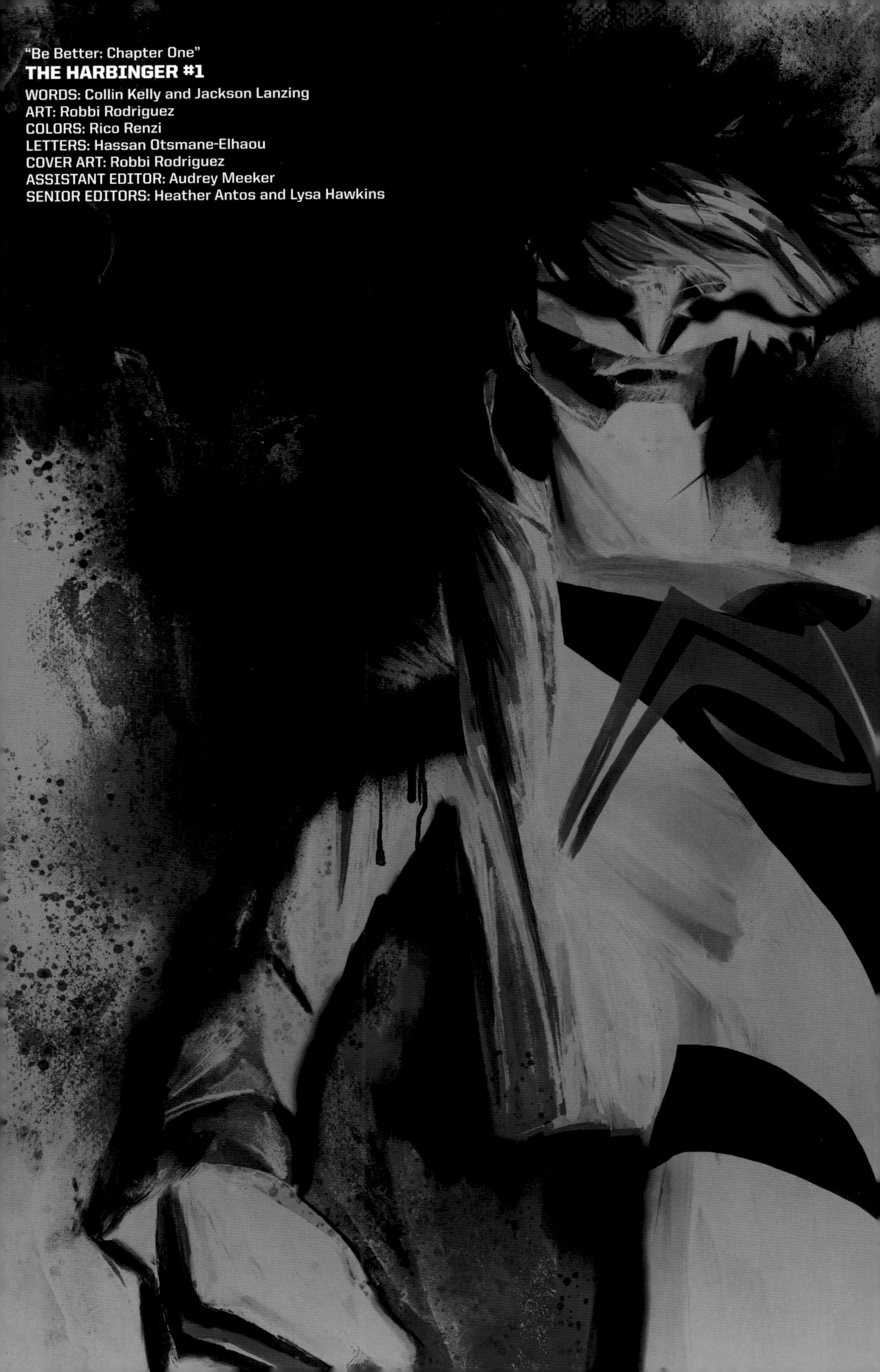

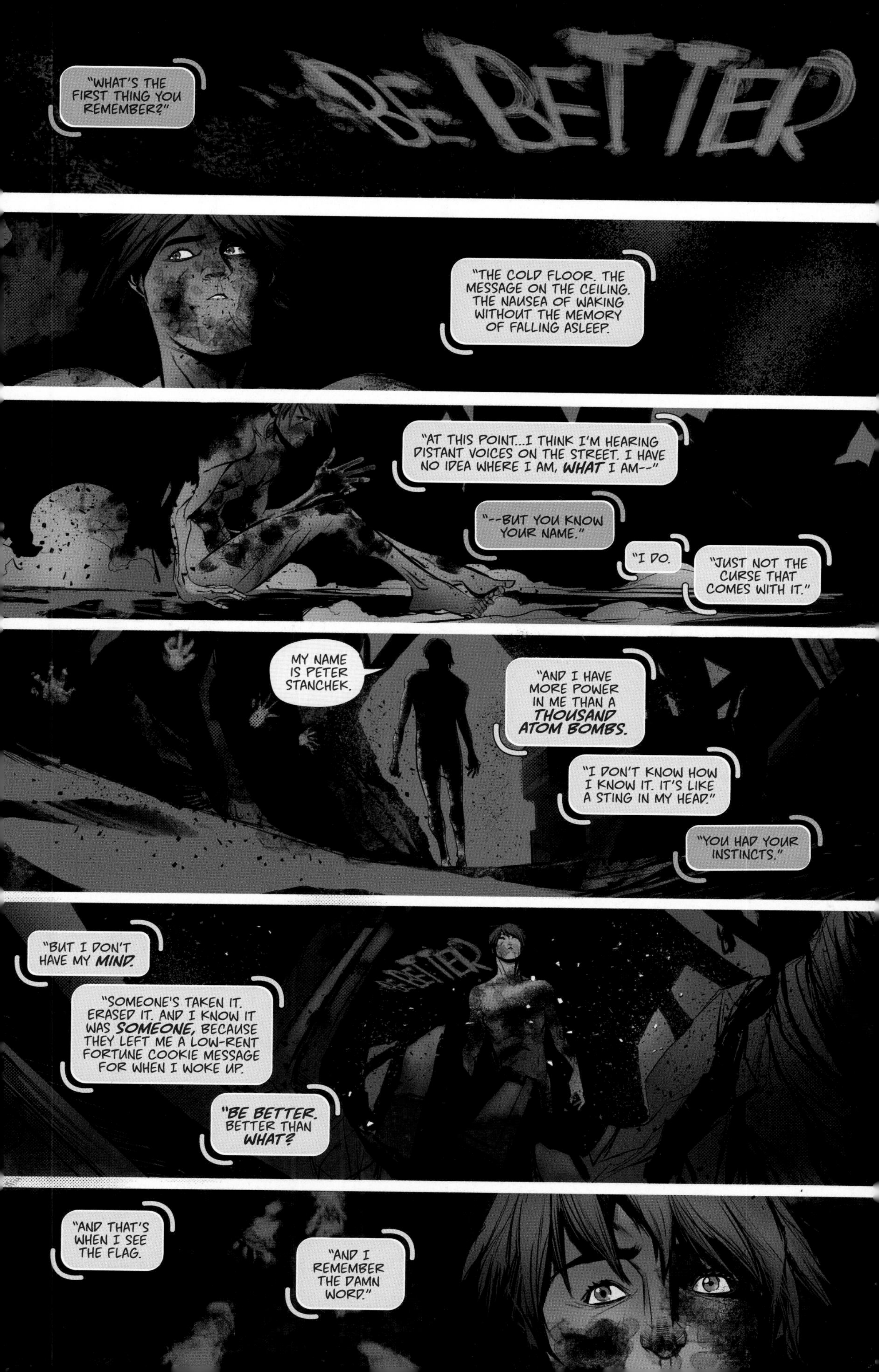
"WHAT'S THE FIRST THING YOU REMEMBER?"
BE BETTER
"THE COLD FLOOR. THE MESSAGE ON THE CEILING. THE NAUSEA OF WAKING WITHOUT THE MEMORY OF FALLING ASLEEP.
"AT THIS POINT...I THINK I'M HEARING DISTANT VOICES ON THE STREET. I HAVE NO IDEA WHERE I AM, WHAT I AM--"
"--BUT YOU KNOW YOUR NAME."
"I DO.
"JUST NOT THE CURSE THAT COMES WITH IT."
MY NAME IS PETER STANCHEK.
"AND I HAVE MORE POWER IN ME THAN A THOUSAND ATOM BOMBS.
"I DON'T KNOW HOW I KNOW IT. IT'S LIKE A STING IN MY HEAD."
"YOU HAD YOUR INSTINCTS."
"BUT I DON'T HAVE MY MIND.
"SOMEONE'S TAKEN IT. ERASED IT. AND I KNOW IT WAS SOMEONE, BECAUSE THEY LEFT ME A LOW-RENT FORTUNE COOKIE MESSAGE FOR WHEN I WOKE UP.
"BE BETTER. BETTER THAN WHAT?
"AND THAT'S WHEN I SEE THE FLAG.
"AND I REMEMBER THE DAMN WORD."

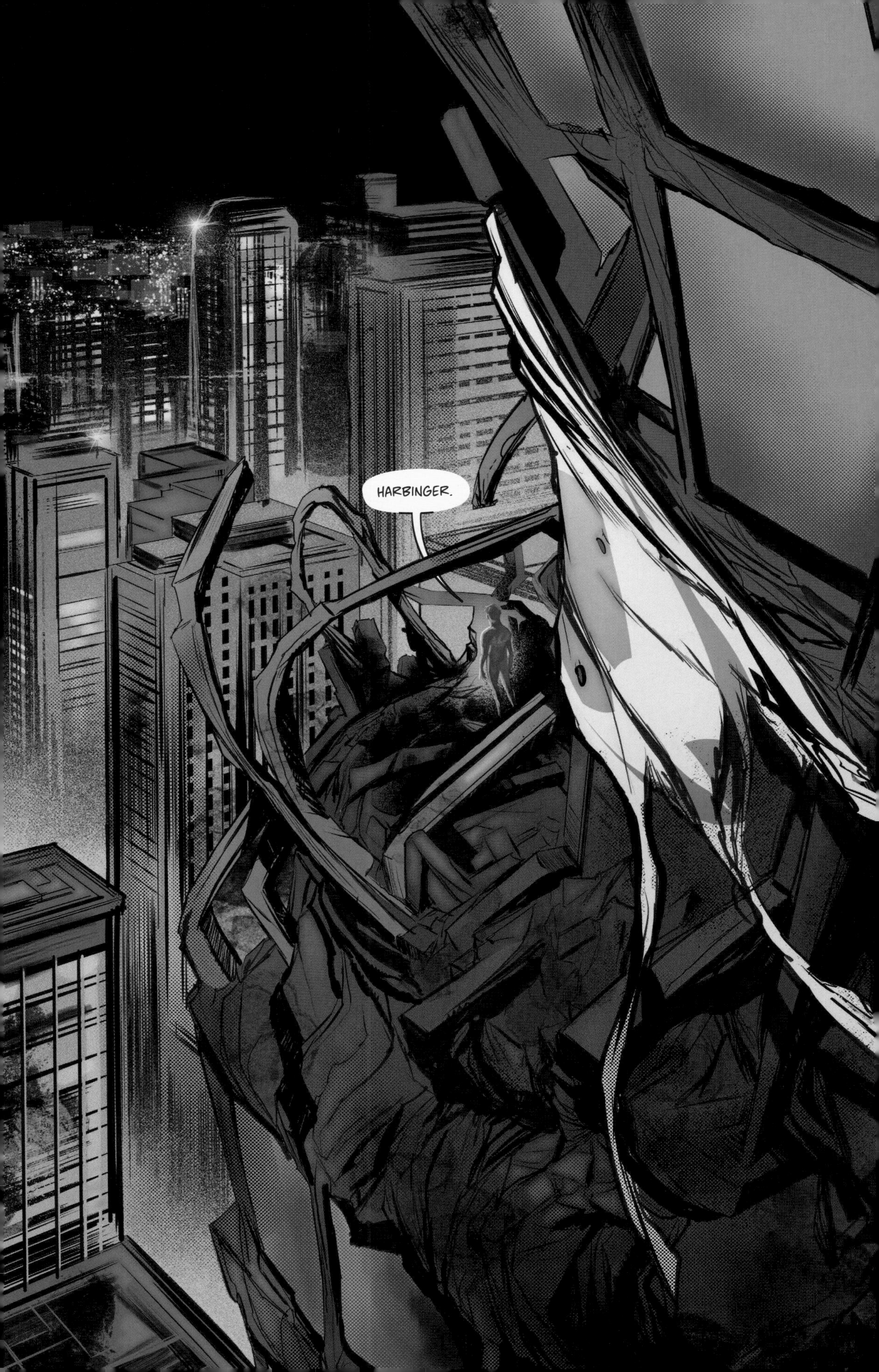
HARBINGER.

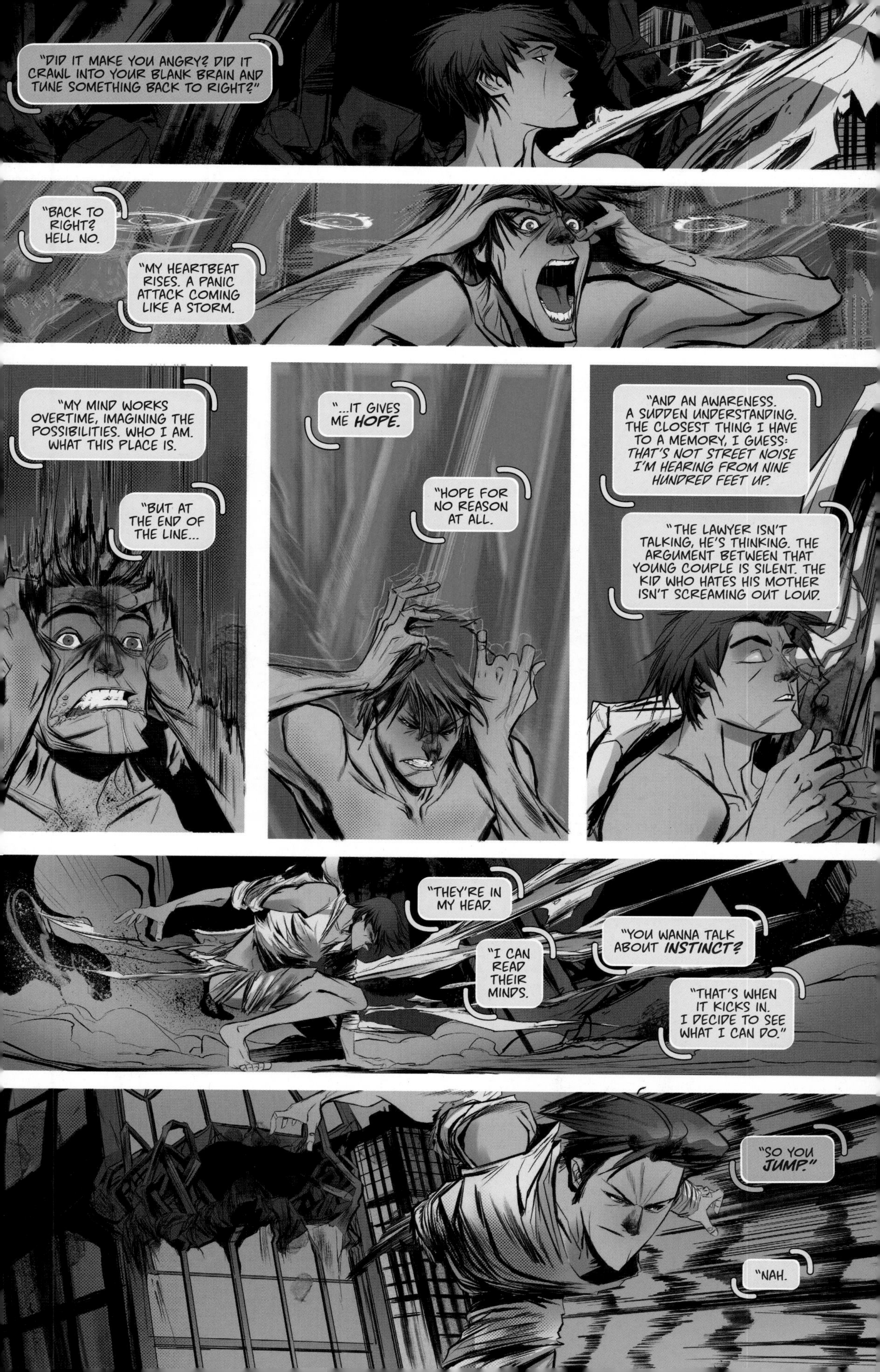
"DID IT MAKE YOU ANGRY? DID IT CRAWL INTO YOUR BLANK BRAIN AND TUNE SOMETHING BACK TO RIGHT?"
"BACK TO RIGHT? HELL NO.
"MY HEARTBEAT RISES. A PANIC ATTACK COMING LIKE A STORM.
"MY MIND WORKS OVERTIME, IMAGINING THE POSSIBILITIES. WHO I AM. WHAT THIS PLACE IS.
"BUT AT THE END OF THE LINE...
"...IT GIVES ME **HOPE.**
"HOPE FOR NO REASON AT ALL.
"AND AN AWARENESS. A SUDDEN UNDERSTANDING. THE CLOSEST THING I HAVE TO A MEMORY, I GUESS: *THAT'S NOT STREET NOISE I'M HEARING FROM NINE HUNDRED FEET UP.*
"THE LAWYER ISN'T TALKING, HE'S THINKING. THE ARGUMENT BETWEEN THAT YOUNG COUPLE IS SILENT. THE KID WHO HATES HIS MOTHER ISN'T SCREAMING OUT LOUD.
"THEY'RE IN MY HEAD.
"I CAN READ THEIR MINDS.
"YOU WANNA TALK ABOUT **INSTINCT?**
"THAT'S WHEN IT KICKS IN. I DECIDE TO SEE WHAT I CAN DO."
"SO YOU **JUMP.**"
"NAH.

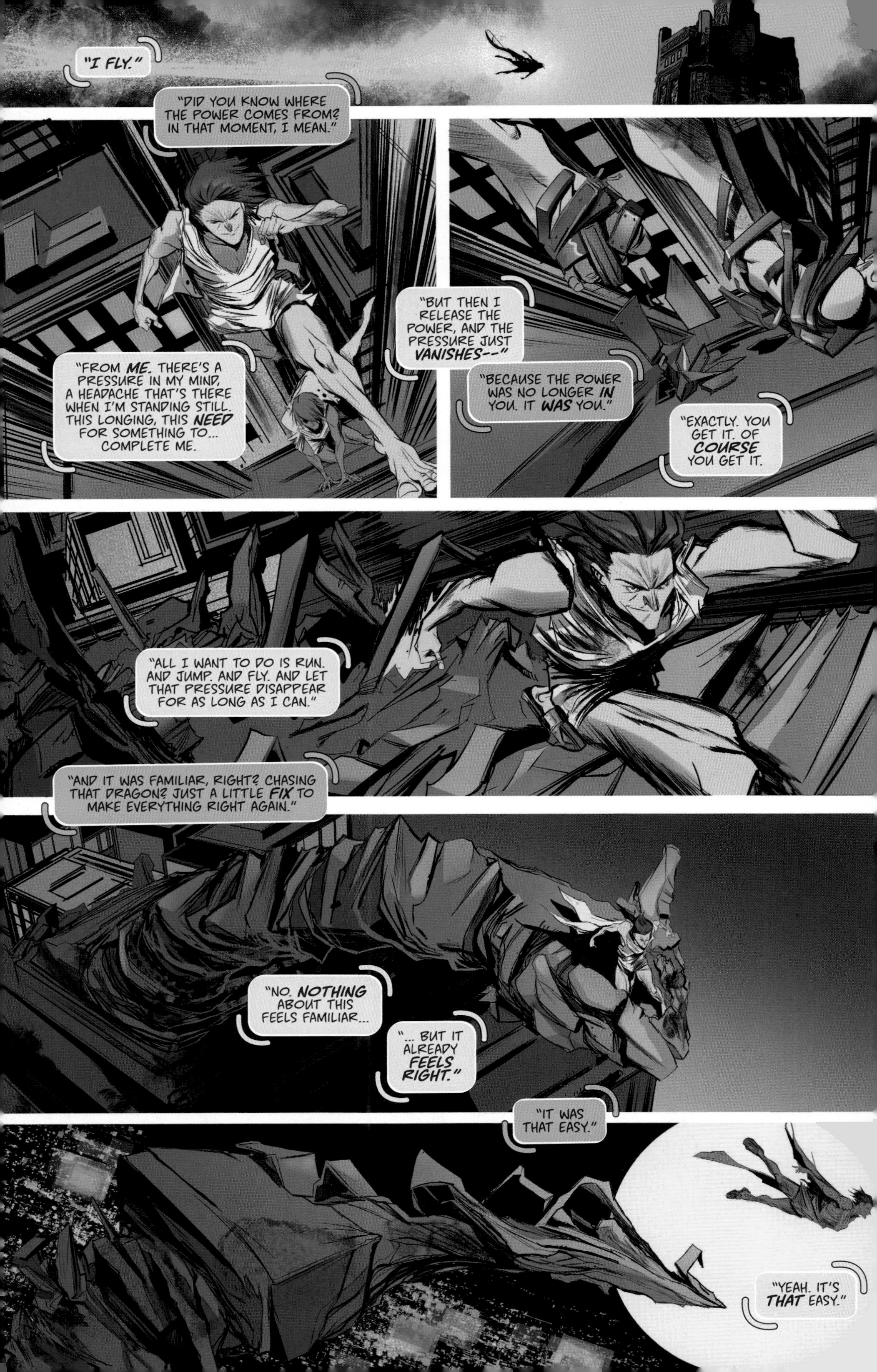
"I FLY."
"DID YOU KNOW WHERE THE POWER COMES FROM? IN THAT MOMENT, I MEAN."
"FROM ME. THERE'S A PRESSURE IN MY MIND, A HEADACHE THAT'S THERE WHEN I'M STANDING STILL. THIS LONGING, THIS NEED FOR SOMETHING TO... COMPLETE ME.
"BUT THEN I RELEASE THE POWER, AND THE PRESSURE JUST VANISHES--"
"BECAUSE THE POWER WAS NO LONGER IN YOU. IT WAS YOU."
"EXACTLY. YOU GET IT. OF COURSE YOU GET IT.
"ALL I WANT TO DO IS RUN. AND JUMP. AND FLY. AND LET THAT PRESSURE DISAPPEAR FOR AS LONG AS I CAN."
"AND IT WAS FAMILIAR, RIGHT? CHASING THAT DRAGON? JUST A LITTLE FIX TO MAKE EVERYTHING RIGHT AGAIN."
"NO. NOTHING ABOUT THIS FEELS FAMILIAR...
"... BUT IT ALREADY FEELS RIGHT."
"IT WAS THAT EASY."
"YEAH. IT'S THAT EASY."

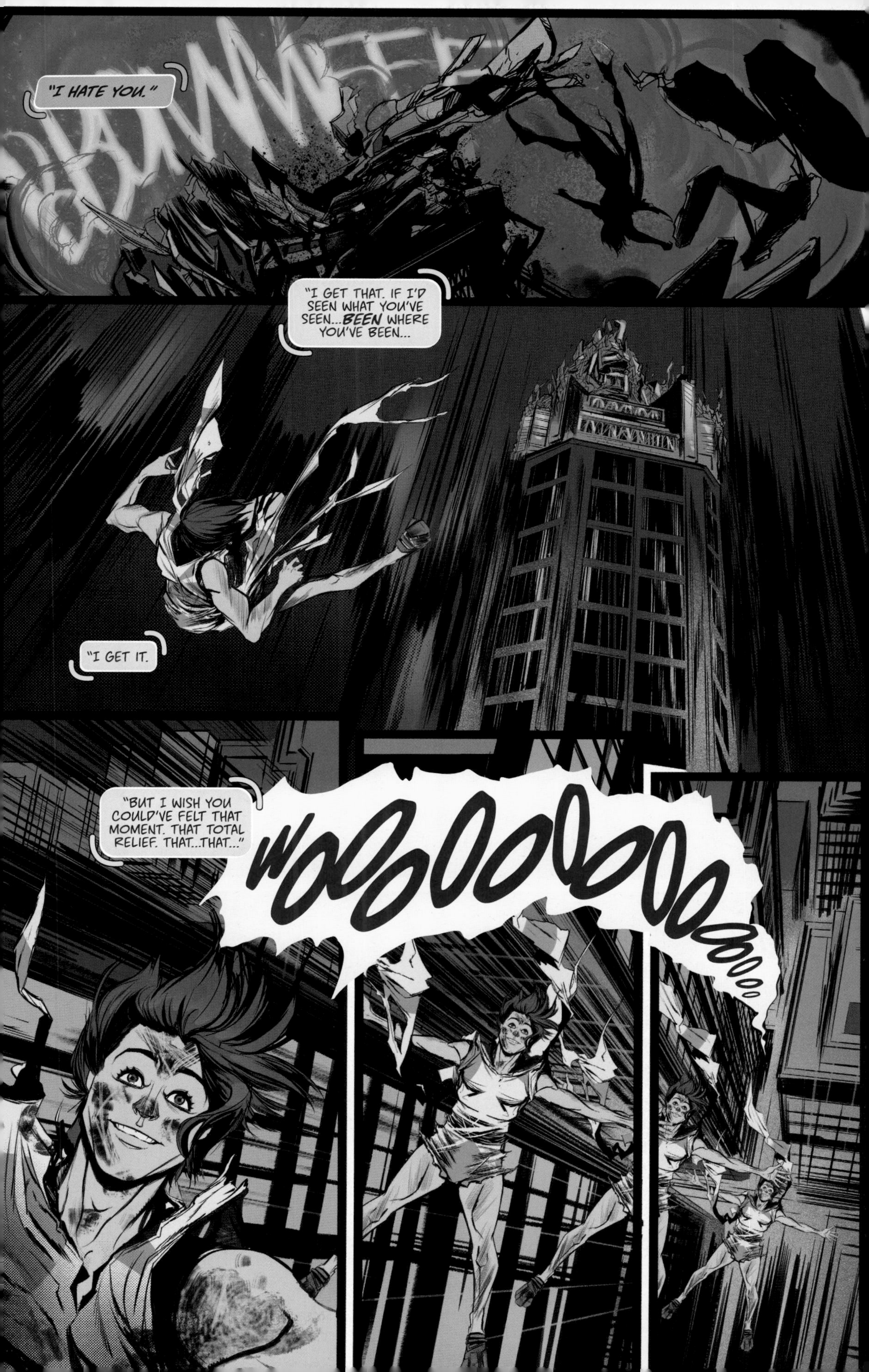
"I HATE YOU."
"I GET THAT. IF I'D SEEN WHAT YOU'VE SEEN...BEEN WHERE YOU'VE BEEN...
"I GET IT.
"BUT I WISH YOU COULD'VE FELT THAT MOMENT. THAT TOTAL RELIEF. THAT...THAT..."
WOOOOOOOOOOOOooooo

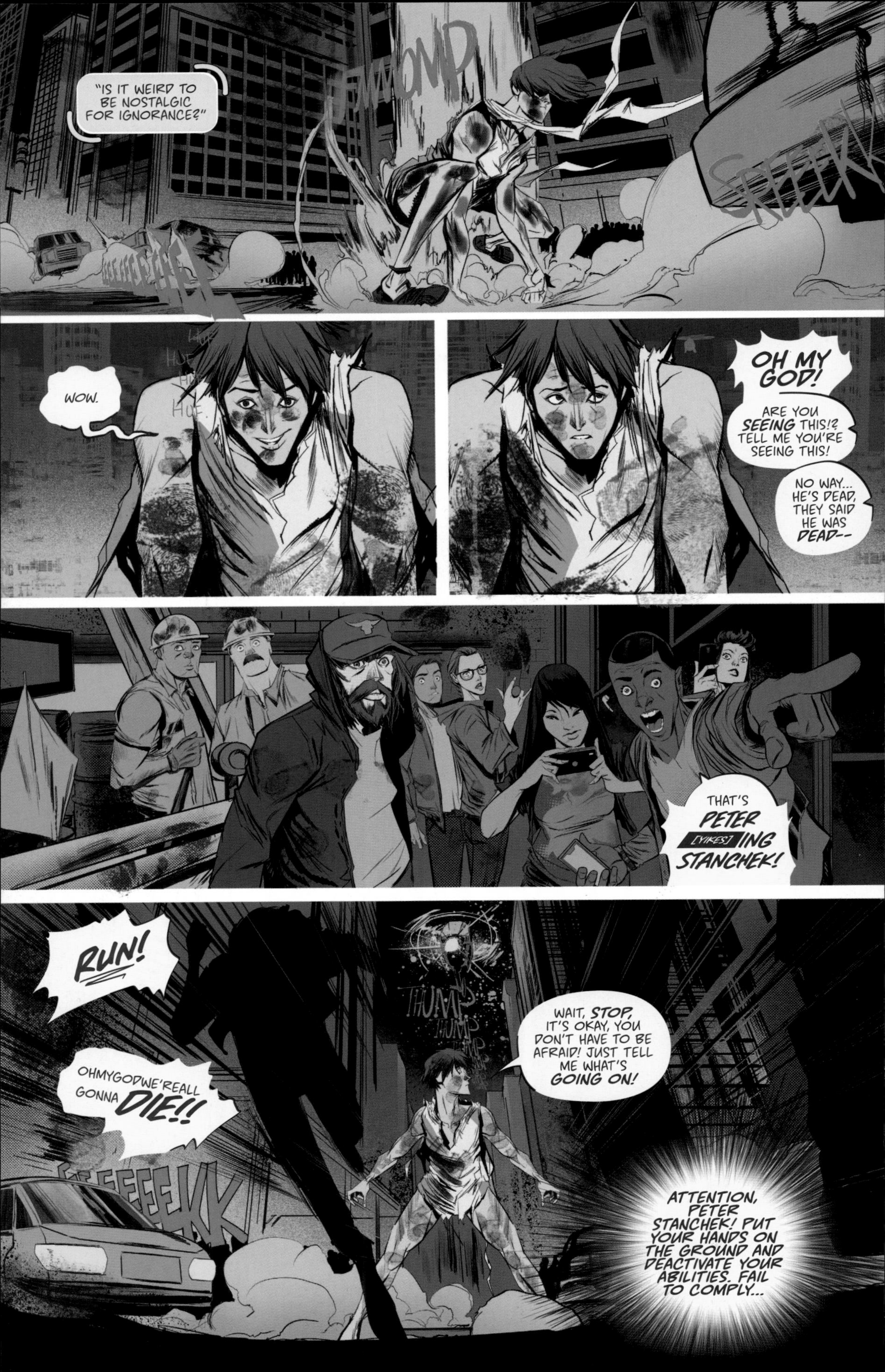
"IS IT WEIRD TO BE NOSTALGIC FOR IGNORANCE?"
THWOMP
SCREEEEEE
SPREEEK
HUF HUF HUF HUF
WOW.
OH MY GOD!
ARE YOU SEEING THIS!? TELL ME YOU'RE SEEING THIS!
NO WAY... HE'S DEAD, THEY SAID HE WAS DEAD--
THAT'S PETER [YIKES] ING STANCHEK!
RUN!
OHMYGODWE'REALL GONNA DIE!!
THUMP THUMP THUMP
WAIT, STOP, IT'S OKAY, YOU DON'T HAVE TO BE AFRAID! JUST TELL ME WHAT'S GOING ON!
SCREEEEEKK
ATTENTION, PETER STANCHEK! PUT YOUR HANDS ON THE GROUND AND DEACTIVATE YOUR ABILITIES. FAIL TO COMPLY...

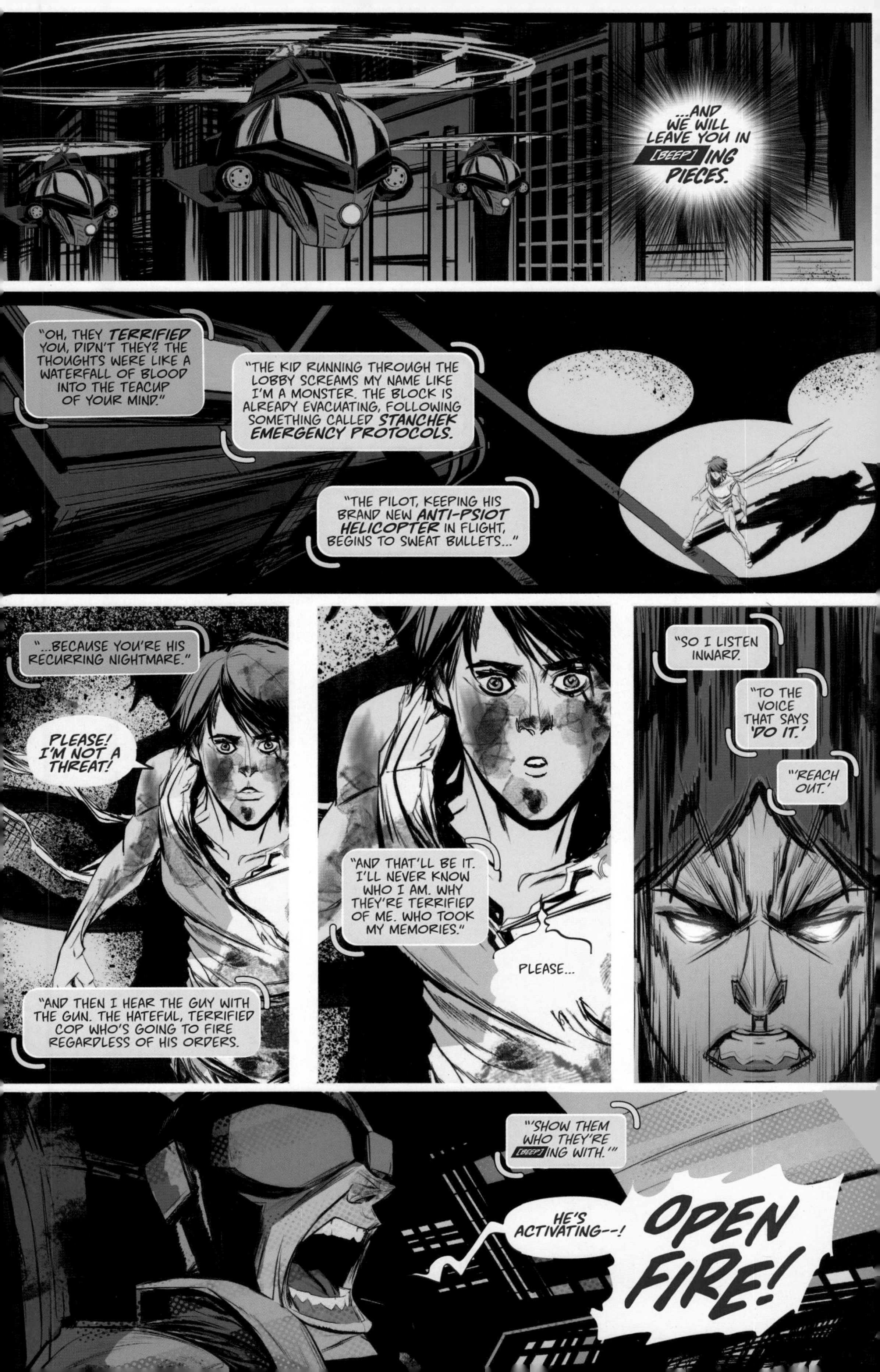
...AND WE WILL LEAVE YOU IN [BEEP] ING PIECES.
"OH, THEY TERRIFIED YOU, DIDN'T THEY? THE THOUGHTS WERE LIKE A WATERFALL OF BLOOD INTO THE TEACUP OF YOUR MIND."
"THE KID RUNNING THROUGH THE LOBBY SCREAMS MY NAME LIKE I'M A MONSTER. THE BLOCK IS ALREADY EVACUATING, FOLLOWING SOMETHING CALLED STANCHEK EMERGENCY PROTOCOLS.
"THE PILOT, KEEPING HIS BRAND NEW ANTI-PSIOT HELICOPTER IN FLIGHT, BEGINS TO SWEAT BULLETS..."
"...BECAUSE YOU'RE HIS RECURRING NIGHTMARE."
PLEASE! I'M NOT A THREAT!
"AND THEN I HEAR THE GUY WITH THE GUN. THE HATEFUL, TERRIFIED COP WHO'S GOING TO FIRE REGARDLESS OF HIS ORDERS.
"AND THAT'LL BE IT. I'LL NEVER KNOW WHO I AM. WHY THEY'RE TERRIFIED OF ME. WHO TOOK MY MEMORIES."
PLEASE...
"SO I LISTEN INWARD.
"TO THE VOICE THAT SAYS 'DO IT.'
"'REACH OUT.'
"'SHOW THEM WHO THEY'RE [BEEP]ING WITH.'"
HE'S ACTIVATING--!
OPEN FIRE!

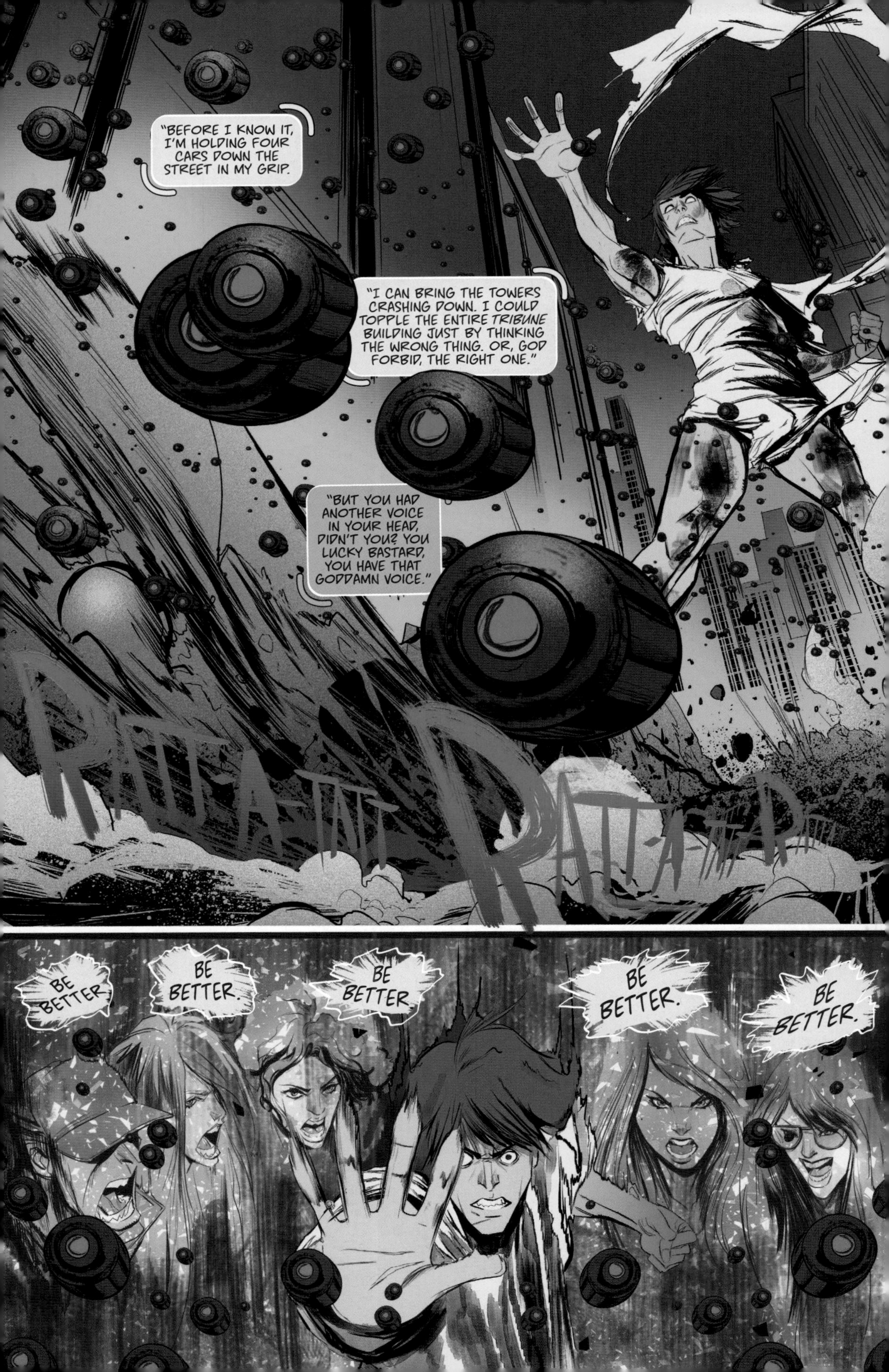
"BEFORE I KNOW IT, I'M HOLDING FOUR CARS DOWN THE STREET IN MY GRIP.
"I CAN BRING THE TOWERS CRASHING DOWN. I COULD TOPPLE THE ENTIRE *TRIBUNE* BUILDING JUST BY THINKING THE WRONG THING. OR, GOD FORBID, THE RIGHT ONE."
"BUT YOU HAD ANOTHER VOICE IN YOUR HEAD, DIDN'T YOU? YOU LUCKY BASTARD, YOU HAVE THAT GODDAMN VOICE."
RATTA-TATT
BE BETTER.
BE BETTER.
BE BETTER.
BE BETTER.
BE BETTER.

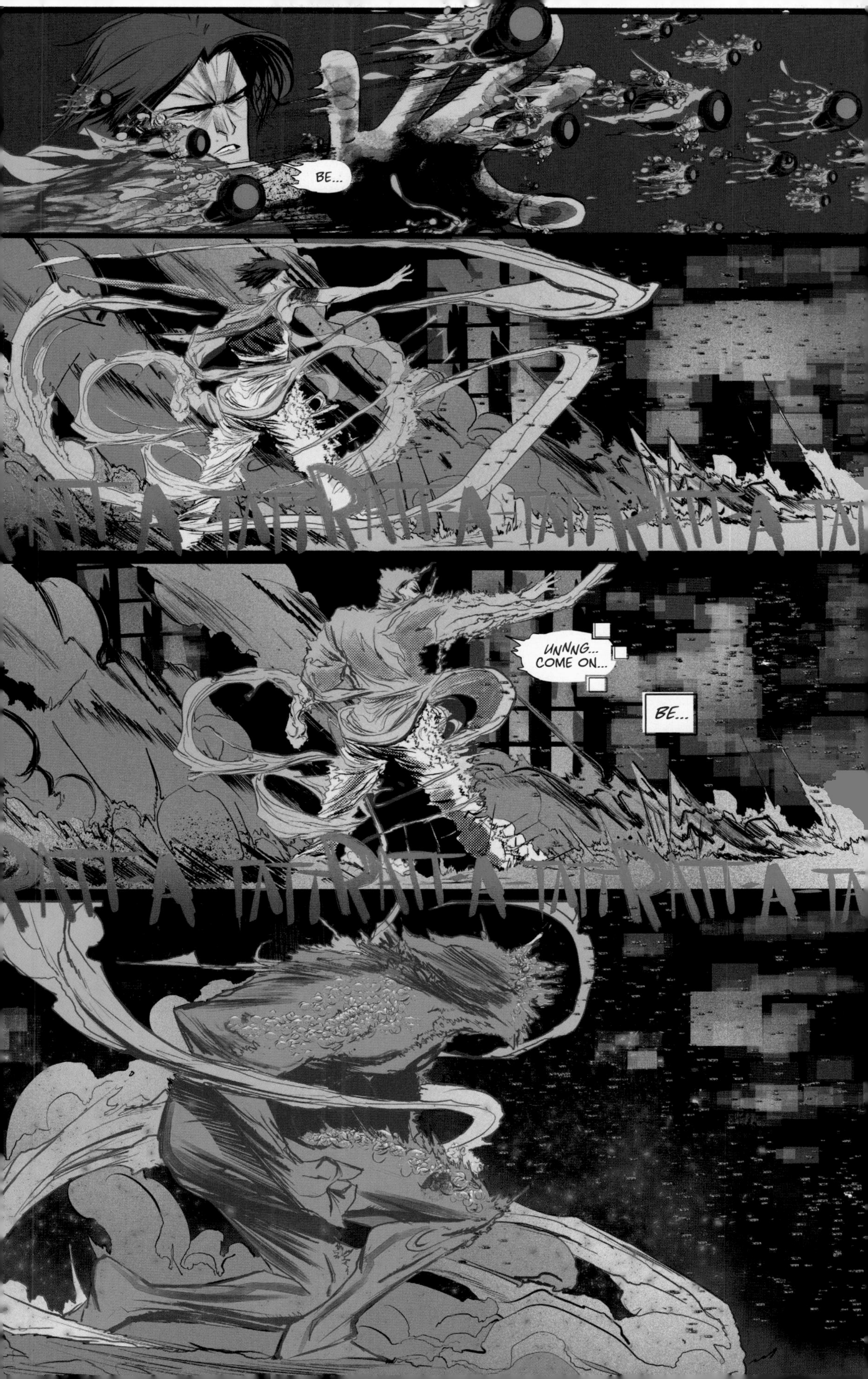

BE...
RATT-A-TAT RATT-A-TAT RATT-A-TAT
UNNNG... COME ON...
BE...
RATT-A-TAT RATT-A-TAT RATT-A-TAT

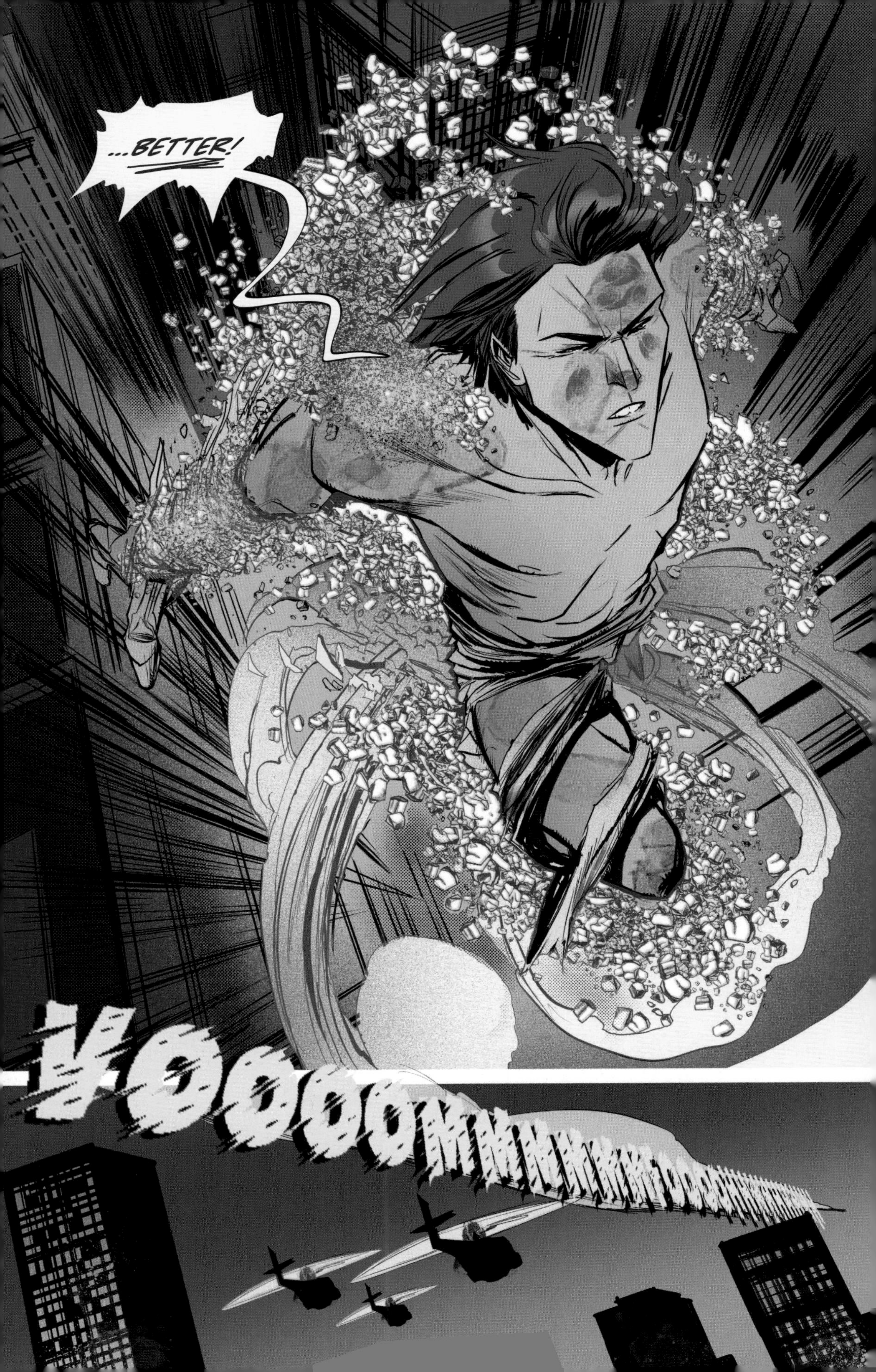
...BETTER!
VOOOOMMMMMMMMMM

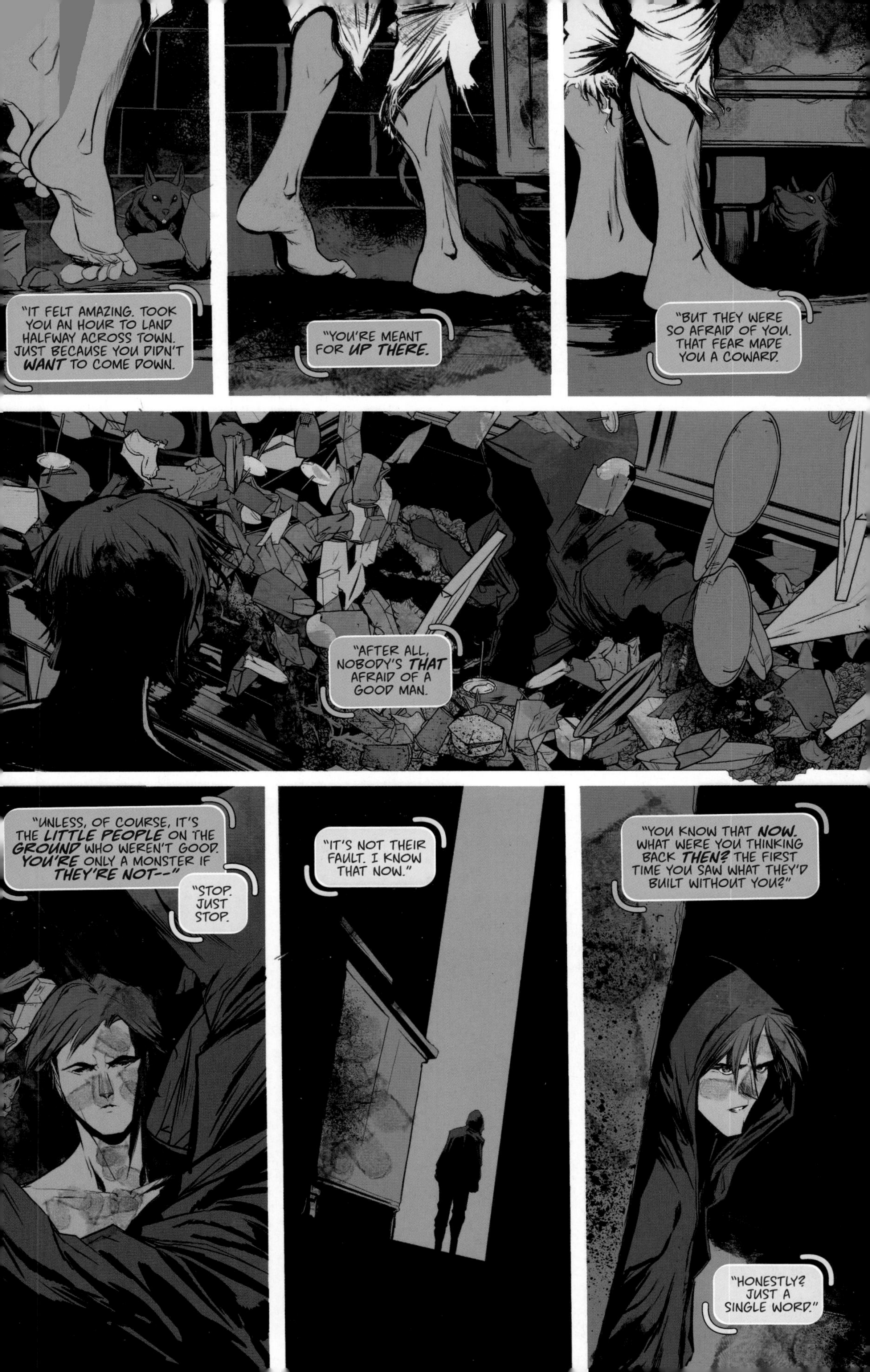
"IT FELT AMAZING. TOOK YOU AN HOUR TO LAND HALFWAY ACROSS TOWN. JUST BECAUSE YOU DIDN'T WANT TO COME DOWN.
"YOU'RE MEANT FOR UP THERE.
"BUT THEY WERE SO AFRAID OF YOU. THAT FEAR MADE YOU A COWARD.
"AFTER ALL, NOBODY'S THAT AFRAID OF A GOOD MAN.
"UNLESS, OF COURSE, IT'S THE LITTLE PEOPLE ON THE GROUND WHO WEREN'T GOOD. YOU'RE ONLY A MONSTER IF THEY'RE NOT--"
"STOP. JUST STOP.
"IT'S NOT THEIR FAULT. I KNOW THAT NOW."
"YOU KNOW THAT NOW. WHAT WERE YOU THINKING BACK THEN? THE FIRST TIME YOU SAW WHAT THEY'D BUILT WITHOUT YOU?"
"HONESTLY? JUST A SINGLE WORD."

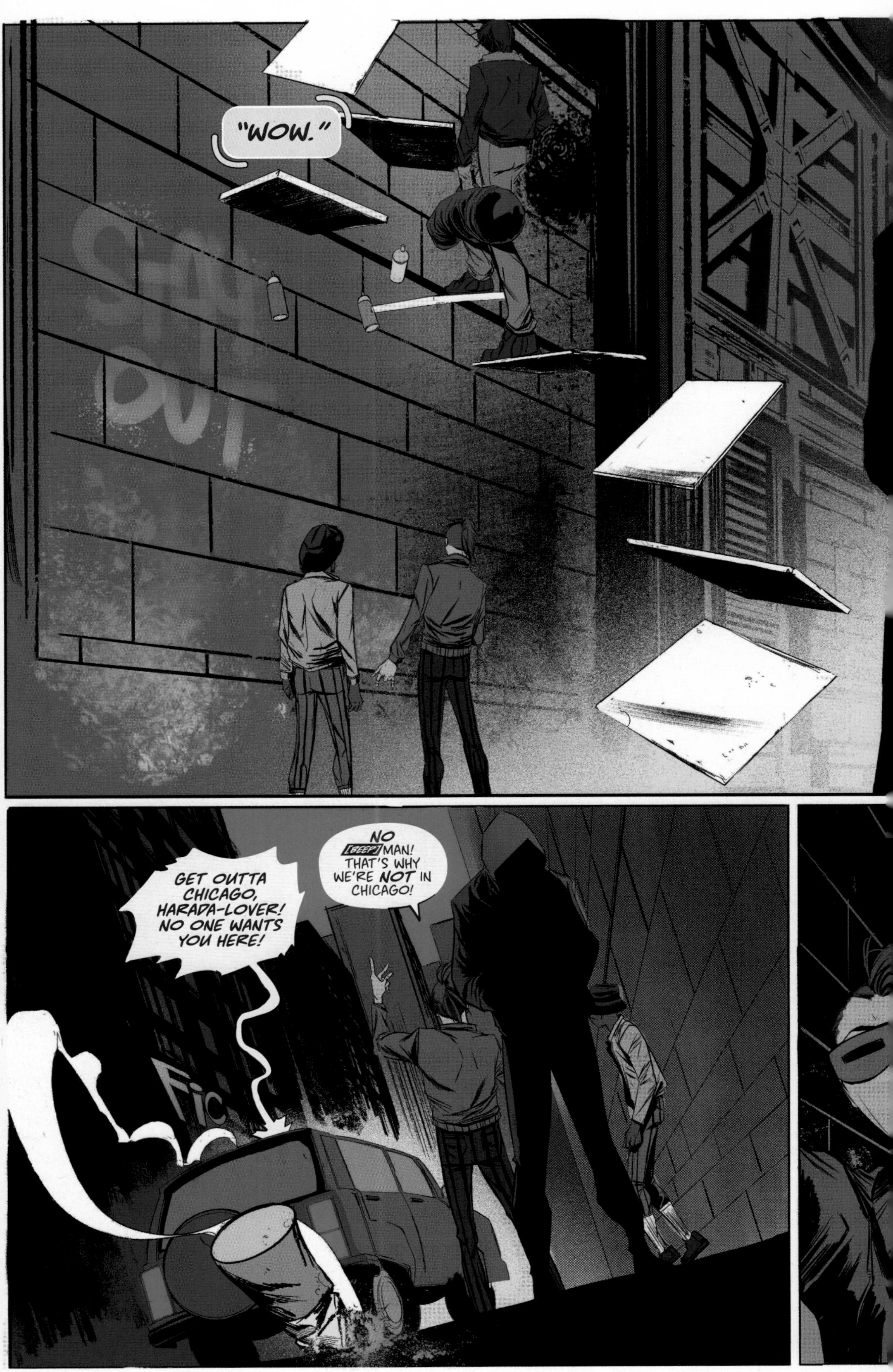
"WOW."
GET OUTTA CHICAGO, HARADA-LOVER! NO ONE WANTS YOU HERE!
NO [BEEP] MAN! THAT'S WHY WE'RE NOT IN CHICAGO!

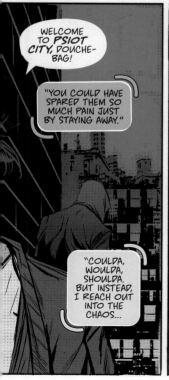

WELCOME TO *PSIOT CITY*, DOUCHE-BAG!

"YOU COULD HAVE SPARED THEM SO MUCH PAIN JUST BY STAYING AWAY."

"COULDA, WOULDA, SHOULDA. BUT INSTEAD, I REACH OUT INTO THE CHAOS..."

"...AND LOOK FOR SOMEONE WHO KNOWS ME..

"...AND WHO ISN'T AFRAID."

"AND THAT'S HOW YOU FIND HER. LUCKY GIRL."

"NO..."

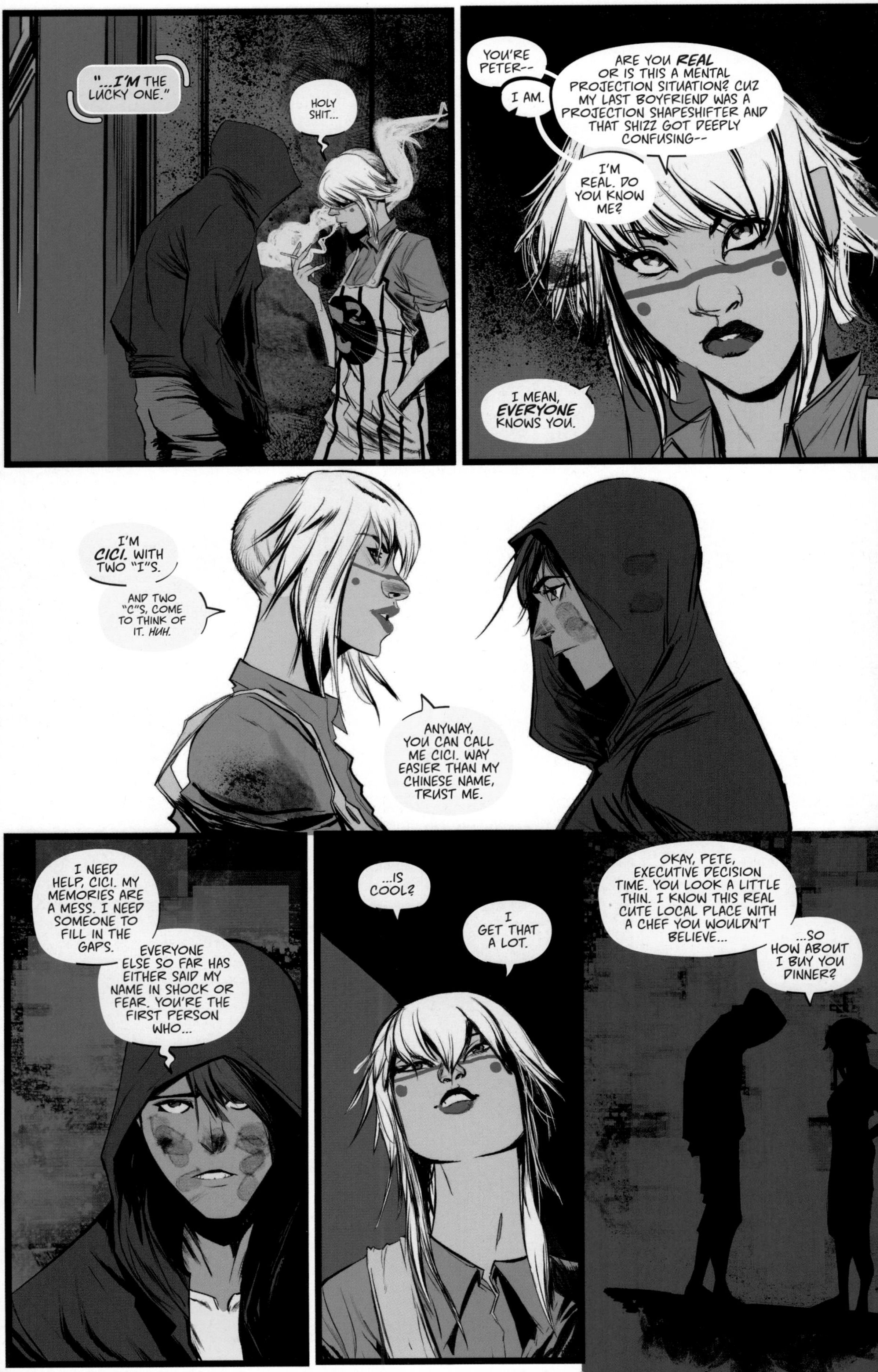
"...I'M THE LUCKY ONE."
HOLY SHIT...
YOU'RE PETER--
ARE YOU REAL OR IS THIS A MENTAL PROJECTION SITUATION? CUZ MY LAST BOYFRIEND WAS A PROJECTION SHAPESHIFTER AND THAT SHIZZ GOT DEEPLY CONFUSING--
I AM.
I'M REAL. DO YOU KNOW ME?
I MEAN, EVERYONE KNOWS YOU.
I'M CICI. WITH TWO "I"S.
AND TWO "C"S, COME TO THINK OF IT. HUH.
ANYWAY, YOU CAN CALL ME CICI. WAY EASIER THAN MY CHINESE NAME, TRUST ME.
I NEED HELP, CICI. MY MEMORIES ARE A MESS. I NEED SOMEONE TO FILL IN THE GAPS.
EVERYONE ELSE SO FAR HAS EITHER SAID MY NAME IN SHOCK OR FEAR. YOU'RE THE FIRST PERSON WHO...
...IS COOL?
I GET THAT A LOT.
OKAY, PETE, EXECUTIVE DECISION TIME. YOU LOOK A LITTLE THIN. I KNOW THIS REAL CUTE LOCAL PLACE WITH A CHEF YOU WOULDN'T BELIEVE...
...SO HOW ABOUT I BUY YOU DINNER?

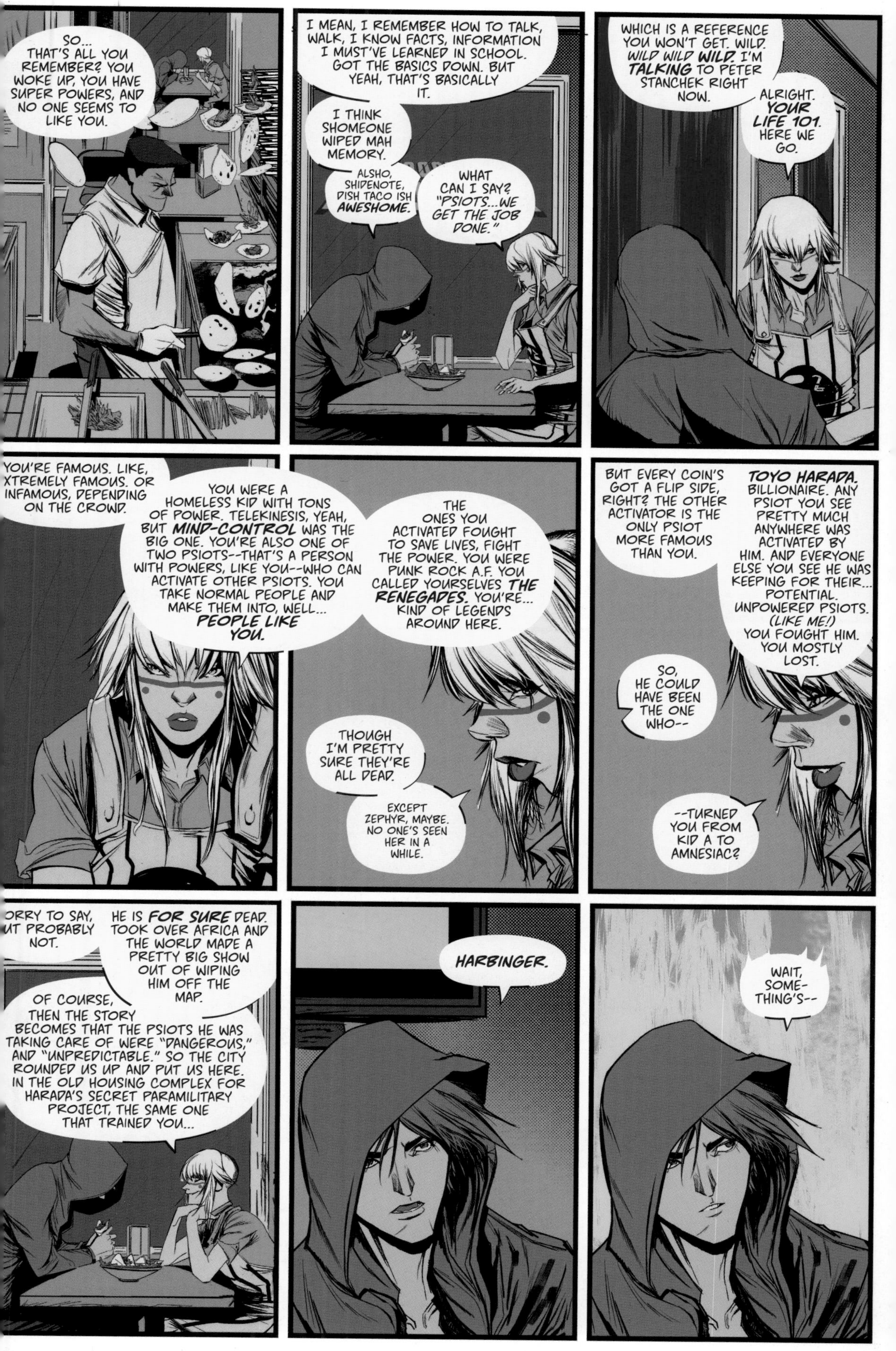
SO... THAT'S ALL YOU REMEMBER? YOU WOKE UP, YOU HAVE SUPER POWERS, AND NO ONE SEEMS TO LIKE YOU.
I MEAN, I REMEMBER HOW TO TALK, WALK, I KNOW FACTS, INFORMATION I MUST'VE LEARNED IN SCHOOL. GOT THE BASICS DOWN. BUT YEAH, THAT'S BASICALLY IT.
I THINK SHOMEONE WIPED MAH MEMORY.
ALSHO, SHIDENOTE, DISH TACO ISH AWESHOME.
WHAT CAN I SAY? "PSIOTS...WE GET THE JOB DONE."
WHICH IS A REFERENCE YOU WON'T GET. WILD. WILD WILD WILD. I'M TALKING TO PETER STANCHEK RIGHT NOW.
ALRIGHT. YOUR LIFE 101. HERE WE GO.
YOU'RE FAMOUS. LIKE, XTREMELY FAMOUS. OR INFAMOUS, DEPENDING ON THE CROWD.
YOU WERE A HOMELESS KID WITH TONS OF POWER. TELEKINESIS, YEAH, BUT MIND-CONTROL WAS THE BIG ONE. YOU'RE ALSO ONE OF TWO PSIOTS--THAT'S A PERSON WITH POWERS, LIKE YOU--WHO CAN ACTIVATE OTHER PSIOTS. YOU TAKE NORMAL PEOPLE AND MAKE THEM INTO, WELL... PEOPLE LIKE YOU.
THE ONES YOU ACTIVATED FOUGHT TO SAVE LIVES, FIGHT THE POWER. YOU WERE PUNK ROCK A.F. YOU CALLED YOURSELVES THE RENEGADES. YOU'RE... KIND OF LEGENDS AROUND HERE.
THOUGH I'M PRETTY SURE THEY'RE ALL DEAD.
EXCEPT ZEPHYR, MAYBE. NO ONE'S SEEN HER IN A WHILE.
BUT EVERY COIN'S GOT A FLIP SIDE, RIGHT? THE OTHER ACTIVATOR IS THE ONLY PSIOT MORE FAMOUS THAN YOU.
TOYO HARADA. BILLIONAIRE. ANY PSIOT YOU SEE PRETTY MUCH ANYWHERE WAS ACTIVATED BY HIM. AND EVERYONE ELSE YOU SEE HE WAS KEEPING FOR THEIR... POTENTIAL. UNPOWERED PSIOTS. (LIKE ME!) YOU FOUGHT HIM. YOU MOSTLY LOST.
SO, HE COULD HAVE BEEN THE ONE WHO--
--TURNED YOU FROM KID A TO AMNESIAC?
ORRY TO SAY, UT PROBABLY NOT.
HE IS FOR SURE DEAD. TOOK OVER AFRICA AND THE WORLD MADE A PRETTY BIG SHOW OUT OF WIPING HIM OFF THE MAP.
OF COURSE, THEN THE STORY BECOMES THAT THE PSIOTS HE WAS TAKING CARE OF WERE "DANGEROUS," AND "UNPREDICTABLE." SO THE CITY ROUNDED US UP AND PUT US HERE. IN THE OLD HOUSING COMPLEX FOR HARADA'S SECRET PARAMILITARY PROJECT, THE SAME ONE THAT TRAINED YOU...
HARBINGER.
WAIT, SOME-THING'S--

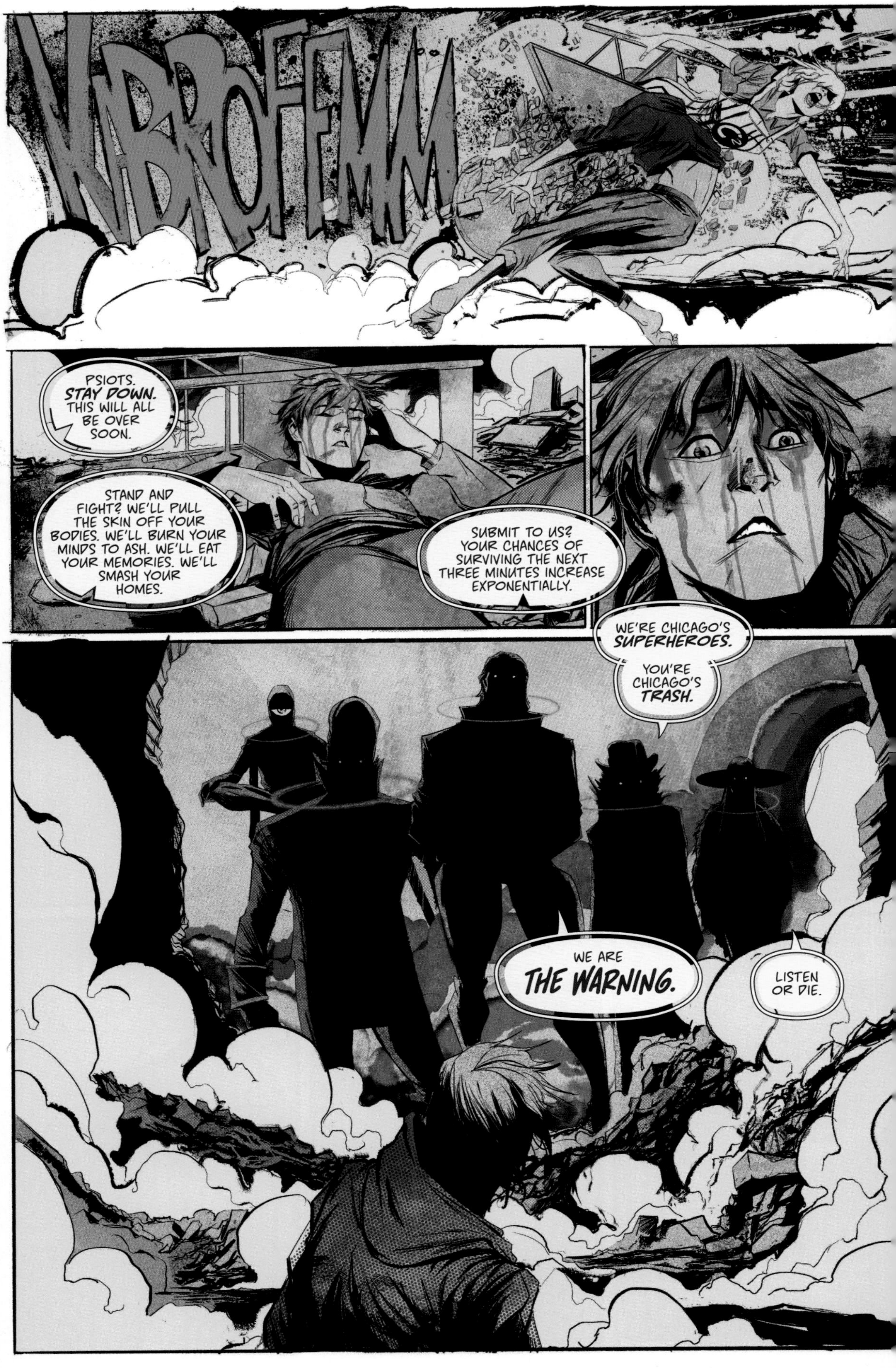
KABROOFMM
PSIOTS. STAY DOWN. THIS WILL ALL BE OVER SOON.
STAND AND FIGHT? WE'LL PULL THE SKIN OFF YOUR BODIES. WE'LL BURN YOUR MINDS TO ASH. WE'LL EAT YOUR MEMORIES. WE'LL SMASH YOUR HOMES.
SUBMIT TO US? YOUR CHANCES OF SURVIVING THE NEXT THREE MINUTES INCREASE EXPONENTIALLY.
WE'RE CHICAGO'S SUPERHEROES.
YOU'RE CHICAGO'S TRASH.
WE ARE THE WARNING.
LISTEN OR DIE.

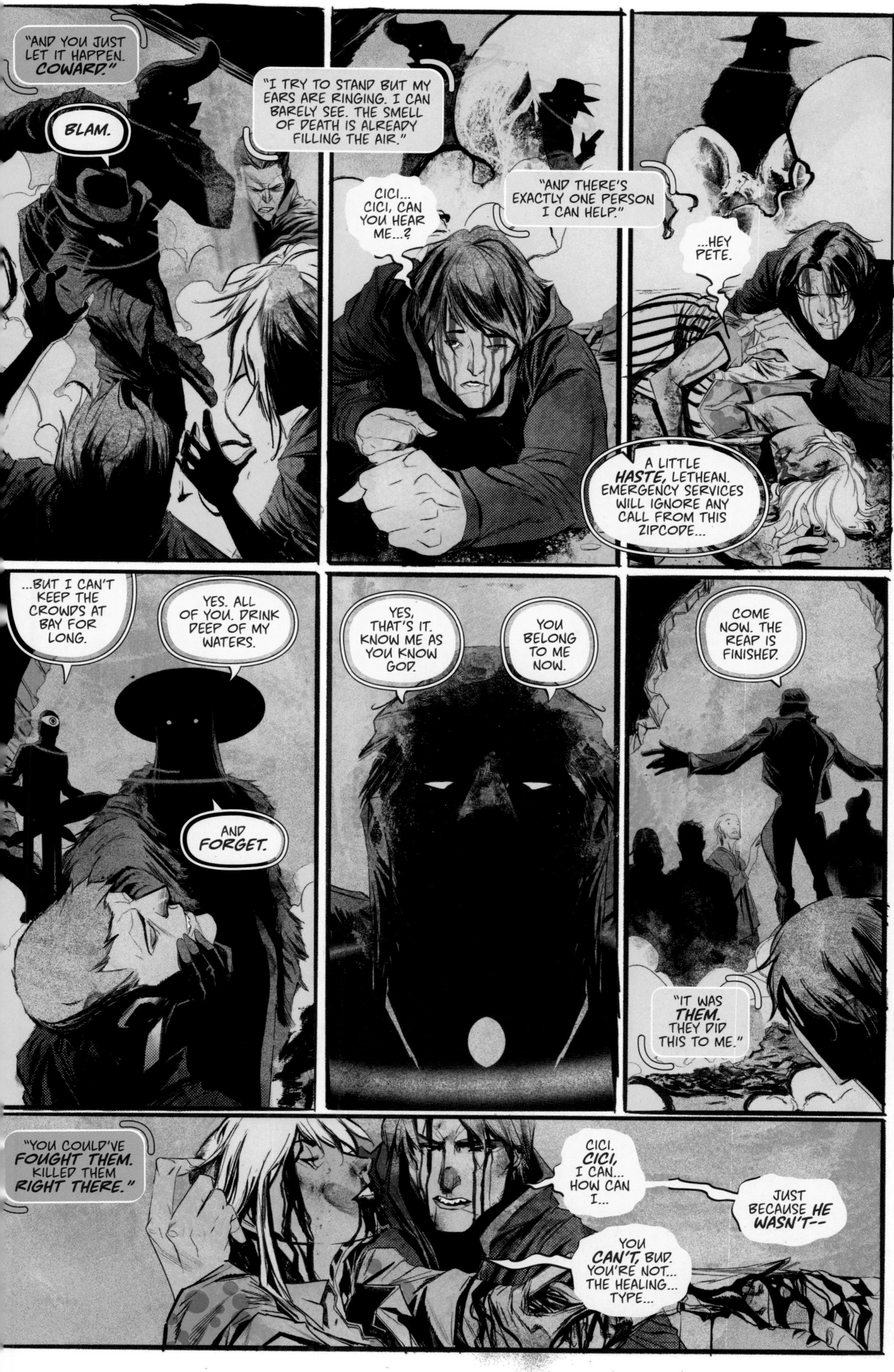
"AND YOU JUST LET IT HAPPEN. COWARD."
BLAM.
"I TRY TO STAND BUT MY EARS ARE RINGING. I CAN BARELY SEE. THE SMELL OF DEATH IS ALREADY FILLING THE AIR."
CICI... CICI, CAN YOU HEAR ME...?
"AND THERE'S EXACTLY ONE PERSON I CAN HELP."
...HEY PETE.
A LITTLE HASTE, LETHEAN. EMERGENCY SERVICES WILL IGNORE ANY CALL FROM THIS ZIPCODE...
...BUT I CAN'T KEEP THE CROWDS AT BAY FOR LONG.
YES. ALL OF YOU. DRINK DEEP OF MY WATERS.
AND FORGET.
YES, THAT'S IT. KNOW ME AS YOU KNOW GOD.
YOU BELONG TO ME NOW.
COME NOW. THE REAP IS FINISHED.
"IT WAS THEM. THEY DID THIS TO ME."
"YOU COULD'VE FOUGHT THEM. KILLED THEM RIGHT THERE."
CICI. CICI, I CAN... HOW CAN I...
JUST BECAUSE HE WASN'T--
YOU CAN'T, BUD. YOU'RE NOT... THE HEALING... TYPE...

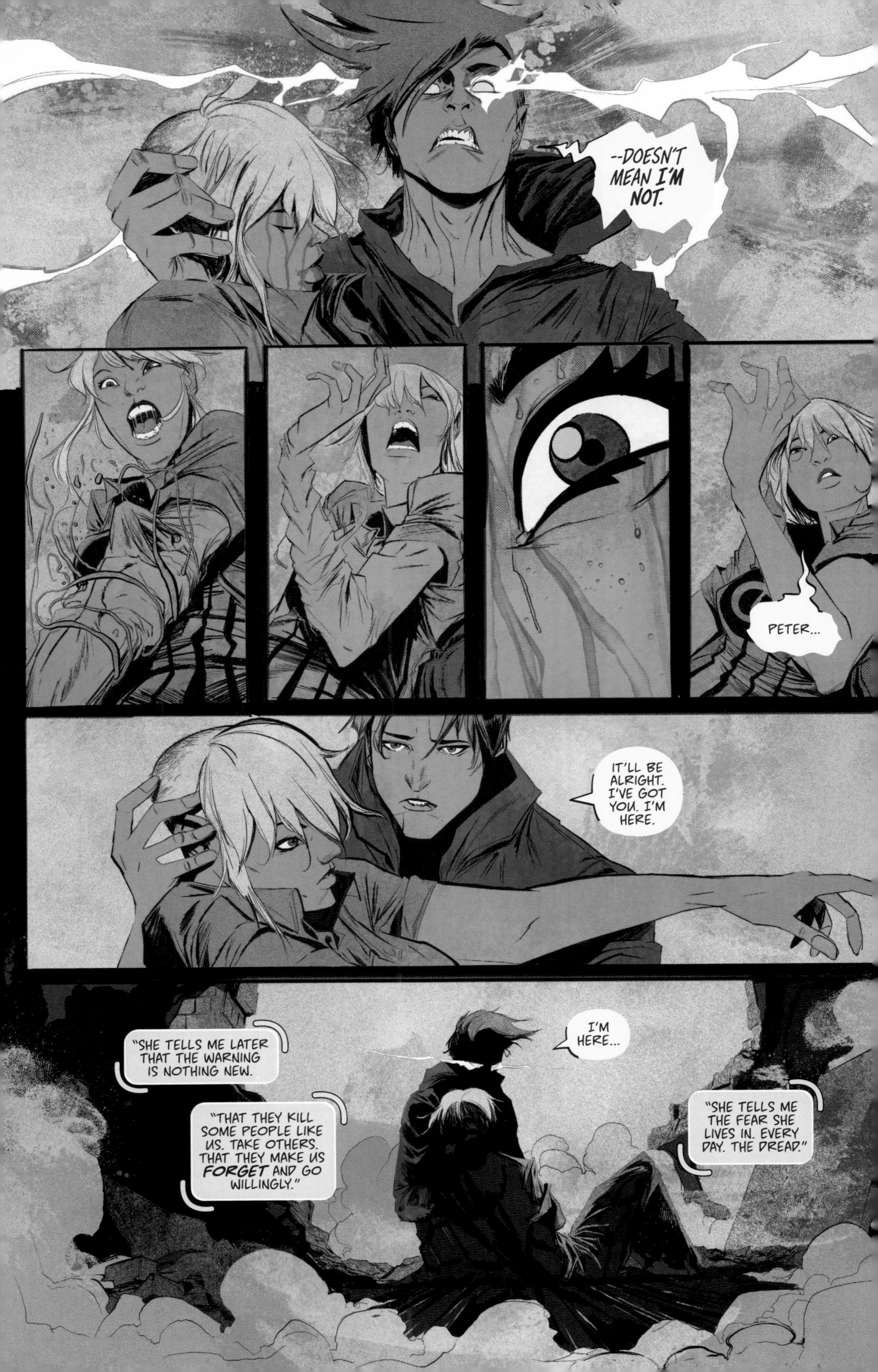
--DOESN'T MEAN I'M NOT.
PETER...
IT'LL BE ALRIGHT. I'VE GOT YOU. I'M HERE.
"SHE TELLS ME LATER THAT THE WARNING IS NOTHING NEW.
"THAT THEY KILL SOME PEOPLE LIKE US. TAKE OTHERS. THAT THEY MAKE US FORGET AND GO WILLINGLY."
I'M HERE...
"SHE TELLS ME THE FEAR SHE LIVES IN. EVERY DAY. THE DREAD."

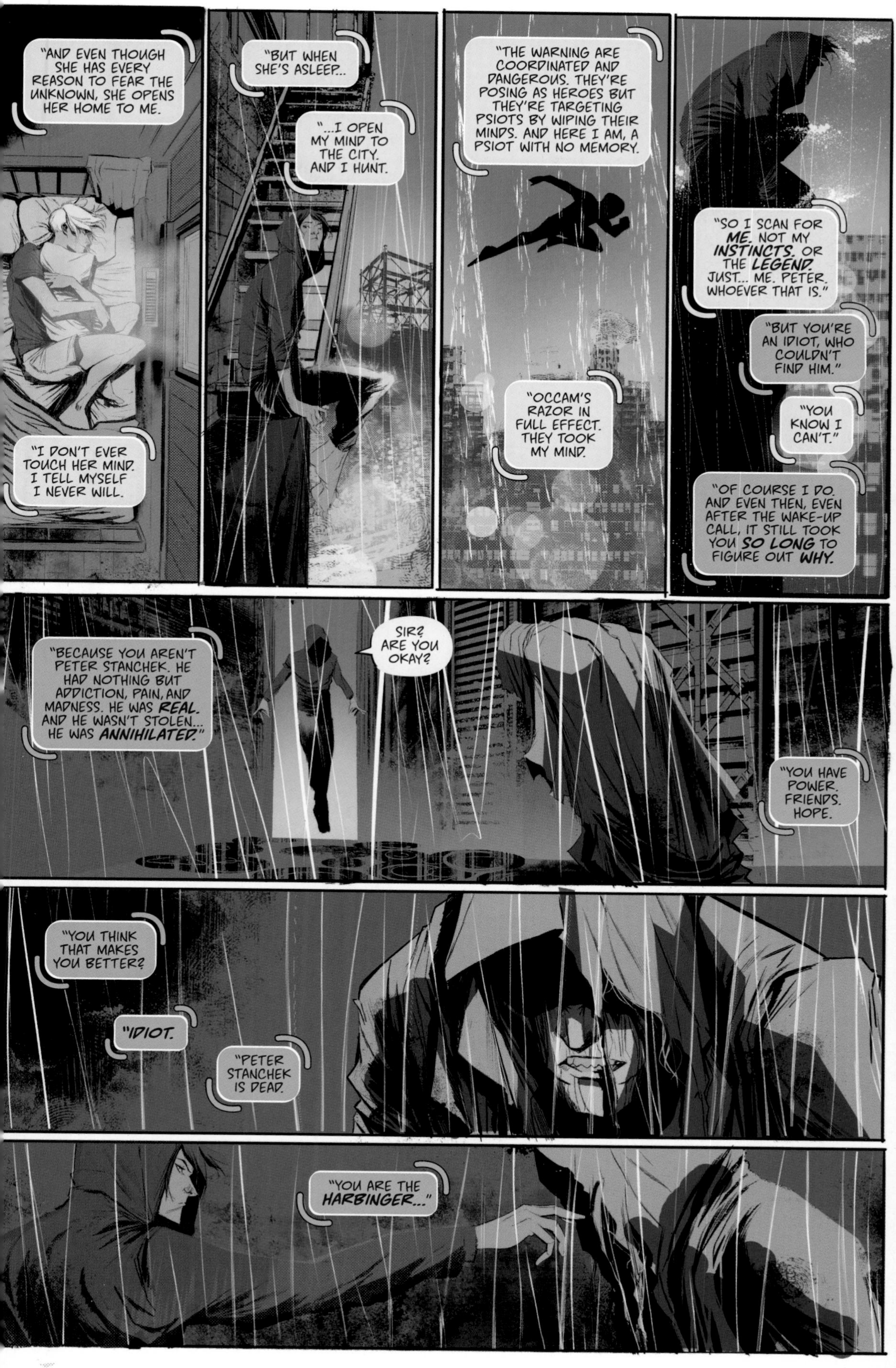
"AND EVEN THOUGH SHE HAS EVERY REASON TO FEAR THE UNKNOWN, SHE OPENS HER HOME TO ME.
"I DON'T EVER TOUCH HER MIND. I TELL MYSELF I NEVER WILL.
"BUT WHEN SHE'S ASLEEP...
"...I OPEN MY MIND TO THE CITY. AND I HUNT.
"THE WARNING ARE COORDINATED AND DANGEROUS. THEY'RE POSING AS HEROES BUT THEY'RE TARGETING PSIOTS BY WIPING THEIR MINDS. AND HERE I AM, A PSIOT WITH NO MEMORY.
"OCCAM'S RAZOR IN FULL EFFECT. THEY TOOK MY MIND.
"SO I SCAN FOR ME. NOT MY INSTINCTS. OR THE LEGEND. JUST... ME. PETER. WHOEVER THAT IS."
"BUT YOU'RE AN IDIOT, WHO COULDN'T FIND HIM."
"YOU KNOW I CAN'T."
"OF COURSE I DO. AND EVEN THEN, EVEN AFTER THE WAKE-UP CALL, IT STILL TOOK YOU SO LONG TO FIGURE OUT WHY.
"BECAUSE YOU AREN'T PETER STANCHEK. HE HAD NOTHING BUT ADDICTION, PAIN, AND MADNESS. HE WAS REAL. AND HE WASN'T STOLEN... HE WAS ANNIHILATED."
SIR? ARE YOU OKAY?
"YOU HAVE POWER. FRIENDS. HOPE.
"YOU THINK THAT MAKES YOU BETTER?
"IDIOT.
"PETER STANCHEK IS DEAD.
"YOU ARE THE HARBINGER..."

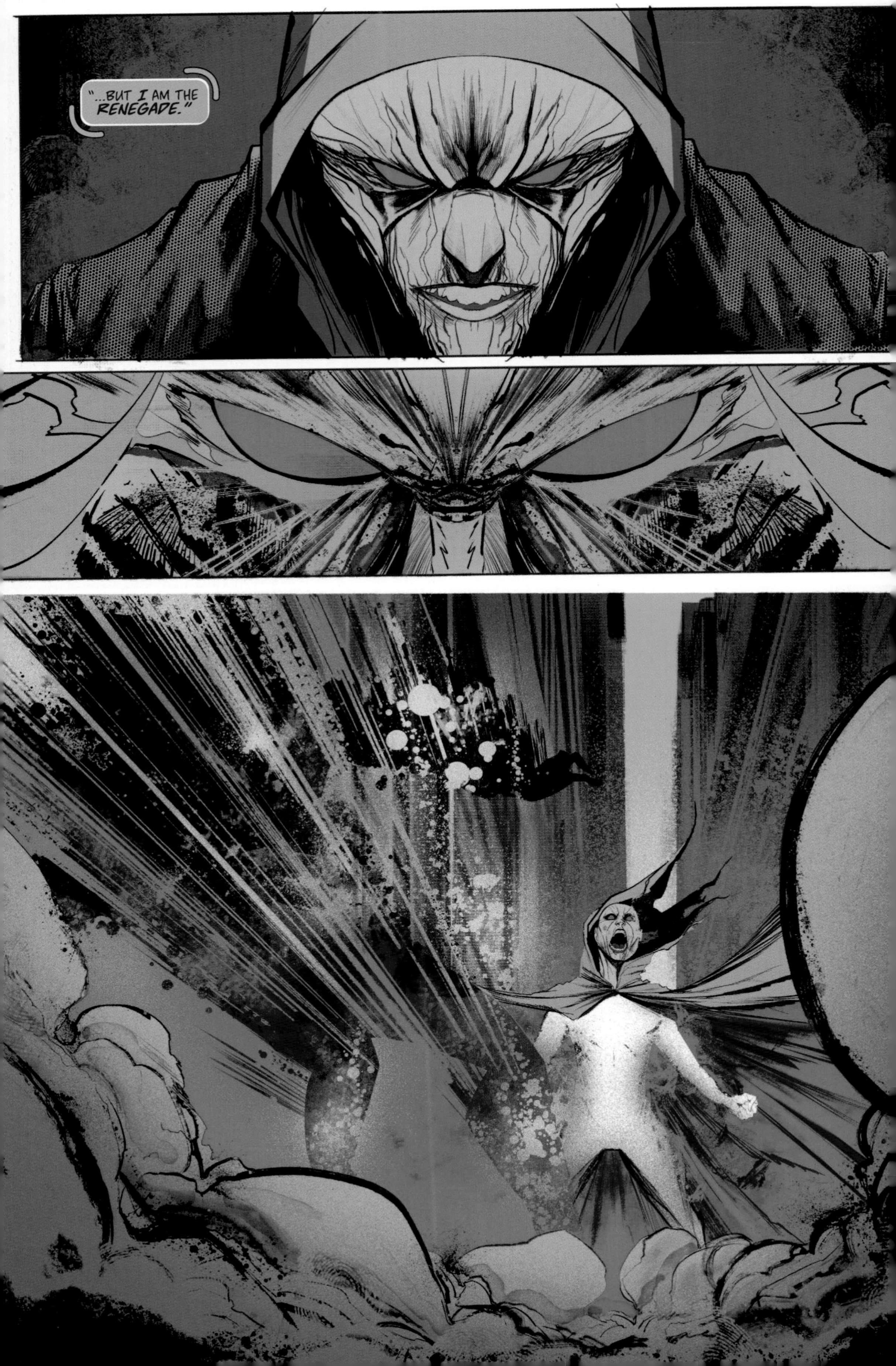
"...BUT I AM THE RENEGADE."

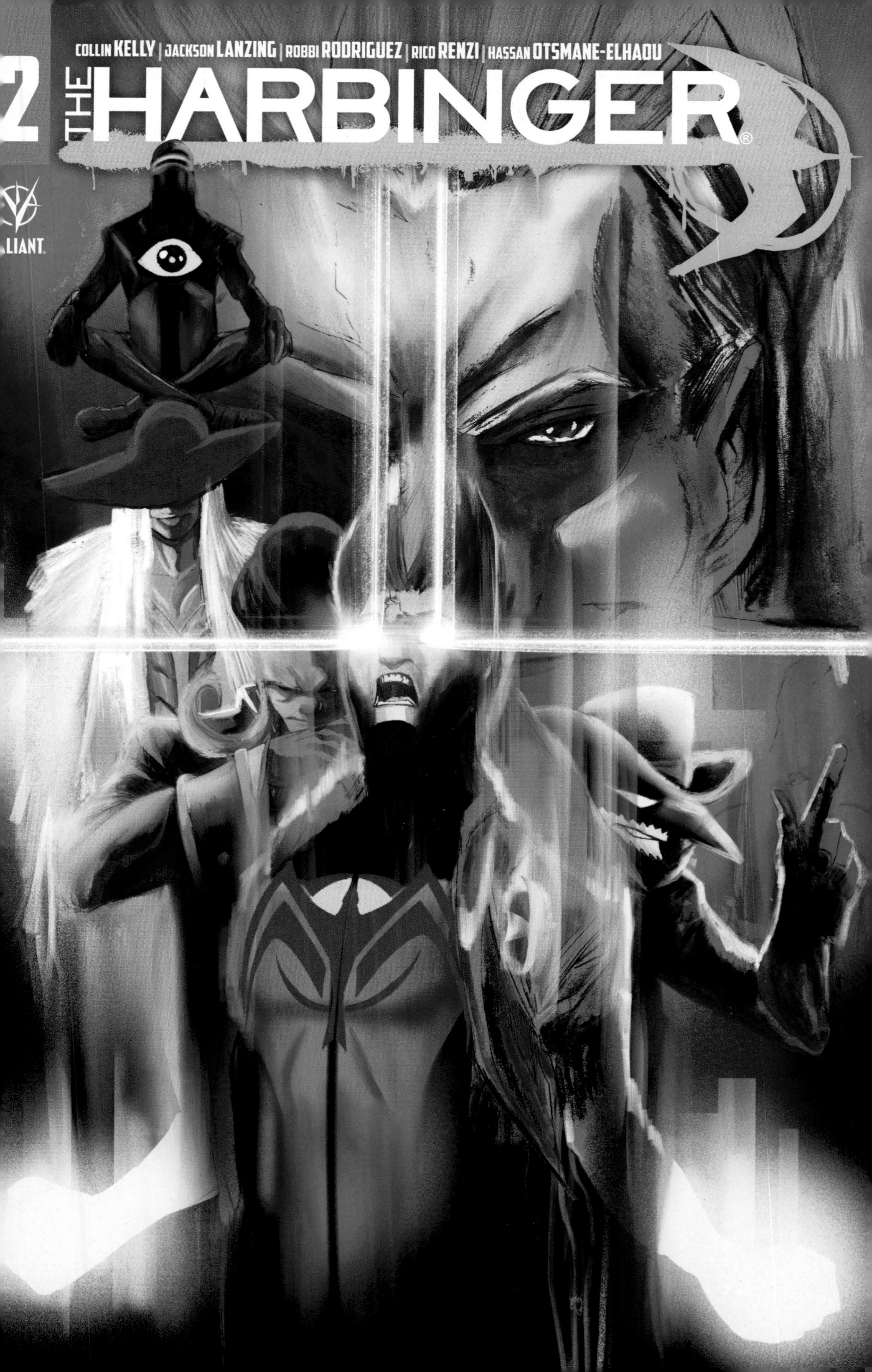
COLLIN KELLY | JACKSON LANZING | ROBBI RODRIGUEZ | RICO RENZI | HASSAN OTSMANE-ELHAOU
2
THE HARBINGER®
LIANT

"Be Better: Chapter Two"

THE HARBINGER #2

WORDS: Collin Kelly and Jackson Lanzing
ART: Robbi Rodriguez
COLORS: Rico Renzi
LETTERS: Hassan Otsmane-Elhaou
COVER ART: Robbi Rodriguez
ASSISTANT EDITOR: Audrey Meeker
SENIOR EDITORS: Lysa Hawkins and Heather Antos

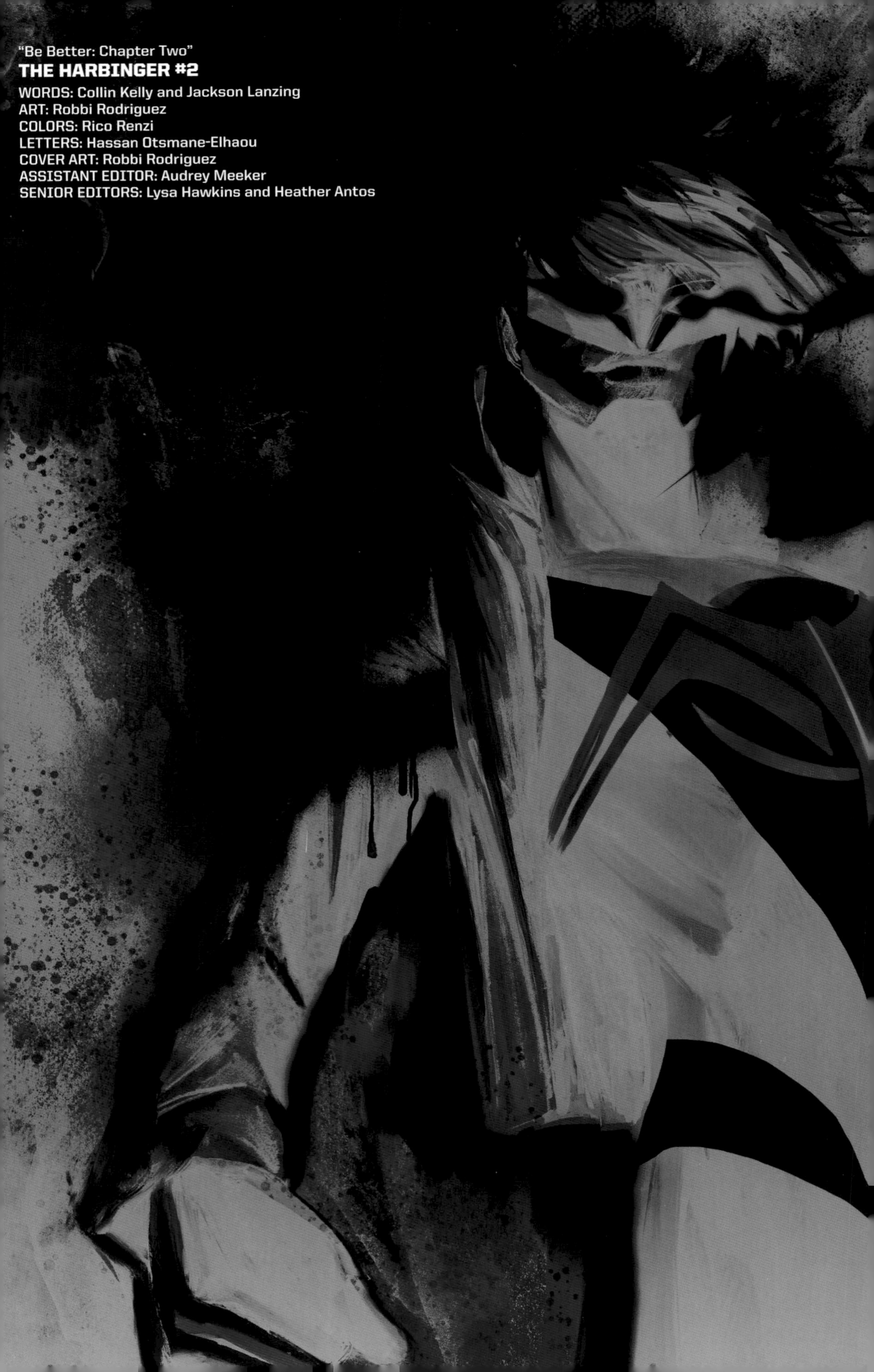

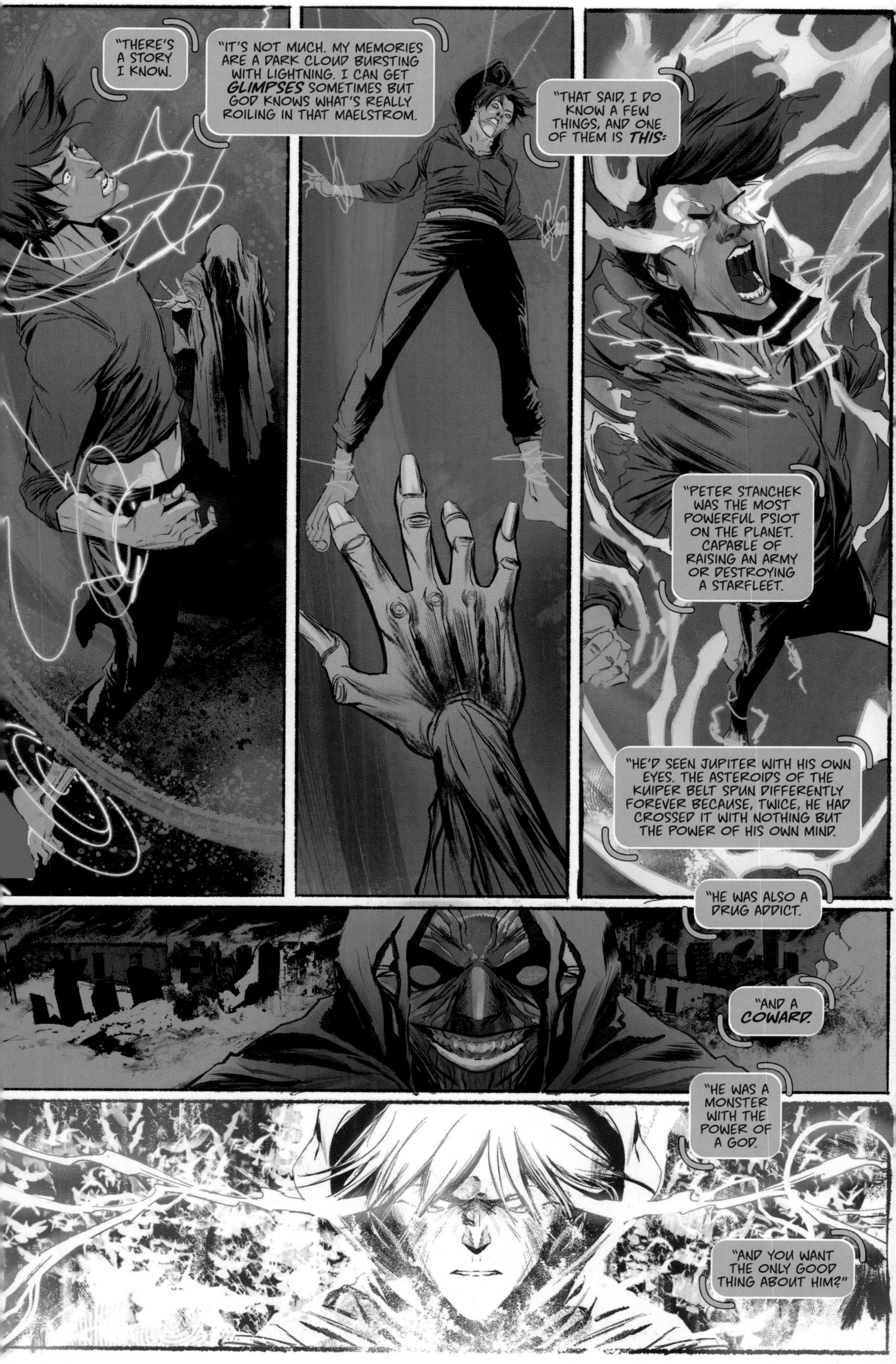
"THERE'S A STORY I KNOW.
"IT'S NOT MUCH. MY MEMORIES ARE A DARK CLOUD BURSTING WITH LIGHTNING. I CAN GET GLIMPSES SOMETIMES BUT GOD KNOWS WHAT'S REALLY ROILING IN THAT MAELSTROM.
"THAT SAID, I DO KNOW A FEW THINGS, AND ONE OF THEM IS THIS:
"PETER STANCHEK WAS THE MOST POWERFUL PSIOT ON THE PLANET. CAPABLE OF RAISING AN ARMY OR DESTROYING A STARFLEET.
"HE'D SEEN JUPITER WITH HIS OWN EYES. THE ASTEROIDS OF THE KUIPER BELT SPUN DIFFERENTLY FOREVER BECAUSE, TWICE, HE HAD CROSSED IT WITH NOTHING BUT THE POWER OF HIS OWN MIND.
"HE WAS ALSO A DRUG ADDICT.
"AND A COWARD.
"HE WAS A MONSTER WITH THE POWER OF A GOD.
"AND YOU WANT THE ONLY GOOD THING ABOUT HIM?"

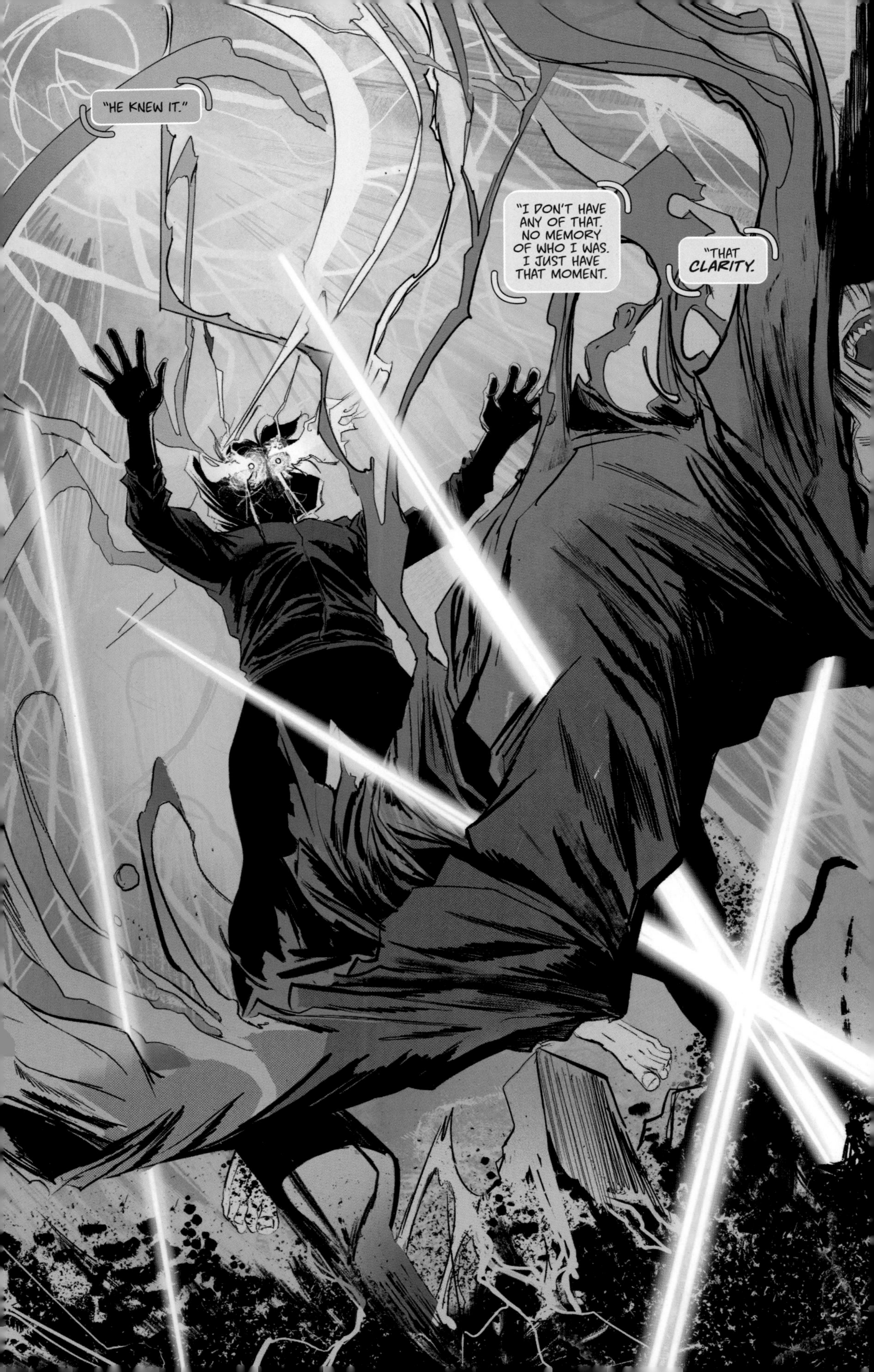
"HE KNEW IT."
"I DON'T HAVE ANY OF THAT. NO MEMORY OF WHO I WAS. I JUST HAVE THAT MOMENT.
"THAT *CLARITY*.

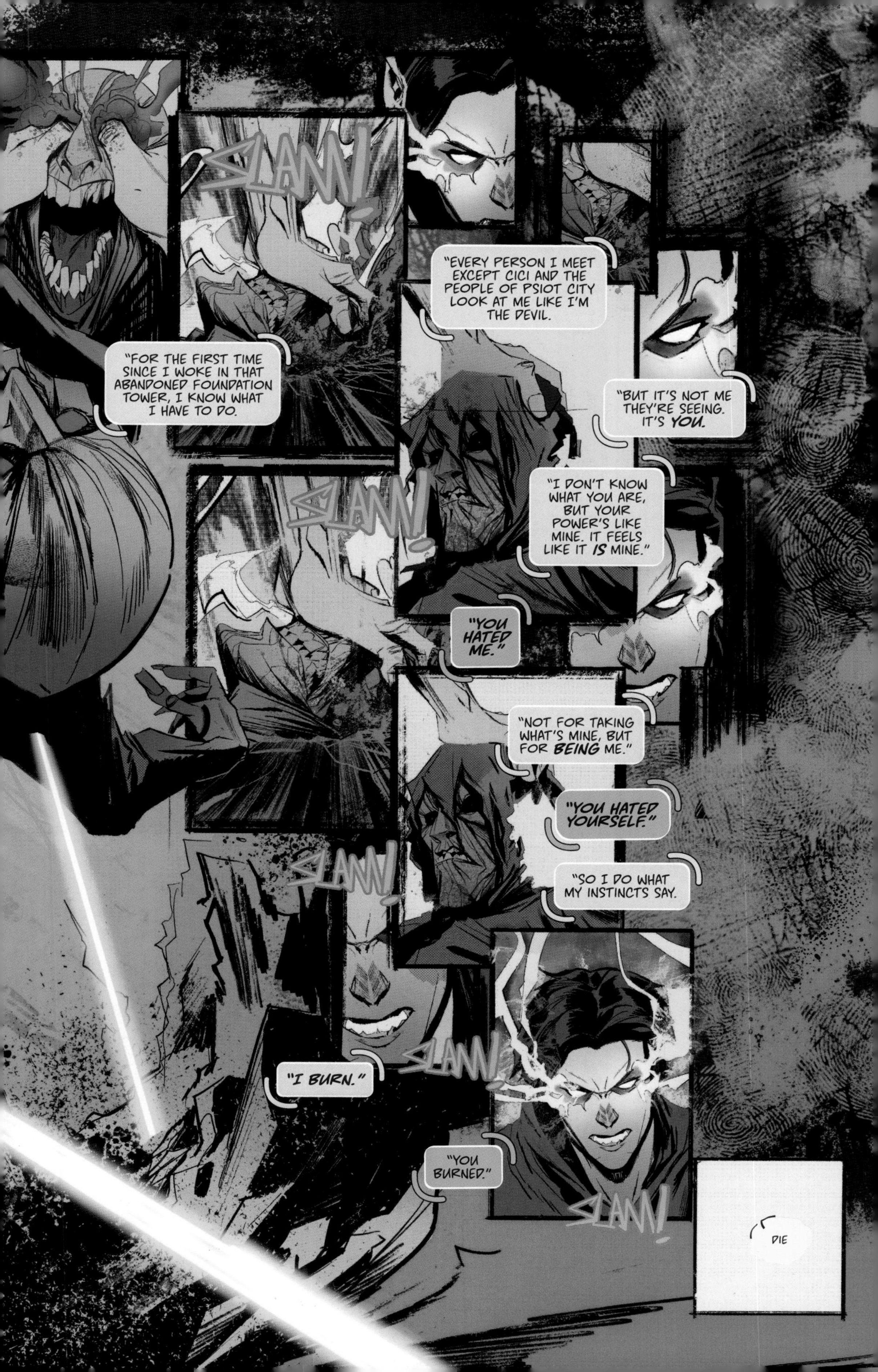

SLAM!
"FOR THE FIRST TIME SINCE I WOKE IN THAT ABANDONED FOUNDATION TOWER, I KNOW WHAT I HAVE TO DO.
"EVERY PERSON I MEET EXCEPT CICI AND THE PEOPLE OF PSIOT CITY LOOK AT ME LIKE I'M THE DEVIL.
"BUT IT'S NOT ME THEY'RE SEEING. IT'S YOU.
"I DON'T KNOW WHAT YOU ARE, BUT YOUR POWER'S LIKE MINE. IT FEELS LIKE IT IS MINE."
SLAM!
"YOU HATED ME."
"NOT FOR TAKING WHAT'S MINE, BUT FOR BEING ME."
"YOU HATED YOURSELF."
SLAM!
"SO I DO WHAT MY INSTINCTS SAY.
SLAM!
"I BURN."
"YOU BURNED."
SLAM!
"DIE

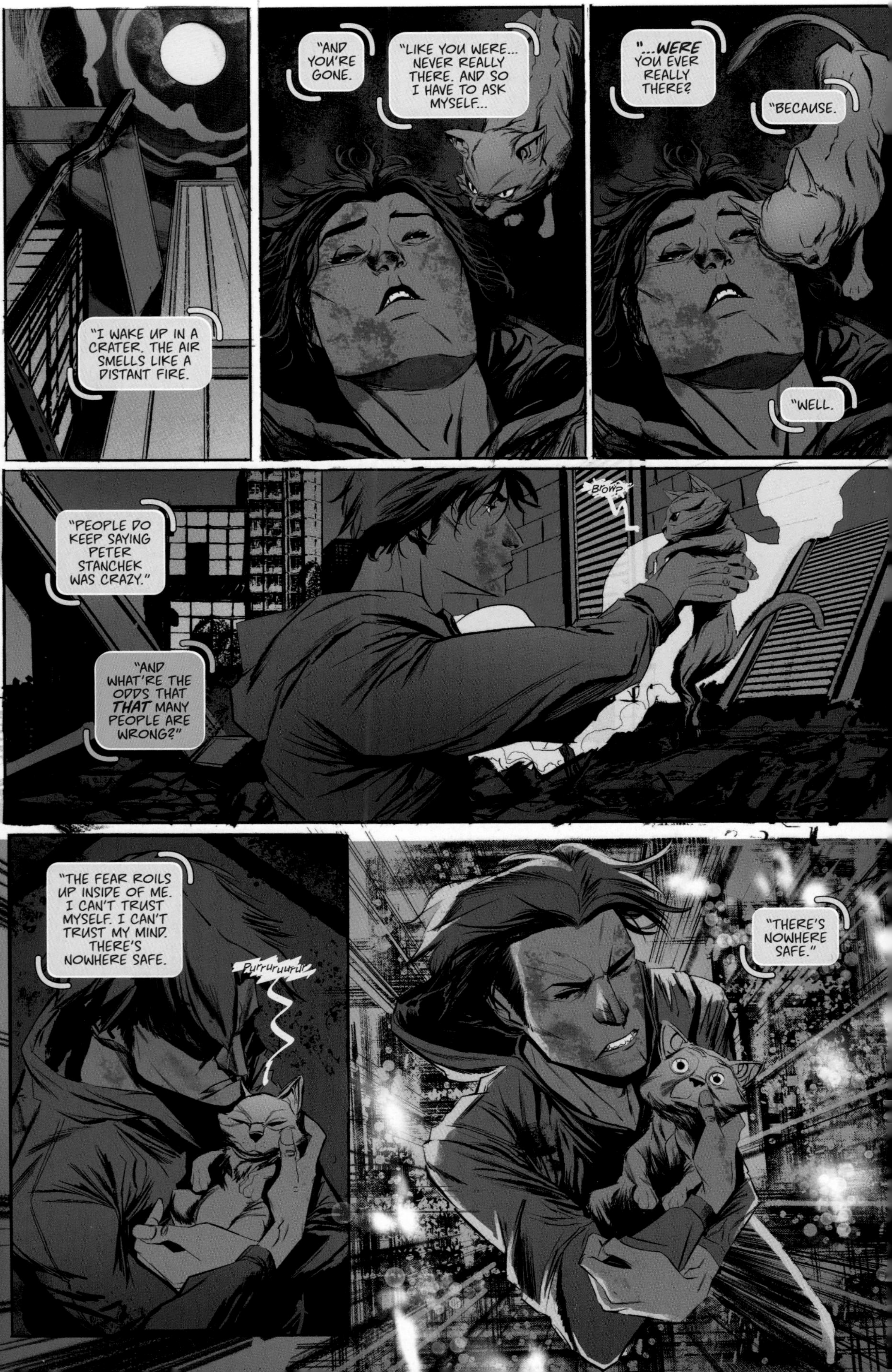
"I WAKE UP IN A CRATER. THE AIR SMELLS LIKE A DISTANT FIRE.
"AND YOU'RE GONE.
"LIKE YOU WERE... NEVER REALLY THERE. AND SO I HAVE TO ASK MYSELF...
"...WERE YOU EVER REALLY THERE?
"BECAUSE.
"WELL.
"PEOPLE DO KEEP SAYING PETER STANCHEK WAS CRAZY."
"AND WHAT'RE THE ODDS THAT THAT MANY PEOPLE ARE WRONG?"
BROW?
"THE FEAR ROILS UP INSIDE OF ME. I CAN'T TRUST MYSELF. I CAN'T TRUST MY MIND. THERE'S NOWHERE SAFE.
Purrruruurur
"THERE'S NOWHERE SAFE."

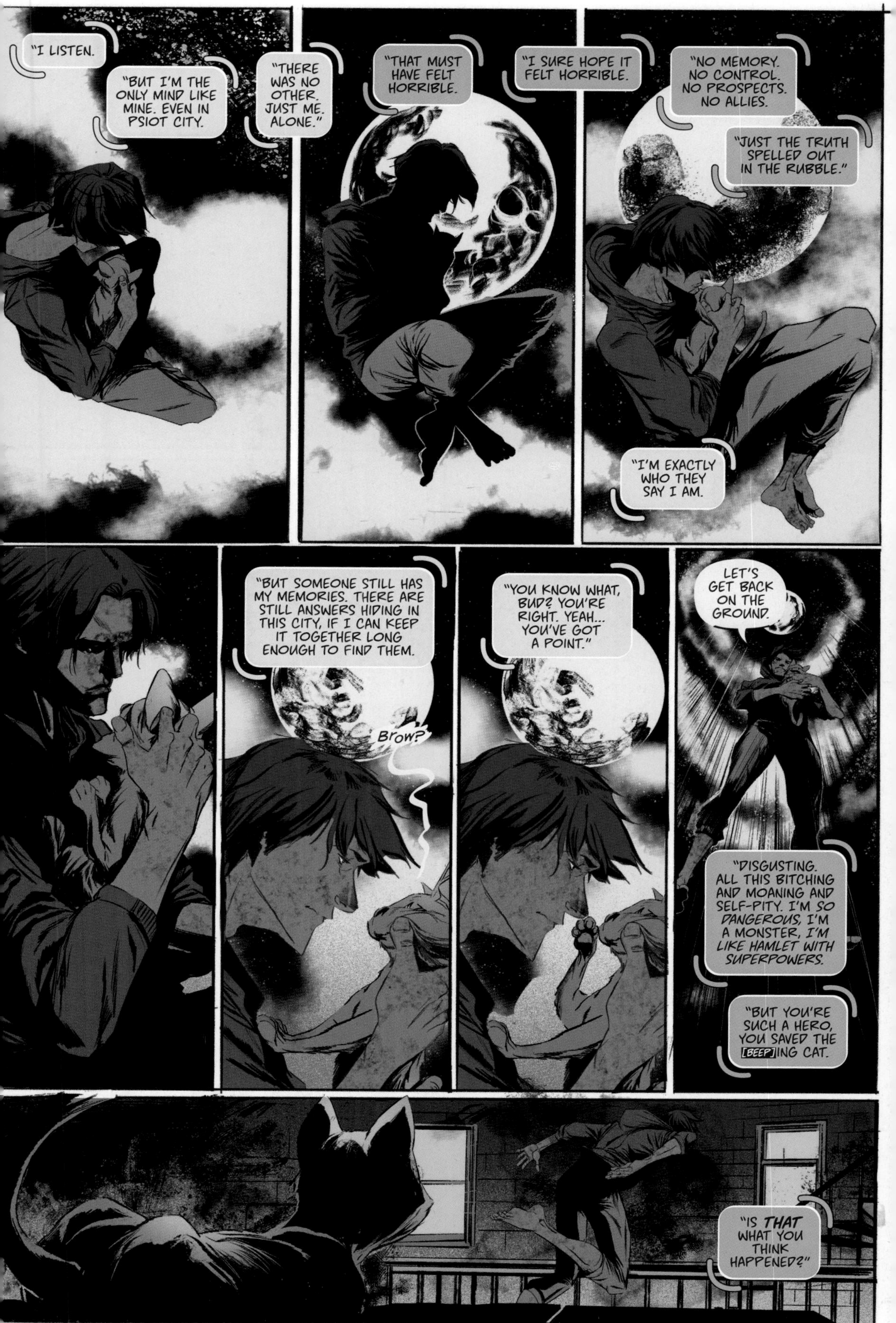
"I LISTEN.
"BUT I'M THE ONLY MIND LIKE MINE. EVEN IN PSIOT CITY.
"THERE WAS NO OTHER. JUST ME. ALONE."
"THAT MUST HAVE FELT HORRIBLE.
"I SURE HOPE IT FELT HORRIBLE.
"NO MEMORY. NO CONTROL. NO PROSPECTS. NO ALLIES.
"JUST THE TRUTH SPELLED OUT IN THE RUBBLE."
"I'M EXACTLY WHO THEY SAY I AM.
"BUT SOMEONE STILL HAS MY MEMORIES. THERE ARE STILL ANSWERS HIDING IN THIS CITY, IF I CAN KEEP IT TOGETHER LONG ENOUGH TO FIND THEM.
Brow?
"YOU KNOW WHAT, BUD? YOU'RE RIGHT. YEAH... YOU'VE GOT A POINT."
LET'S GET BACK ON THE GROUND.
"DISGUSTING. ALL THIS BITCHING AND MOANING AND SELF-PITY. I'M SO DANGEROUS, I'M A MONSTER, I'M LIKE HAMLET WITH SUPERPOWERS.
"BUT YOU'RE SUCH A HERO, YOU SAVED THE [BEEP]ING CAT.
"IS THAT WHAT YOU THINK HAPPENED?"

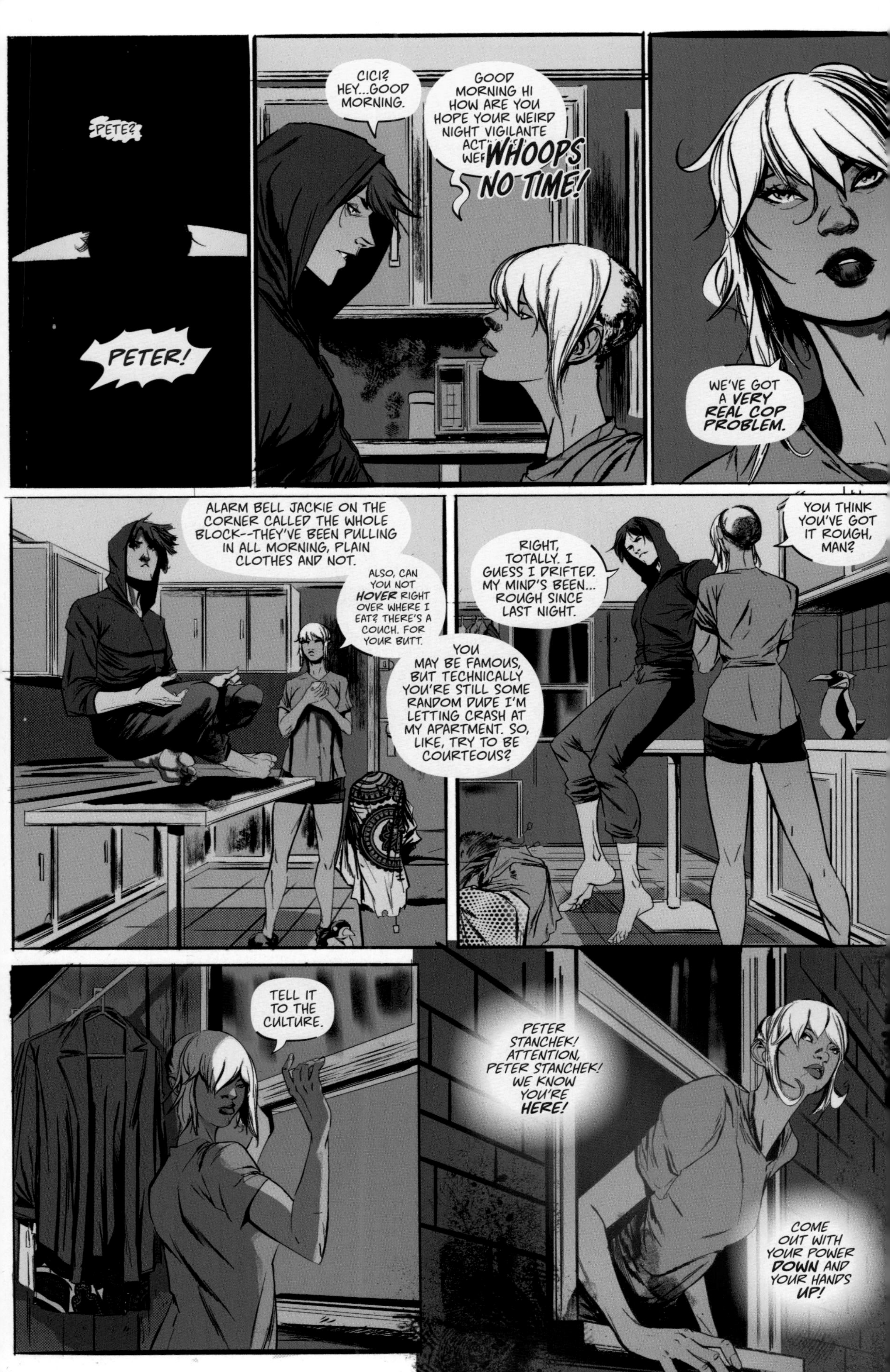
PETE?
PETER!
CICI? HEY...GOOD MORNING.
GOOD MORNING HI HOW ARE YOU HOPE YOUR WEIRD NIGHT VIGILANTE
WHOOPS NO TIME!
WE'VE GOT A VERY REAL COP PROBLEM.
ALARM BELL JACKIE ON THE CORNER CALLED THE WHOLE BLOCK--THEY'VE BEEN PULLING IN ALL MORNING, PLAIN CLOTHES AND NOT.
ALSO, CAN YOU NOT HOVER RIGHT OVER WHERE I EAT? THERE'S A COUCH. FOR YOUR BUTT.
YOU MAY BE FAMOUS, BUT TECHNICALLY YOU'RE STILL SOME RANDOM DUDE I'M LETTING CRASH AT MY APARTMENT. SO, LIKE, TRY TO BE COURTEOUS?
RIGHT, TOTALLY. I GUESS I DRIFTED. MY MIND'S BEEN... ROUGH SINCE LAST NIGHT.
YOU THINK YOU'VE GOT IT ROUGH, MAN?
TELL IT TO THE CULTURE.
PETER STANCHEK! ATTENTION, PETER STANCHEK! WE KNOW YOU'RE HERE!
COME OUT WITH YOUR POWER DOWN AND YOUR HANDS UP!

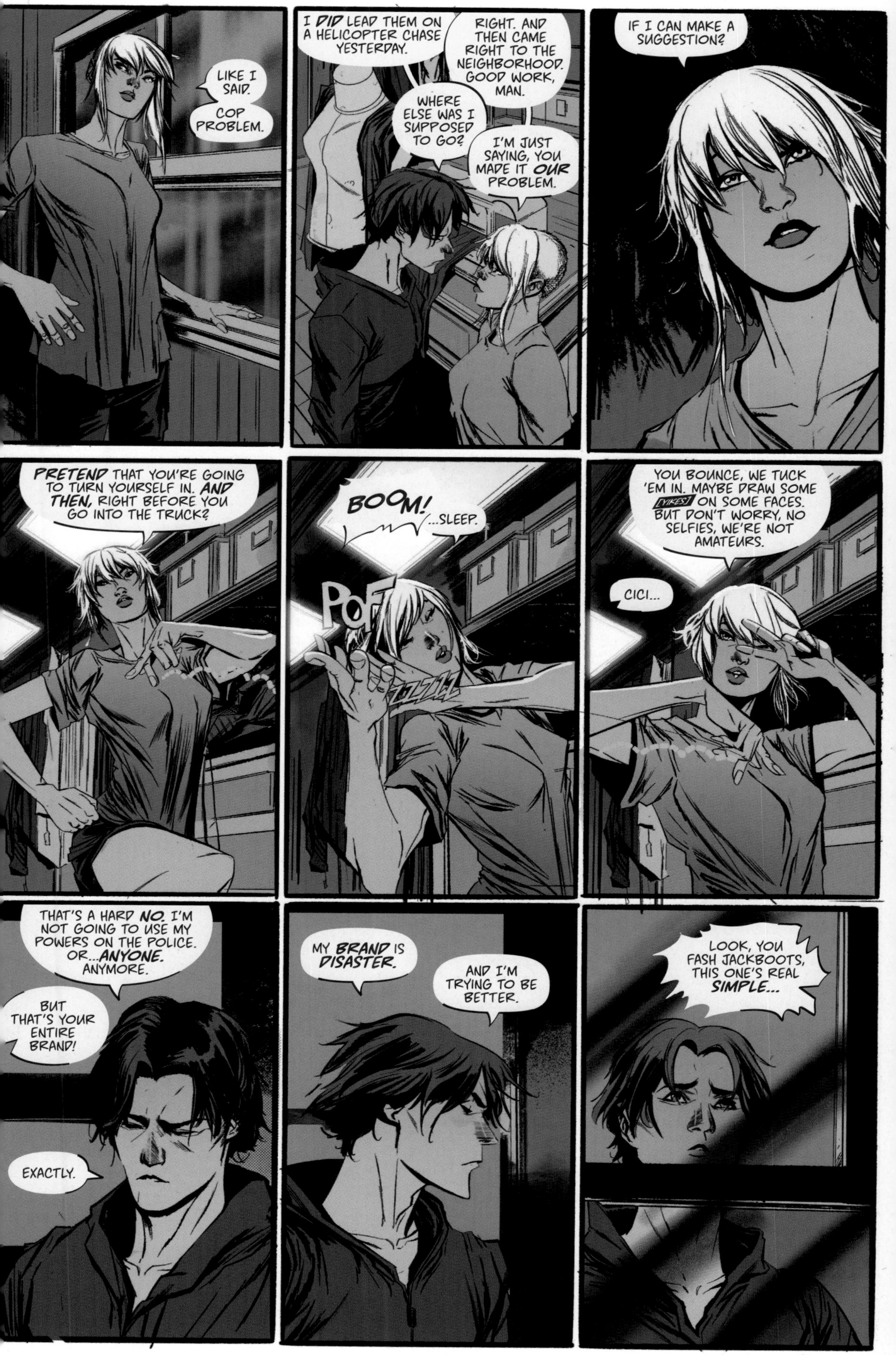
LIKE I SAID.
COP PROBLEM.
I DID LEAD THEM ON A HELICOPTER CHASE YESTERDAY.
RIGHT. AND THEN CAME RIGHT TO THE NEIGHBORHOOD. GOOD WORK, MAN.
WHERE ELSE WAS I SUPPOSED TO GO?
I'M JUST SAYING, YOU MADE IT OUR PROBLEM.
IF I CAN MAKE A SUGGESTION?
PRETEND THAT YOU'RE GOING TO TURN YOURSELF IN. AND THEN, RIGHT BEFORE YOU GO INTO THE TRUCK?
BOOM!
...SLEEP.
POF
YOU BOUNCE, WE TUCK 'EM IN. MAYBE DRAW SOME [YIKES] ON SOME FACES. BUT DON'T WORRY, NO SELFIES, WE'RE NOT AMATEURS.
CICI...
THAT'S A HARD NO. I'M NOT GOING TO USE MY POWERS ON THE POLICE. OR...ANYONE. ANYMORE.
BUT THAT'S YOUR ENTIRE BRAND!
EXACTLY.
MY BRAND IS DISASTER.
AND I'M TRYING TO BE BETTER.
LOOK, YOU FASH JACKBOOTS, THIS ONE'S REAL SIMPLE...

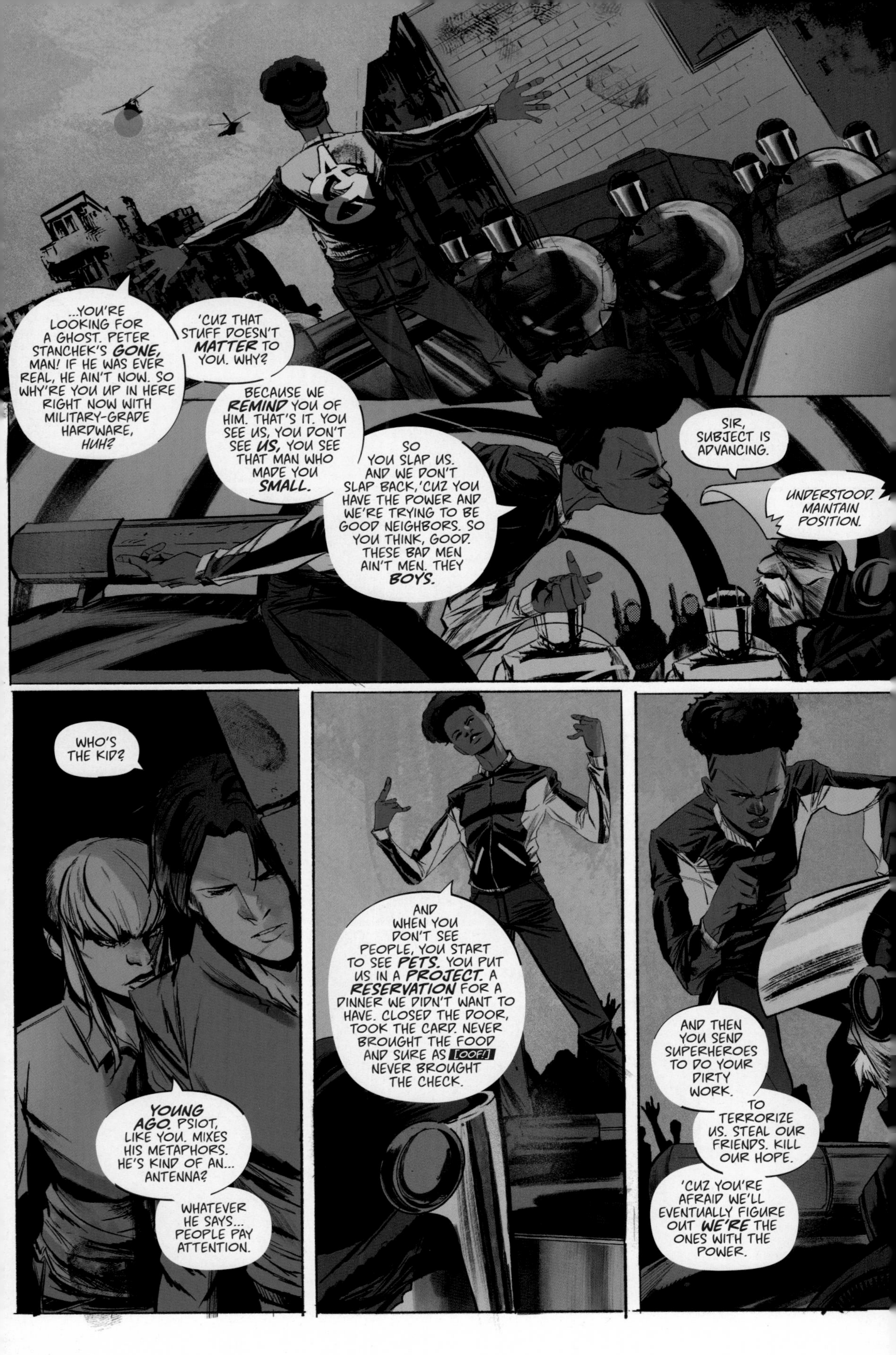
...YOU'RE LOOKING FOR A GHOST. PETER STANCHEK'S GONE, MAN! IF HE WAS EVER REAL, HE AIN'T NOW. SO WHY'RE YOU UP IN HERE RIGHT NOW WITH MILITARY-GRADE HARDWARE, HUH?
'CUZ THAT STUFF DOESN'T MATTER TO YOU. WHY?
BECAUSE WE REMIND YOU OF HIM. THAT'S IT. YOU SEE US, YOU DON'T SEE US, YOU SEE THAT MAN WHO MADE YOU SMALL.
SO YOU SLAP US. AND WE DON'T SLAP BACK, 'CUZ YOU HAVE THE POWER AND WE'RE TRYING TO BE GOOD NEIGHBORS. SO YOU THINK, GOOD. THESE BAD MEN AIN'T MEN. THEY BOYS.
SIR, SUBJECT IS ADVANCING.
UNDERSTOOD. MAINTAIN POSITION.
WHO'S THE KID?
YOUNG AGO. PSIOT, LIKE YOU. MIXES HIS METAPHORS. HE'S KIND OF AN... ANTENNA?
WHATEVER HE SAYS... PEOPLE PAY ATTENTION.
AND WHEN YOU DON'T SEE PEOPLE, YOU START TO SEE PETS. YOU PUT US IN A PROJECT. A RESERVATION FOR A DINNER WE DIDN'T WANT TO HAVE. CLOSED THE DOOR, TOOK THE CARD. NEVER BROUGHT THE FOOD AND SURE AS [OOF!] NEVER BROUGHT THE CHECK.
AND THEN YOU SEND SUPERHEROES TO DO YOUR DIRTY WORK.
TO TERRORIZE US. STEAL OUR FRIENDS. KILL OUR HOPE.
'CUZ YOU'RE AFRAID WE'LL EVENTUALLY FIGURE OUT WE'RE THE ONES WITH THE POWER.

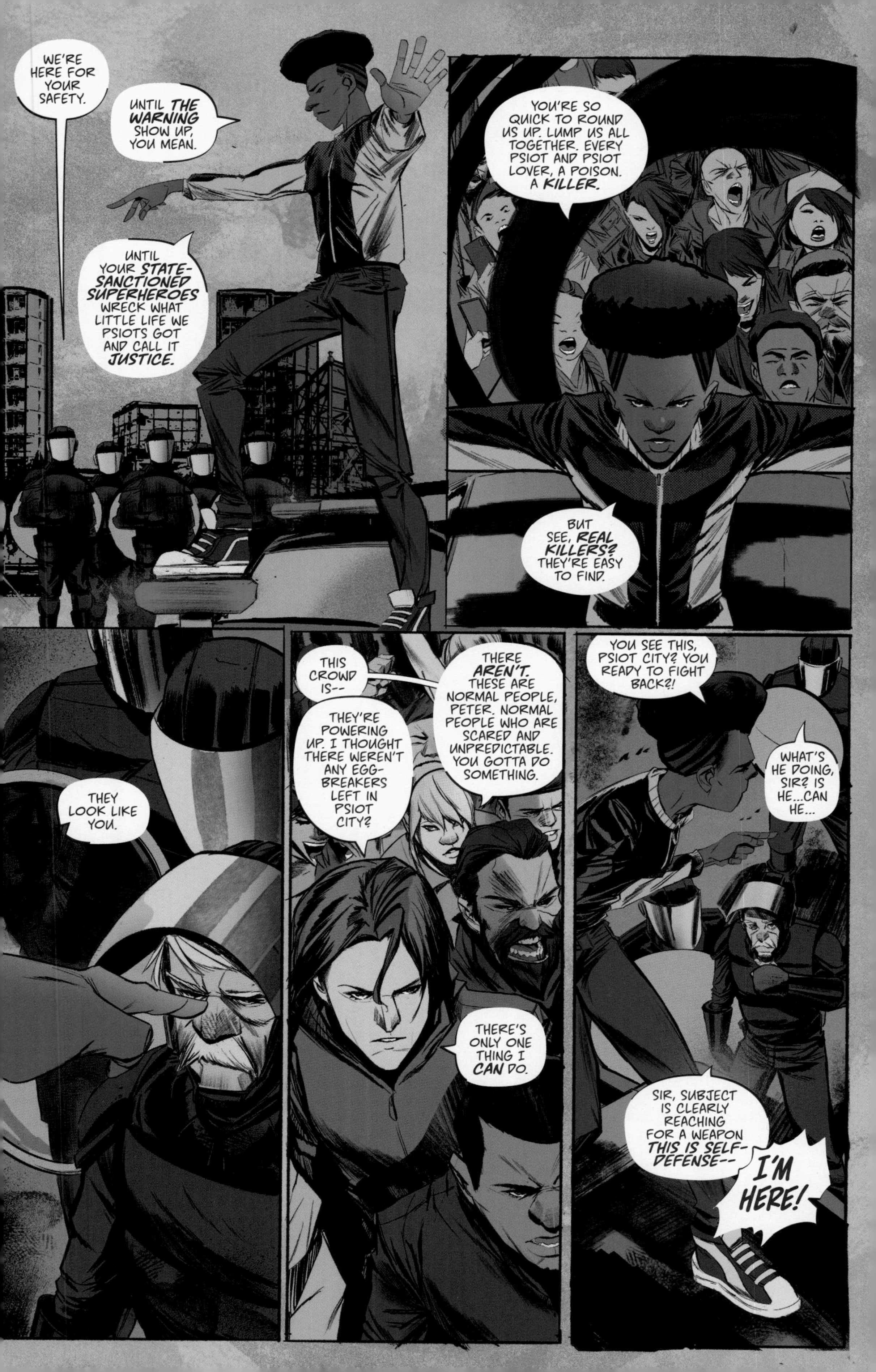
WE'RE HERE FOR YOUR SAFETY.
UNTIL THE WARNING SHOW UP, YOU MEAN.
UNTIL YOUR STATE-SANCTIONED SUPERHEROES WRECK WHAT LITTLE LIFE WE PSIOTS GOT AND CALL IT JUSTICE.
YOU'RE SO QUICK TO ROUND US UP. LUMP US ALL TOGETHER. EVERY PSIOT AND PSIOT LOVER, A POISON. A KILLER.
BUT SEE, REAL KILLERS? THEY'RE EASY TO FIND.
THEY LOOK LIKE YOU.
THIS CROWD IS--
THEY'RE POWERING UP. I THOUGHT THERE WEREN'T ANY EGG-BREAKERS LEFT IN PSIOT CITY?
THERE AREN'T. THESE ARE NORMAL PEOPLE, PETER. NORMAL PEOPLE WHO ARE SCARED AND UNPREDICTABLE. YOU GOTTA DO SOMETHING.
THERE'S ONLY ONE THING I CAN DO.
YOU SEE THIS, PSIOT CITY? YOU READY TO FIGHT BACK?!
WHAT'S HE DOING, SIR? IS HE...CAN HE...
SIR, SUBJECT IS CLEARLY REACHING FOR A WEAPON THIS IS SELF-DEFENSE--
I'M HERE!

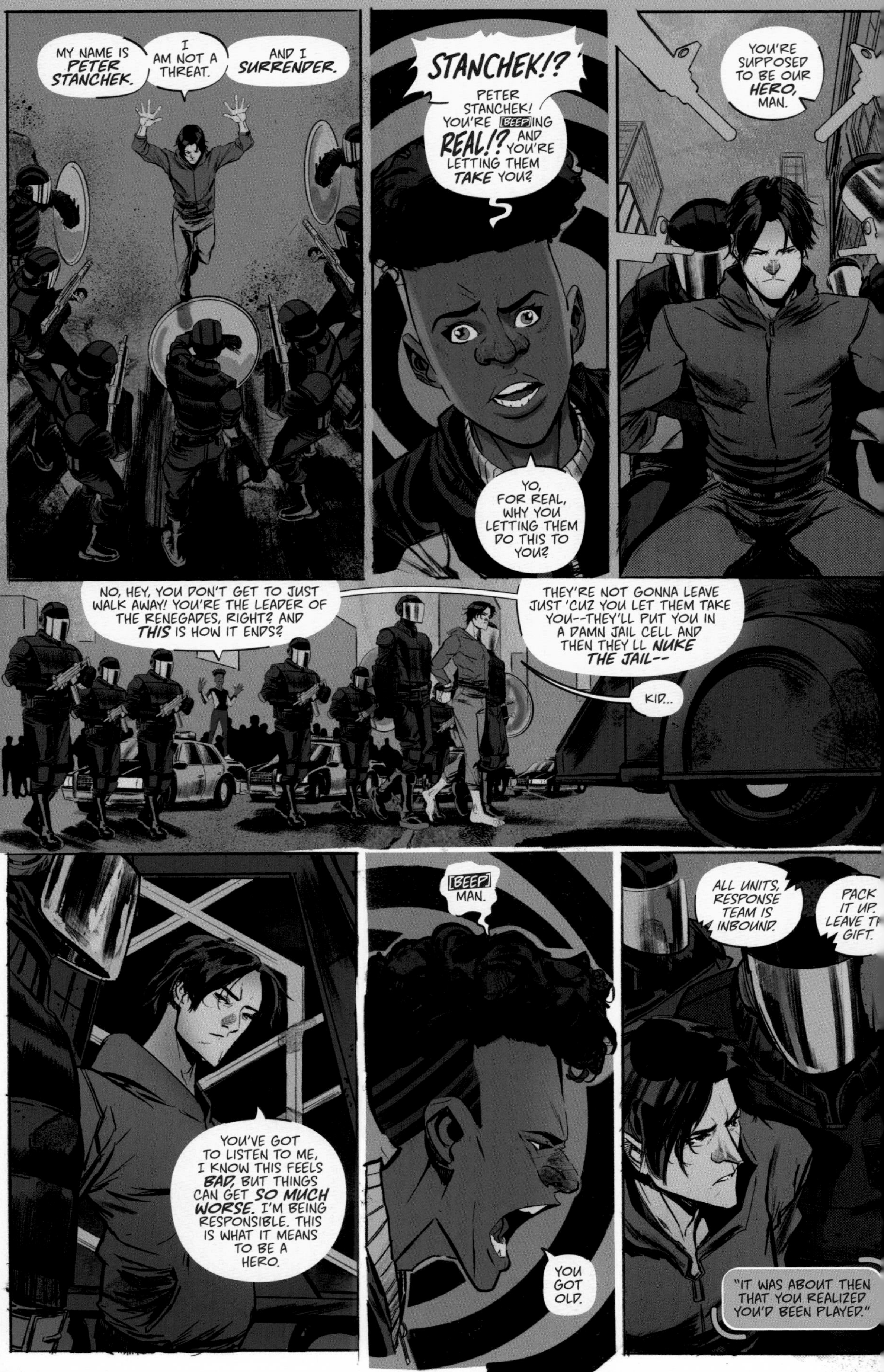
MY NAME IS PETER STANCHEK.
I AM NOT A THREAT.
AND I SURRENDER.
STANCHEK!?
PETER STANCHEK! YOU'RE [BEEP]ING REAL!? AND YOU'RE LETTING THEM TAKE YOU?
YO, FOR REAL, WHY YOU LETTING THEM DO THIS TO YOU?
YOU'RE SUPPOSED TO BE OUR HERO, MAN.
NO, HEY, YOU DON'T GET TO JUST WALK AWAY! YOU'RE THE LEADER OF THE RENEGADES, RIGHT? AND THIS IS HOW IT ENDS?
THEY'RE NOT GONNA LEAVE JUST 'CUZ YOU LET THEM TAKE YOU--THEY'LL PUT YOU IN A DAMN JAIL CELL AND THEN THEY'LL NUKE THE JAIL--
KID...
YOU'VE GOT TO LISTEN TO ME, I KNOW THIS FEELS BAD, BUT THINGS CAN GET SO MUCH WORSE. I'M BEING RESPONSIBLE. THIS IS WHAT IT MEANS TO BE A HERO.
[BEEP] MAN.
YOU GOT OLD.
ALL UNITS, RESPONSE TEAM IS INBOUND.
PACK IT UP. LEAVE TH GIFT.
"IT WAS ABOUT THEN THAT YOU REALIZED YOU'D BEEN PLAYED."

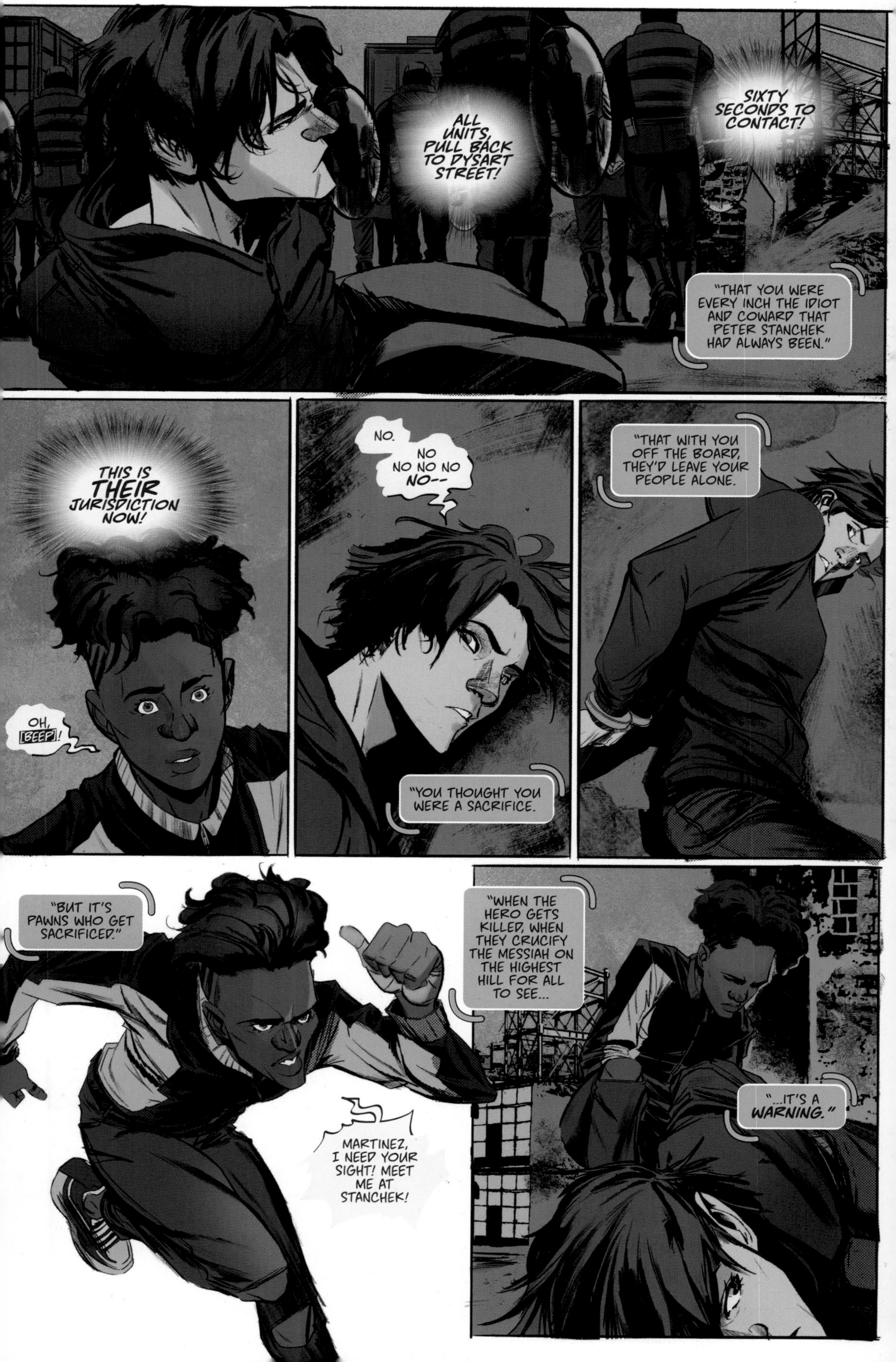
ALL UNITS, PULL BACK TO DYSART STREET!
SIXTY SECONDS TO CONTACT!
"THAT YOU WERE EVERY INCH THE IDIOT AND COWARD THAT PETER STANCHEK HAD ALWAYS BEEN."
THIS IS THEIR JURISDICTION NOW!
OH, [BEEP]!
NO.
NO NO NO NO NO--
"YOU THOUGHT YOU WERE A SACRIFICE.
"THAT WITH YOU OFF THE BOARD, THEY'D LEAVE YOUR PEOPLE ALONE.
"BUT IT'S PAWNS WHO GET SACRIFICED."
MARTINEZ, I NEED YOUR SIGHT! MEET ME AT STANCHEK!
"WHEN THE HERO GETS KILLED, WHEN THEY CRUCIFY THE MESSIAH ON THE HIGHEST HILL FOR ALL TO SEE...
"...IT'S A WARNING."

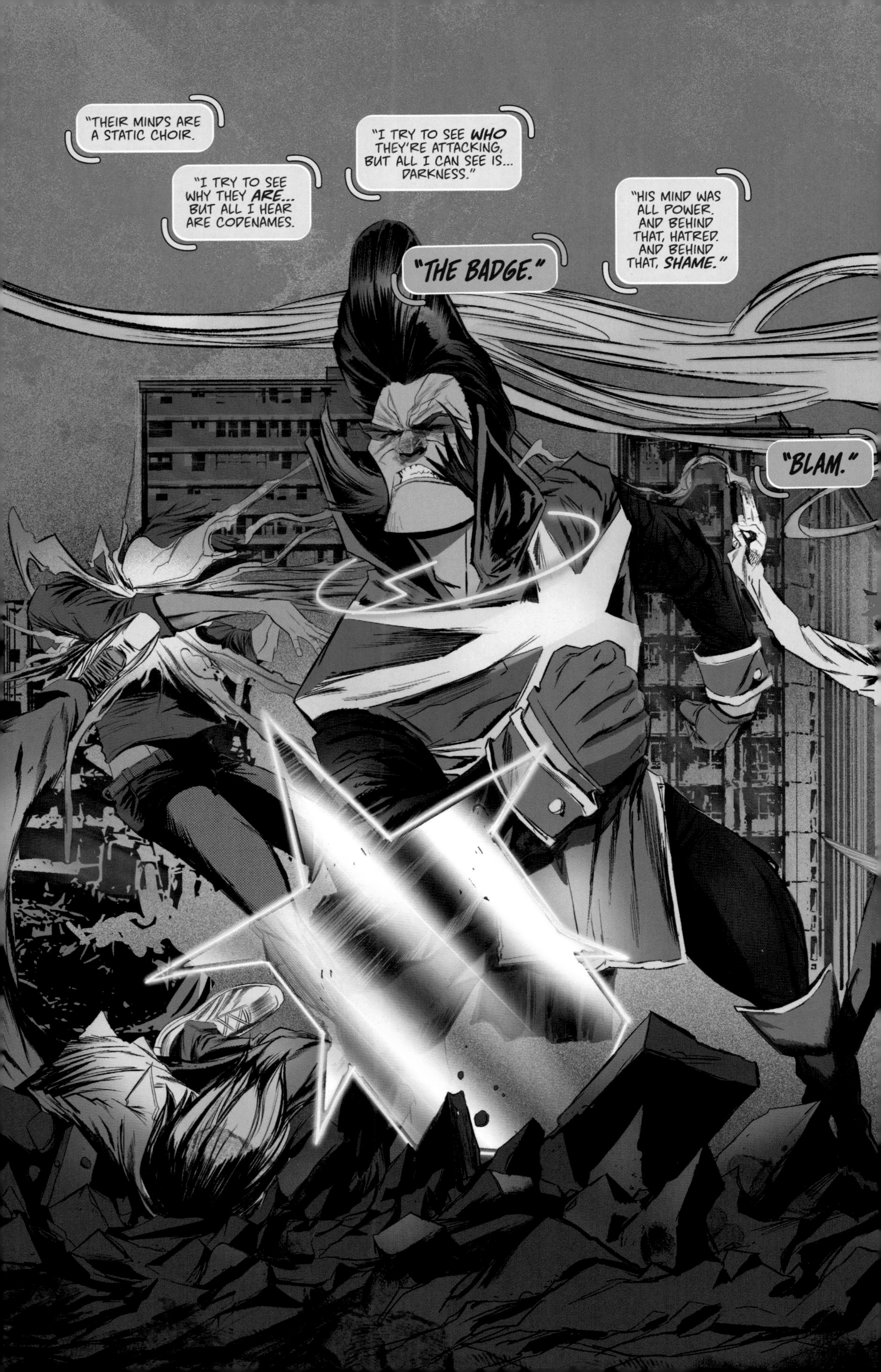
"THEIR MINDS ARE A STATIC CHOIR.
"I TRY TO SEE WHY THEY ARE... BUT ALL I HEAR ARE CODENAMES.
"I TRY TO SEE WHO THEY'RE ATTACKING, BUT ALL I CAN SEE IS... DARKNESS."
"THE BADGE."
"HIS MIND WAS ALL POWER. AND BEHIND THAT, HATRED. AND BEHIND THAT, SHAME."
"BLAM."

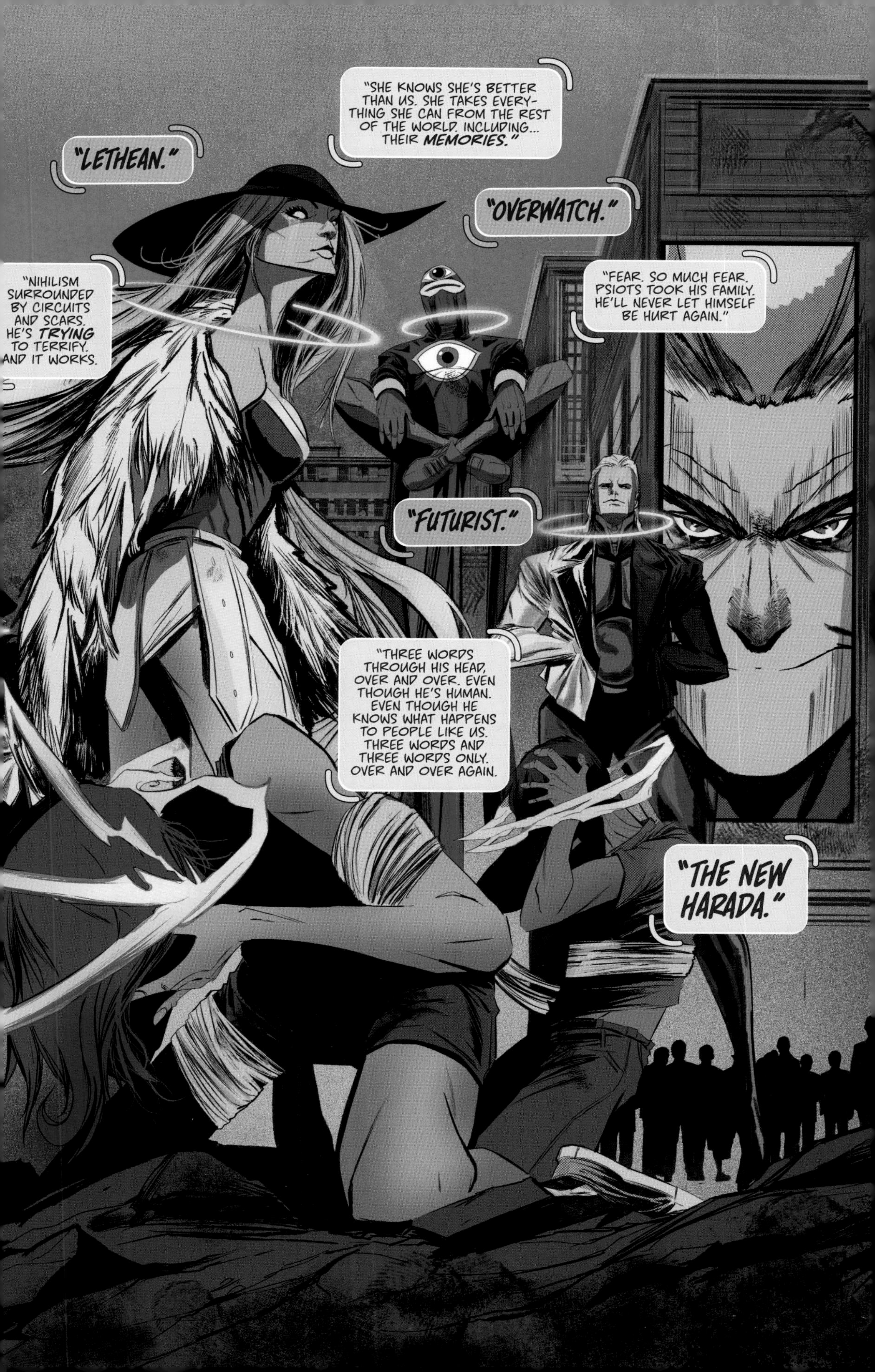
"LETHEAN."
"SHE KNOWS SHE'S BETTER THAN US. SHE TAKES EVERYTHING SHE CAN FROM THE REST OF THE WORLD. INCLUDING... THEIR MEMORIES."
"NIHILISM SURROUNDED BY CIRCUITS AND SCARS. HE'S TRYING TO TERRIFY. AND IT WORKS.
"OVERWATCH."
"FEAR. SO MUCH FEAR. PSIOTS TOOK HIS FAMILY. HE'LL NEVER LET HIMSELF BE HURT AGAIN."
"FUTURIST."
"THREE WORDS THROUGH HIS HEAD, OVER AND OVER. EVEN THOUGH HE'S HUMAN. EVEN THOUGH HE KNOWS WHAT HAPPENS TO PEOPLE LIKE US. THREE WORDS AND THREE WORDS ONLY. OVER AND OVER AGAIN.
"THE NEW HARADA."

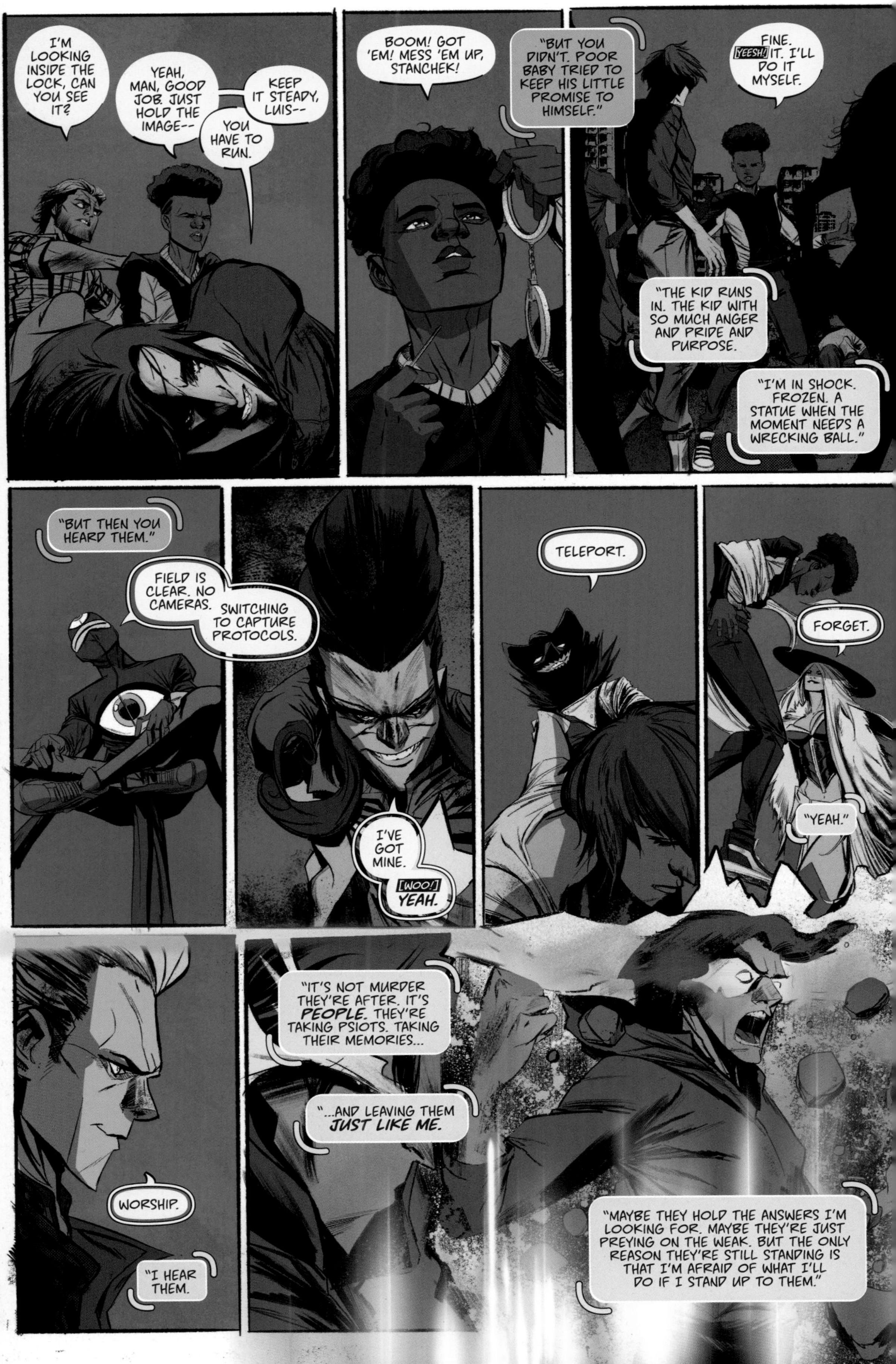
I'M LOOKING INSIDE THE LOCK, CAN YOU SEE IT?
YEAH, MAN, GOOD JOB. JUST HOLD THE IMAGE--
KEEP IT STEADY, LUIS--
YOU HAVE TO RUN.
BOOM! GOT 'EM! MESS 'EM UP, STANCHEK!
"BUT YOU DIDN'T. POOR BABY TRIED TO KEEP HIS LITTLE PROMISE TO HIMSELF."
FINE. YEESH! IT. I'LL DO IT MYSELF.
"THE KID RUNS IN. THE KID WITH SO MUCH ANGER AND PRIDE AND PURPOSE.
"I'M IN SHOCK. FROZEN. A STATUE WHEN THE MOMENT NEEDS A WRECKING BALL."
"BUT THEN YOU HEARD THEM."
FIELD IS CLEAR. NO CAMERAS.
SWITCHING TO CAPTURE PROTOCOLS.
I'VE GOT MINE.
WOO! YEAH.
TELEPORT.
FORGET.
"YEAH."
WORSHIP.
"I HEAR THEM.
"IT'S NOT MURDER THEY'RE AFTER. IT'S PEOPLE. THEY'RE TAKING PSIOTS. TAKING THEIR MEMORIES...
"...AND LEAVING THEM JUST LIKE ME.
"MAYBE THEY HOLD THE ANSWERS I'M LOOKING FOR. MAYBE THEY'RE JUST PREYING ON THE WEAK. BUT THE ONLY REASON THEY'RE STILL STANDING IS THAT I'M AFRAID OF WHAT I'LL DO IF I STAND UP TO THEM."

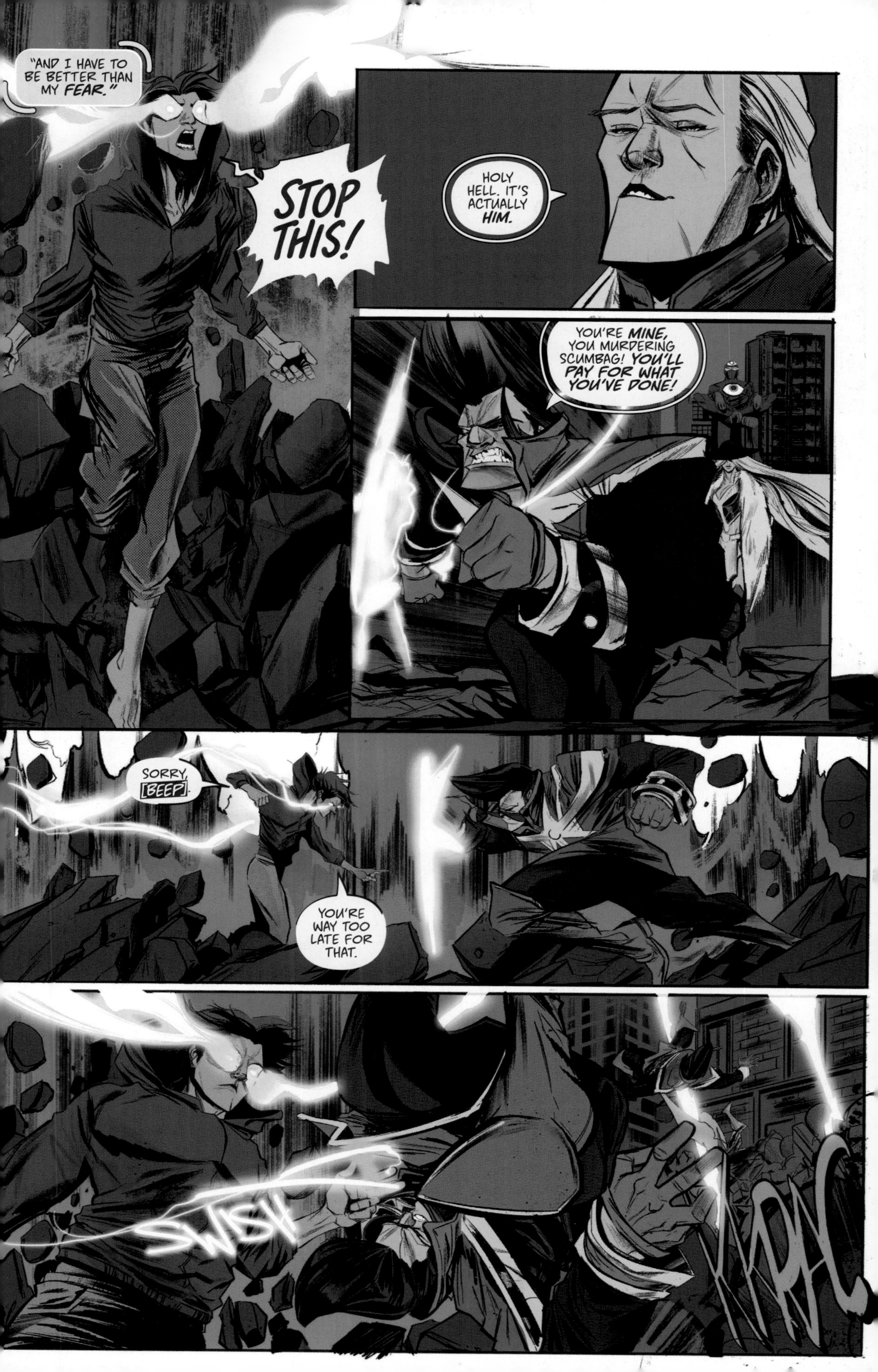
"AND I HAVE TO BE BETTER THAN MY FEAR."
STOP THIS!
HOLY HELL. IT'S ACTUALLY HIM.
YOU'RE MINE, YOU MURDERING SCUMBAG! YOU'LL PAY FOR WHAT YOU'VE DONE!
SORRY, [BEEP].
YOU'RE WAY TOO LATE FOR THAT.
SWISH

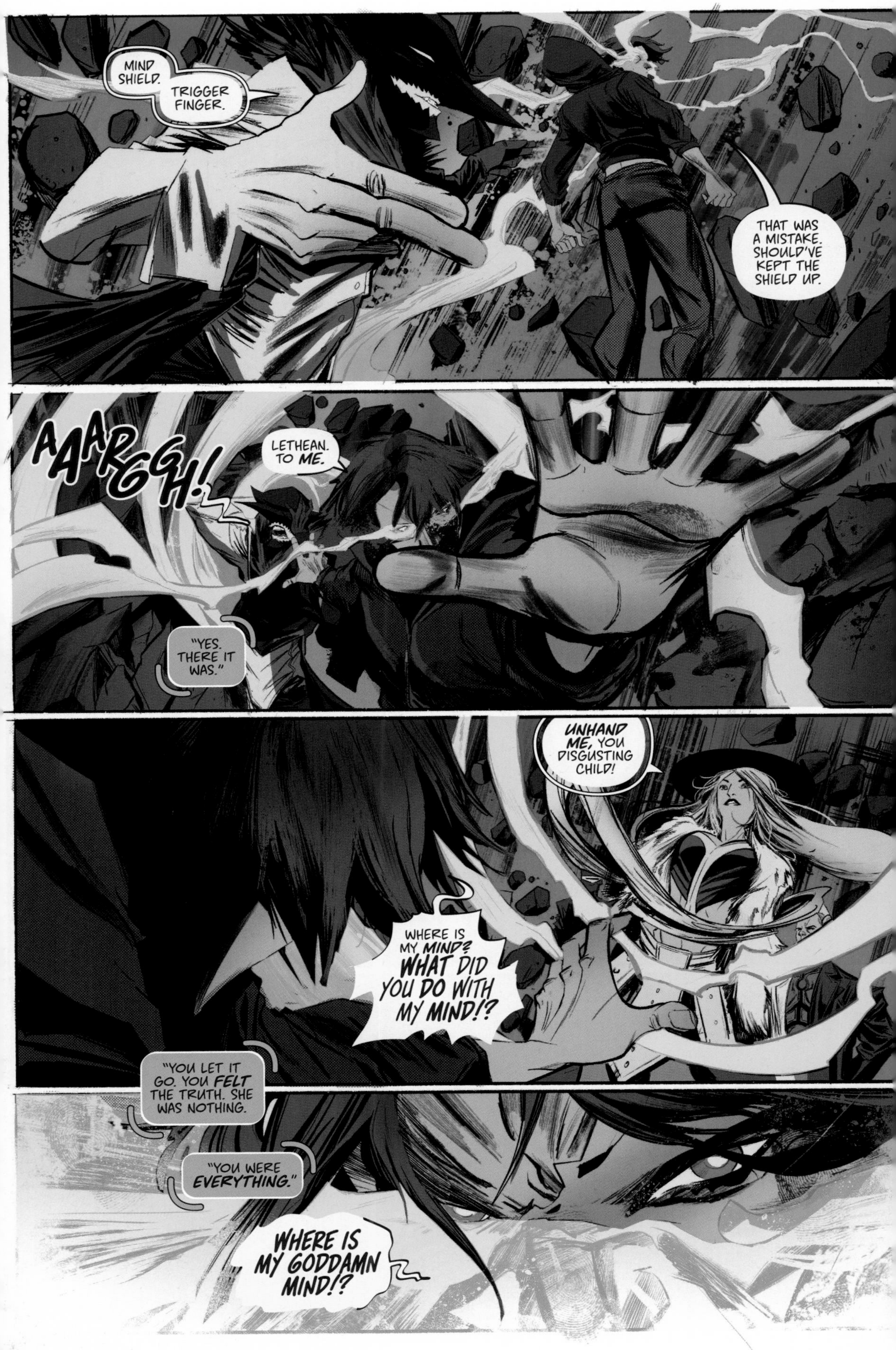
MIND SHIELD.
TRIGGER FINGER.
THAT WAS A MISTAKE. SHOULD'VE KEPT THE SHIELD UP.
AAARGGH!
LETHEAN. TO ME.
"YES. THERE IT WAS."
UNHAND ME, YOU DISGUSTING CHILD!
WHERE IS MY MIND? WHAT DID YOU DO WITH MY MIND!?
"YOU LET IT GO. YOU FELT THE TRUTH. SHE WAS NOTHING.
"YOU WERE EVERYTHING."
WHERE IS MY GODDAMN MIND!?

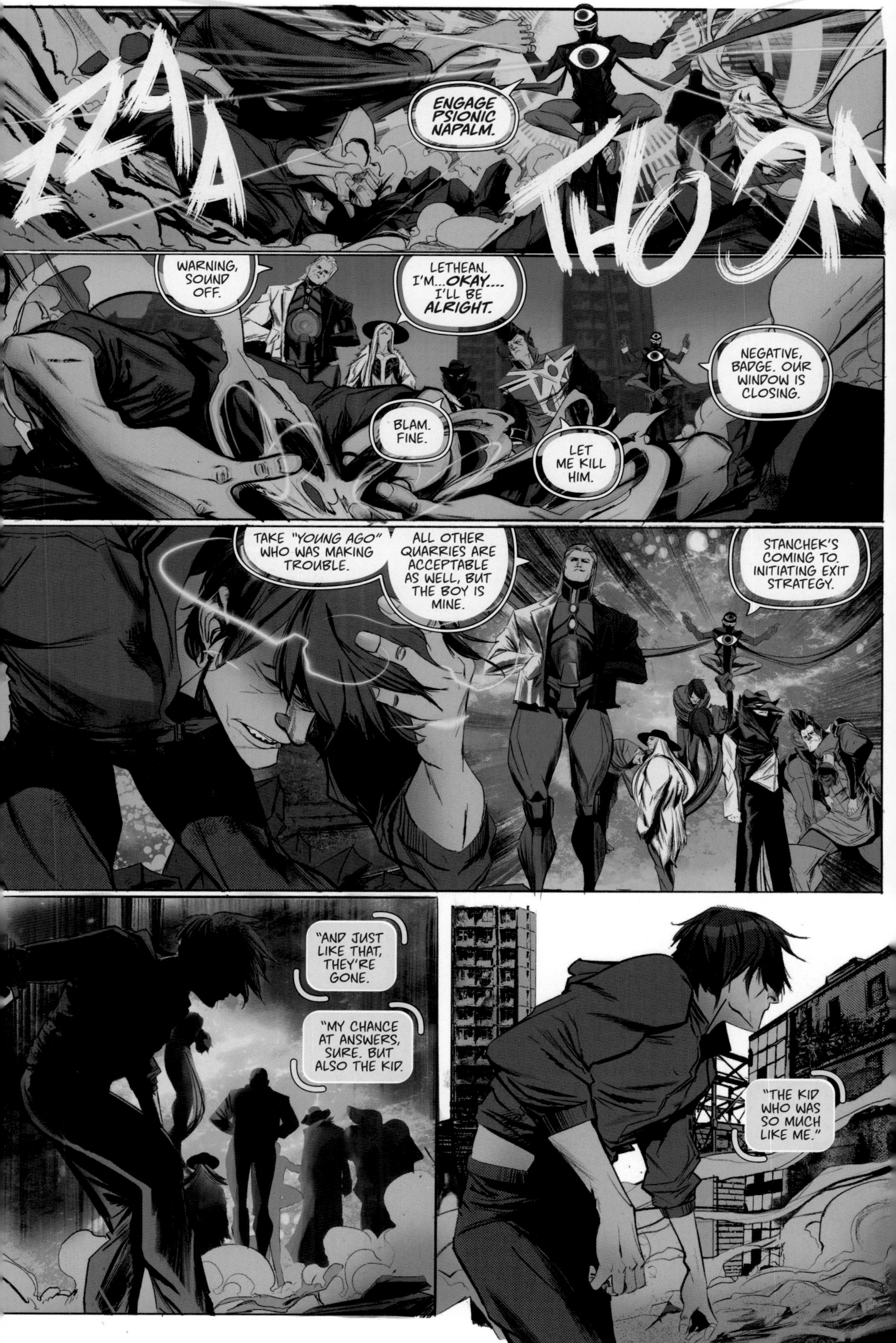
ENGAGE PSIONIC NAPALM.
ZZA ZZA
THOOM
WARNING, SOUND OFF.
LETHEAN. I'M...OKAY.... I'LL BE ALRIGHT.
NEGATIVE, BADGE. OUR WINDOW IS CLOSING.
BLAM. FINE.
LET ME KILL HIM.
TAKE "YOUNG AGO" WHO WAS MAKING TROUBLE.
ALL OTHER QUARRIES ARE ACCEPTABLE AS WELL, BUT THE BOY IS MINE.
STANCHEK'S COMING TO. INITIATING EXIT STRATEGY.
"AND JUST LIKE THAT, THEY'RE GONE.
"MY CHANCE AT ANSWERS, SURE. BUT ALSO THE KID.
"THE KID WHO WAS SO MUCH LIKE ME."

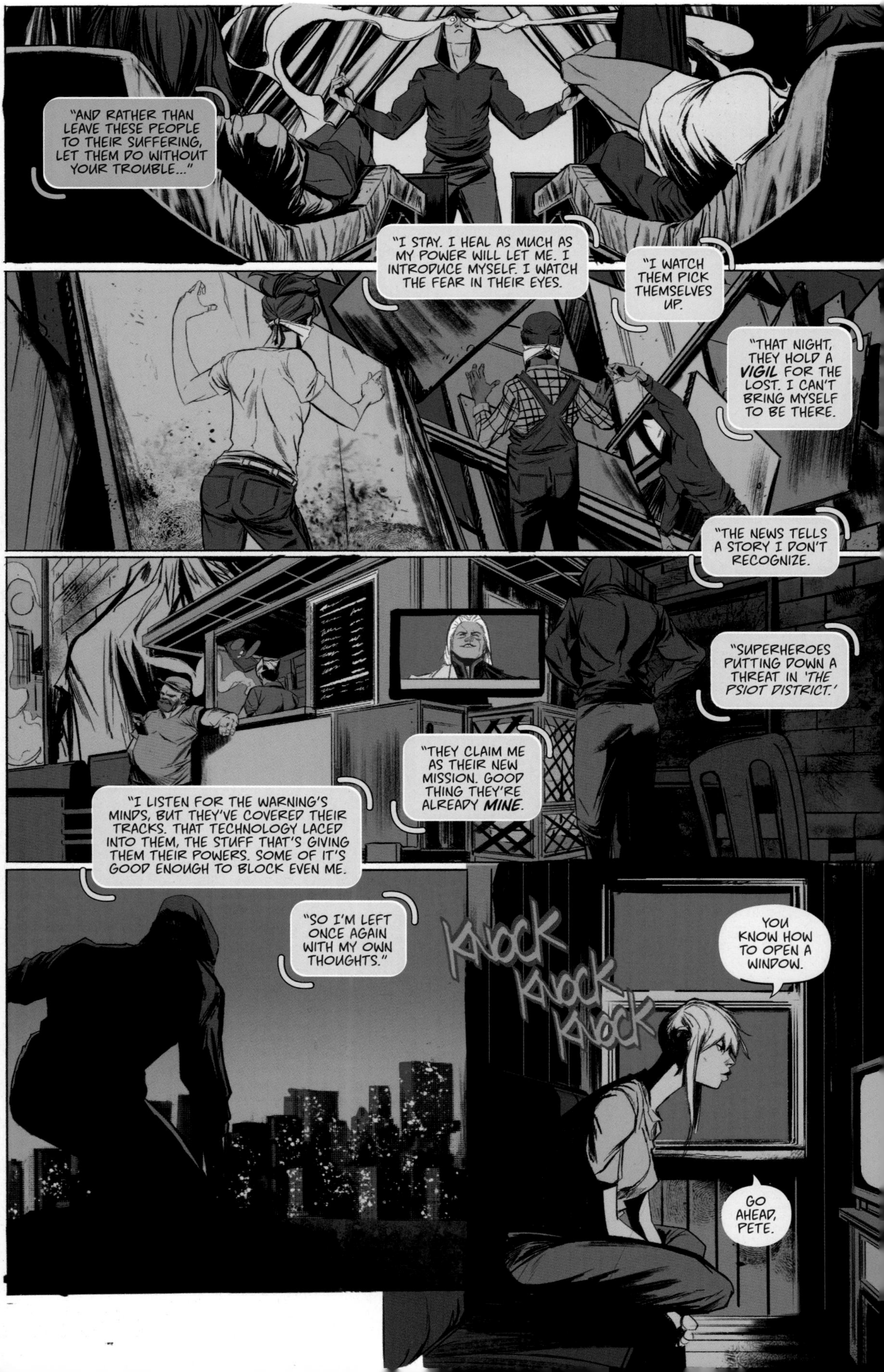
"AND RATHER THAN LEAVE THESE PEOPLE TO THEIR SUFFERING, LET THEM DO WITHOUT YOUR TROUBLE..."
"I STAY. I HEAL AS MUCH AS MY POWER WILL LET ME. I INTRODUCE MYSELF. I WATCH THE FEAR IN THEIR EYES.
"I WATCH THEM PICK THEMSELVES UP.
"THAT NIGHT, THEY HOLD A VIGIL FOR THE LOST. I CAN'T BRING MYSELF TO BE THERE.
"THE NEWS TELLS A STORY I DON'T RECOGNIZE.
"SUPERHEROES PUTTING DOWN A THREAT IN 'THE PSIOT DISTRICT.'
"THEY CLAIM ME AS THEIR NEW MISSION. GOOD THING THEY'RE ALREADY MINE.
"I LISTEN FOR THE WARNING'S MINDS, BUT THEY'VE COVERED THEIR TRACKS. THAT TECHNOLOGY LACED INTO THEM, THE STUFF THAT'S GIVING THEM THEIR POWERS. SOME OF IT'S GOOD ENOUGH TO BLOCK EVEN ME.
"SO I'M LEFT ONCE AGAIN WITH MY OWN THOUGHTS."
KNOCK KNOCK KNOCK
YOU KNOW HOW TO OPEN A WINDOW.
GO AHEAD, PETE.

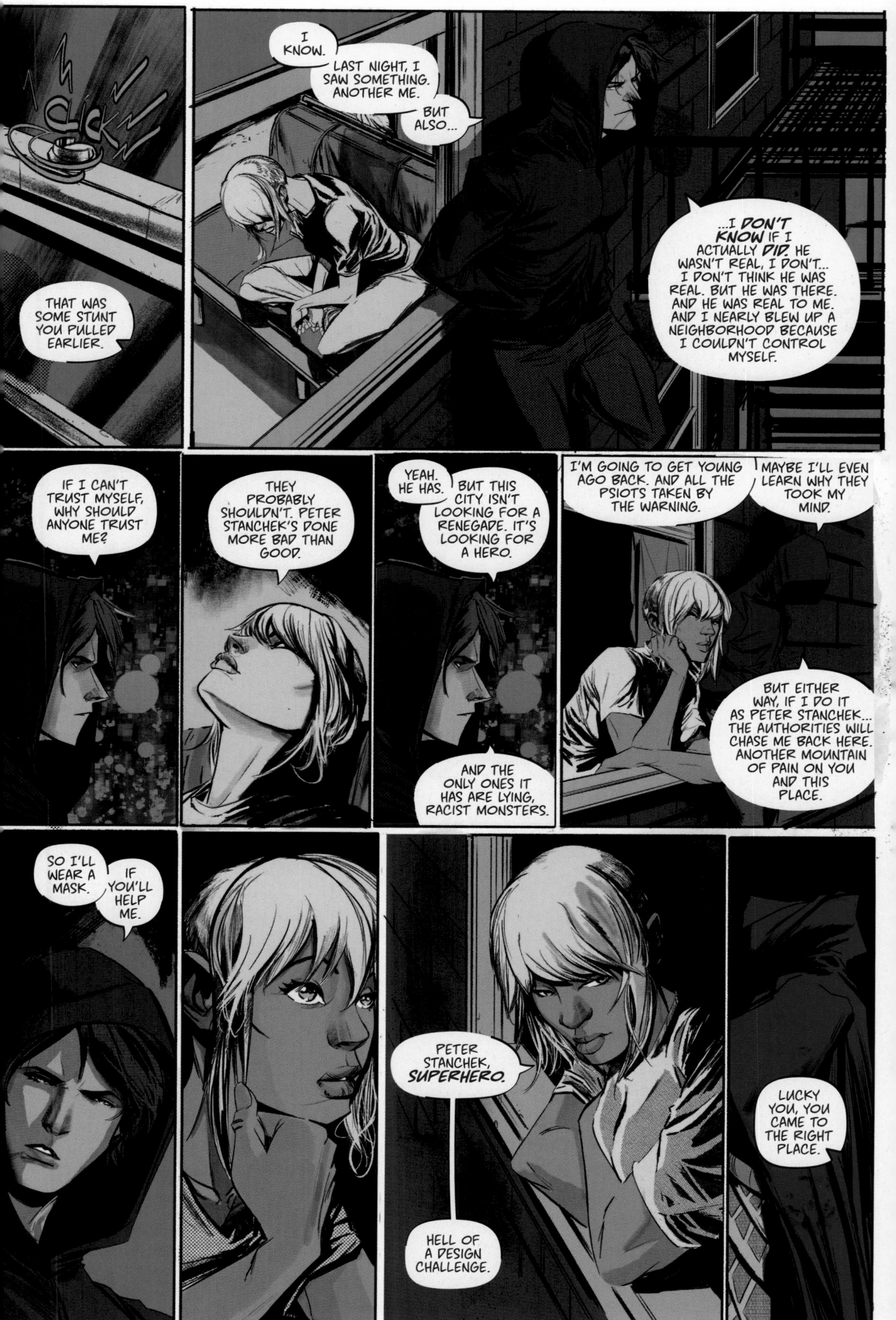
CLICK
THAT WAS SOME STUNT YOU PULLED EARLIER.
I KNOW.
LAST NIGHT, I SAW SOMETHING. ANOTHER ME.
BUT ALSO...
...I DON'T KNOW IF I ACTUALLY DID. HE WASN'T REAL, I DON'T... I DON'T THINK HE WAS REAL. BUT HE WAS THERE. AND HE WAS REAL TO ME. AND I NEARLY BLEW UP A NEIGHBORHOOD BECAUSE I COULDN'T CONTROL MYSELF.
IF I CAN'T TRUST MYSELF, WHY SHOULD ANYONE TRUST ME?
THEY PROBABLY SHOULDN'T. PETER STANCHEK'S DONE MORE BAD THAN GOOD.
YEAH. HE HAS.
BUT THIS CITY ISN'T LOOKING FOR A RENEGADE. IT'S LOOKING FOR A HERO.
AND THE ONLY ONES IT HAS ARE LYING, RACIST MONSTERS.
I'M GOING TO GET YOUNG AGO BACK. AND ALL THE PSIOTS TAKEN BY THE WARNING.
MAYBE I'LL EVEN LEARN WHY THEY TOOK MY MIND.
BUT EITHER WAY, IF I DO IT AS PETER STANCHEK... THE AUTHORITIES WILL CHASE ME BACK HERE. ANOTHER MOUNTAIN OF PAIN ON YOU AND THIS PLACE.
SO I'LL WEAR A MASK.
IF YOU'LL HELP ME.
PETER STANCHEK, SUPERHERO.
HELL OF A DESIGN CHALLENGE.
LUCKY YOU, YOU CAME TO THE RIGHT PLACE.

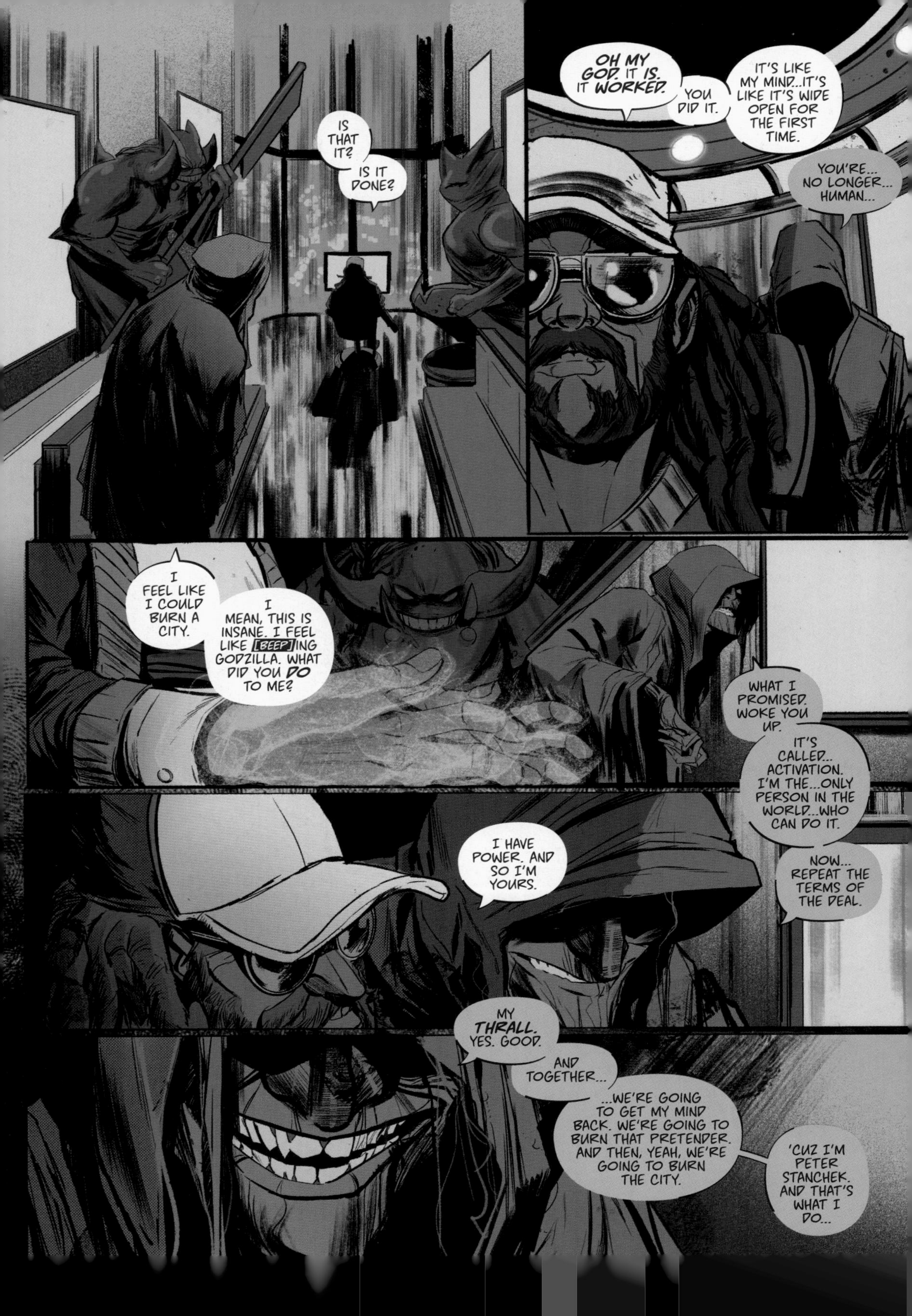
IS THAT IT?
IS IT DONE?
OH MY GOD. IT IS. IT WORKED.
YOU DID IT.
IT'S LIKE MY MIND...IT'S LIKE IT'S WIDE OPEN FOR THE FIRST TIME.
YOU'RE... NO LONGER... HUMAN...
I FEEL LIKE I COULD BURN A CITY.
I MEAN, THIS IS INSANE. I FEEL LIKE [BEEP]ING GODZILLA. WHAT DID YOU DO TO ME?
WHAT I PROMISED. WOKE YOU UP.
IT'S CALLED... ACTIVATION. I'M THE...ONLY PERSON IN THE WORLD...WHO CAN DO IT.
NOW... REPEAT THE TERMS OF THE DEAL.
I HAVE POWER. AND SO I'M YOURS.
MY THRALL. YES. GOOD.
AND TOGETHER...
...WE'RE GOING TO GET MY MIND BACK. WE'RE GOING TO BURN THAT PRETENDER. AND THEN, YEAH, WE'RE GOING TO BURN THE CITY.
'CUZ I'M PETER STANCHEK. AND THAT'S WHAT I DO...

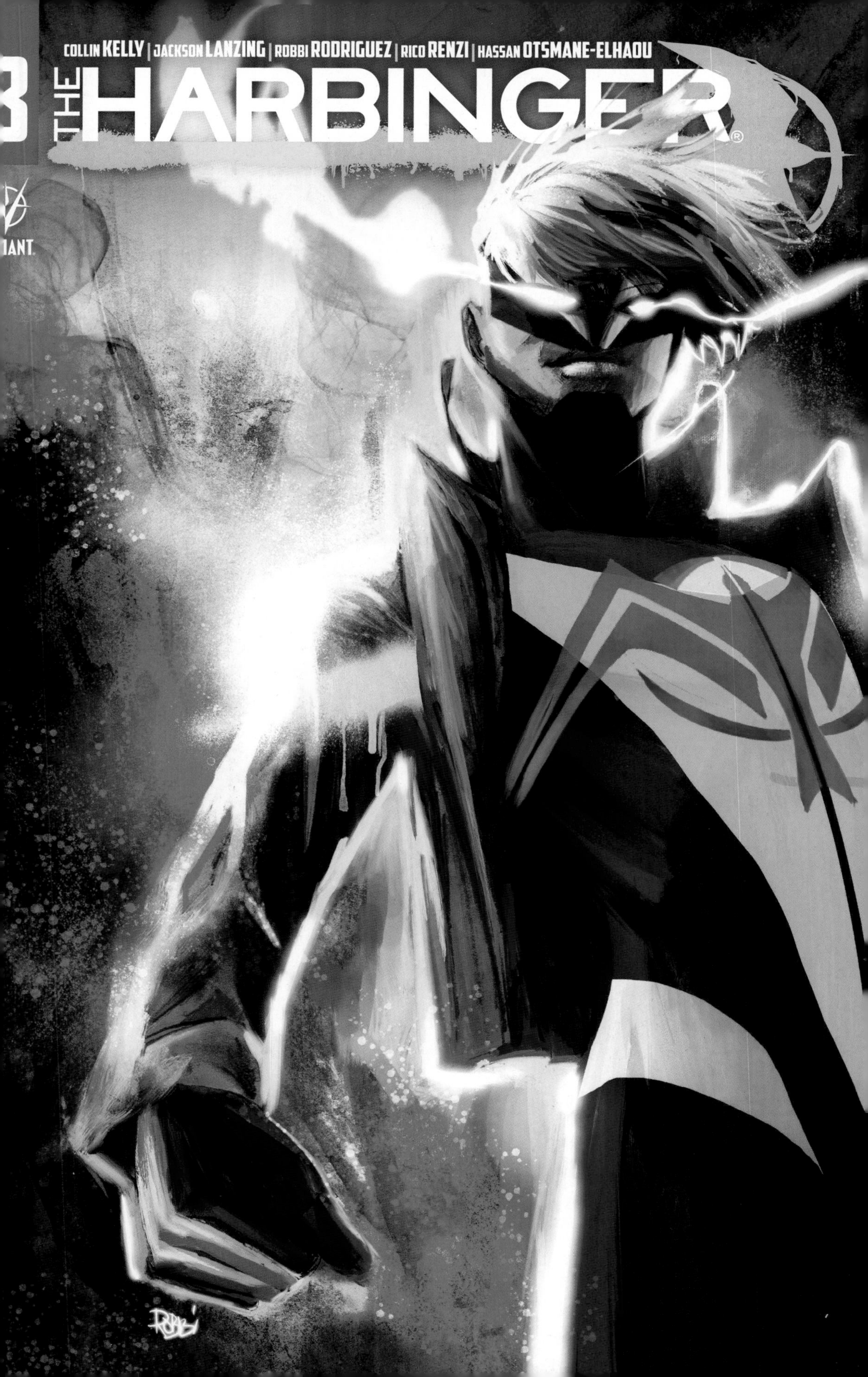
COLLIN KELLY | JACKSON LANZING | ROBBI RODRIGUEZ | RICO RENZI | HASSAN OTSMANE-ELHAOU
3
THE HARBINGER®
VALIANT.
ROBBI

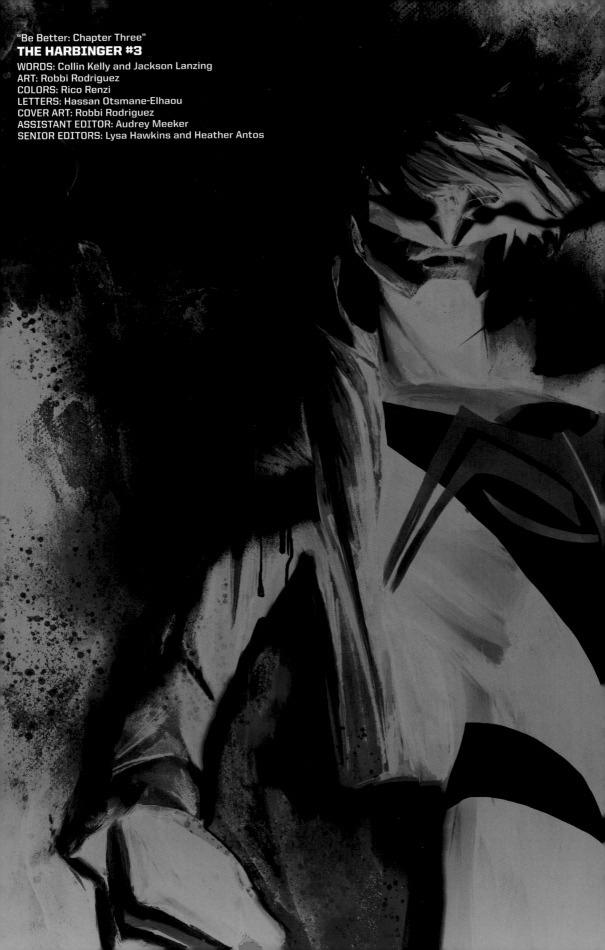

"Be Better: Chapter Three"
THE HARBINGER #3
WORDS: Collin Kelly and Jackson Lanzing
ART: Robbi Rodriguez
COLORS: Rico Renzi
LETTERS: Hassan Otsmane-Elhaou
COVER ART: Robbi Rodriguez
ASSISTANT EDITOR: Audrey Meeker
SENIOR EDITORS: Lysa Hawkins and Heather Antos

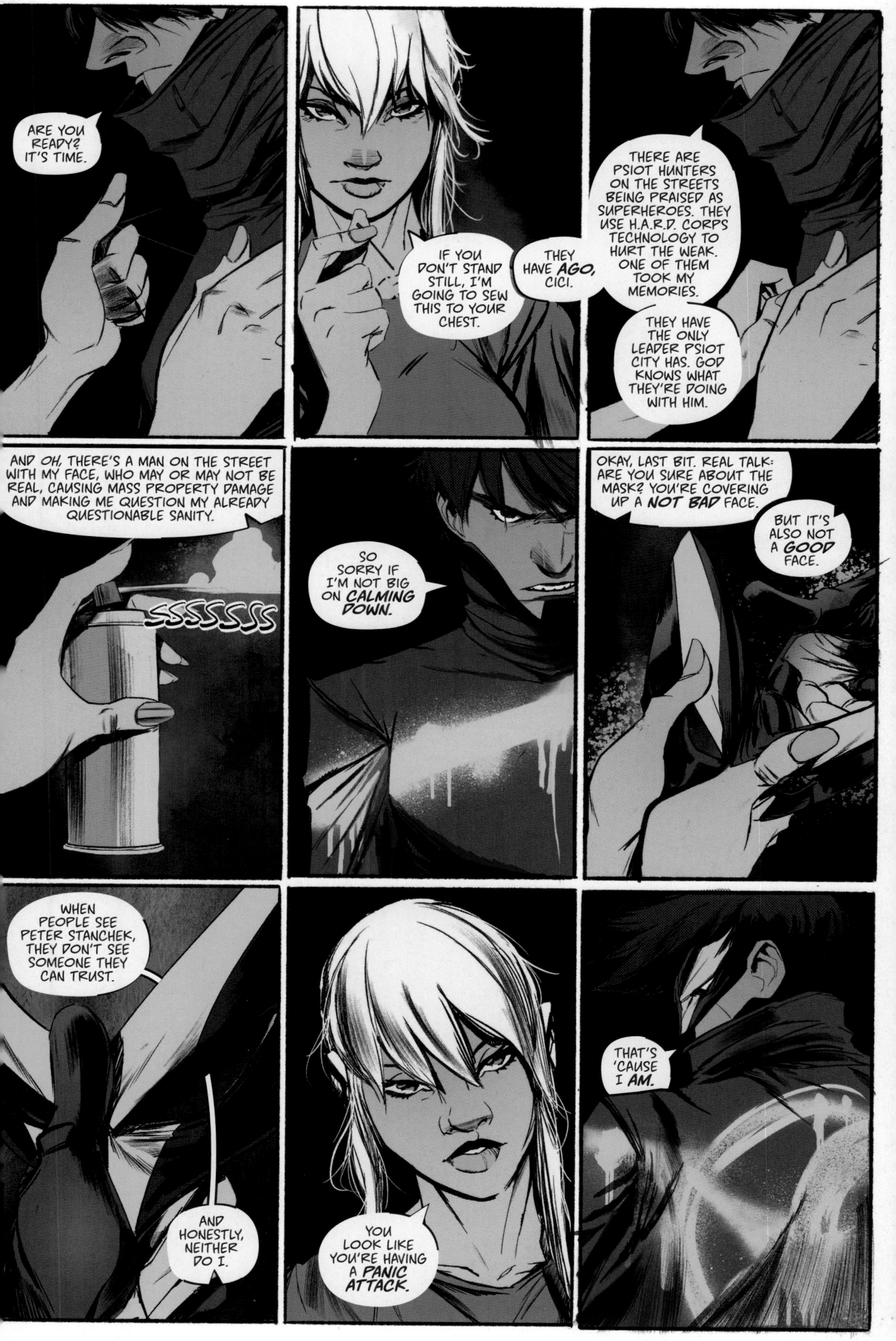
ARE YOU READY? IT'S TIME.
IF YOU DON'T STAND STILL, I'M GOING TO SEW THIS TO YOUR CHEST.
THEY HAVE AGO, CICI.
THERE ARE PSIOT HUNTERS ON THE STREETS BEING PRAISED AS SUPERHEROES. THEY USE H.A.R.D. CORPS TECHNOLOGY TO HURT THE WEAK. ONE OF THEM TOOK MY MEMORIES.
THEY HAVE THE ONLY LEADER PSIOT CITY HAS. GOD KNOWS WHAT THEY'RE DOING WITH HIM.
AND OH, THERE'S A MAN ON THE STREET WITH MY FACE, WHO MAY OR MAY NOT BE REAL, CAUSING MASS PROPERTY DAMAGE AND MAKING ME QUESTION MY ALREADY QUESTIONABLE SANITY.
SSSSSSS
SO SORRY IF I'M NOT BIG ON CALMING DOWN.
OKAY, LAST BIT. REAL TALK: ARE YOU SURE ABOUT THE MASK? YOU'RE COVERING UP A NOT BAD FACE.
BUT IT'S ALSO NOT A GOOD FACE.
WHEN PEOPLE SEE PETER STANCHEK, THEY DON'T SEE SOMEONE THEY CAN TRUST.
AND HONESTLY, NEITHER DO I.
YOU LOOK LIKE YOU'RE HAVING A PANIC ATTACK.
THAT'S 'CAUSE I AM.

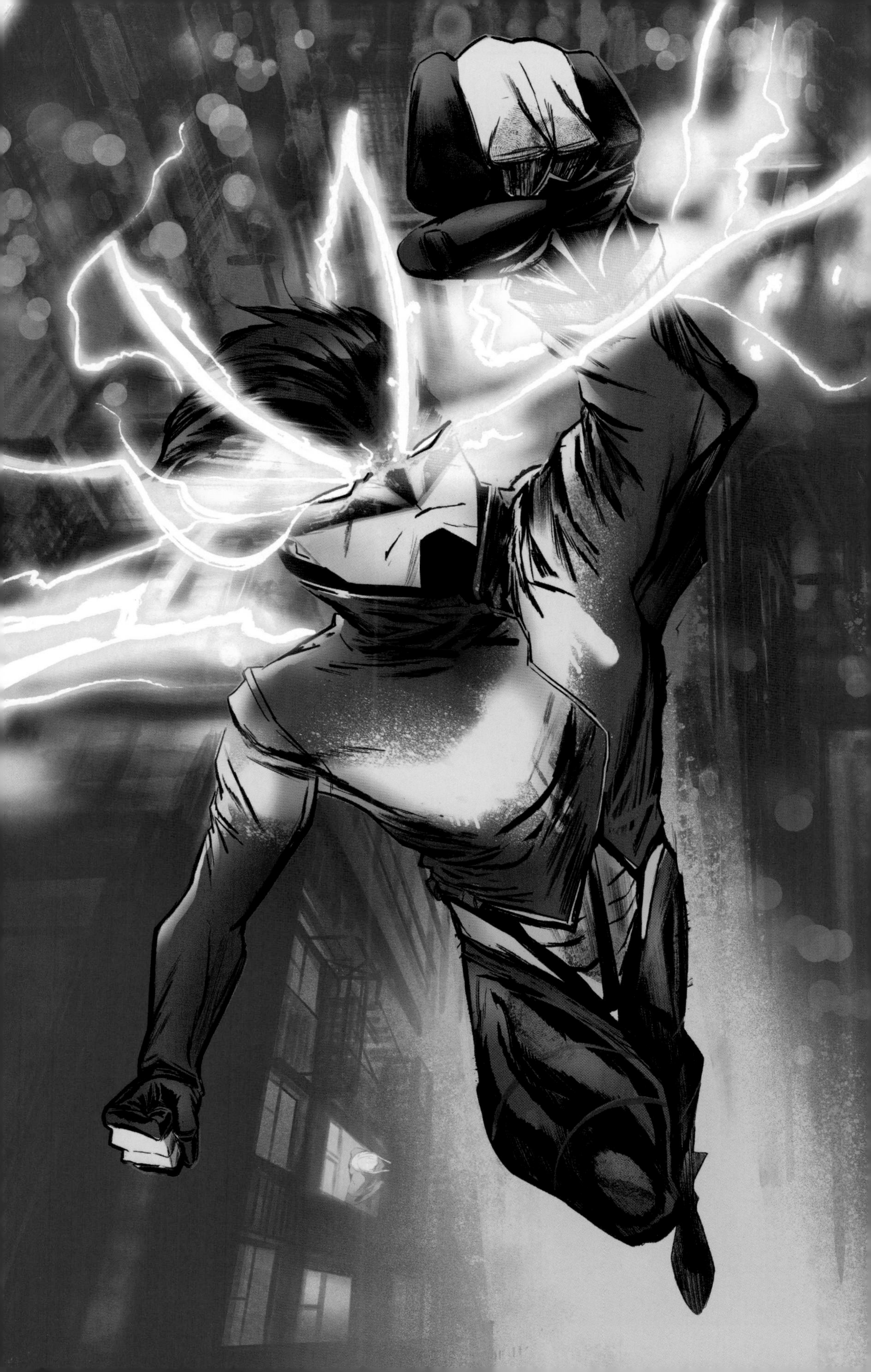

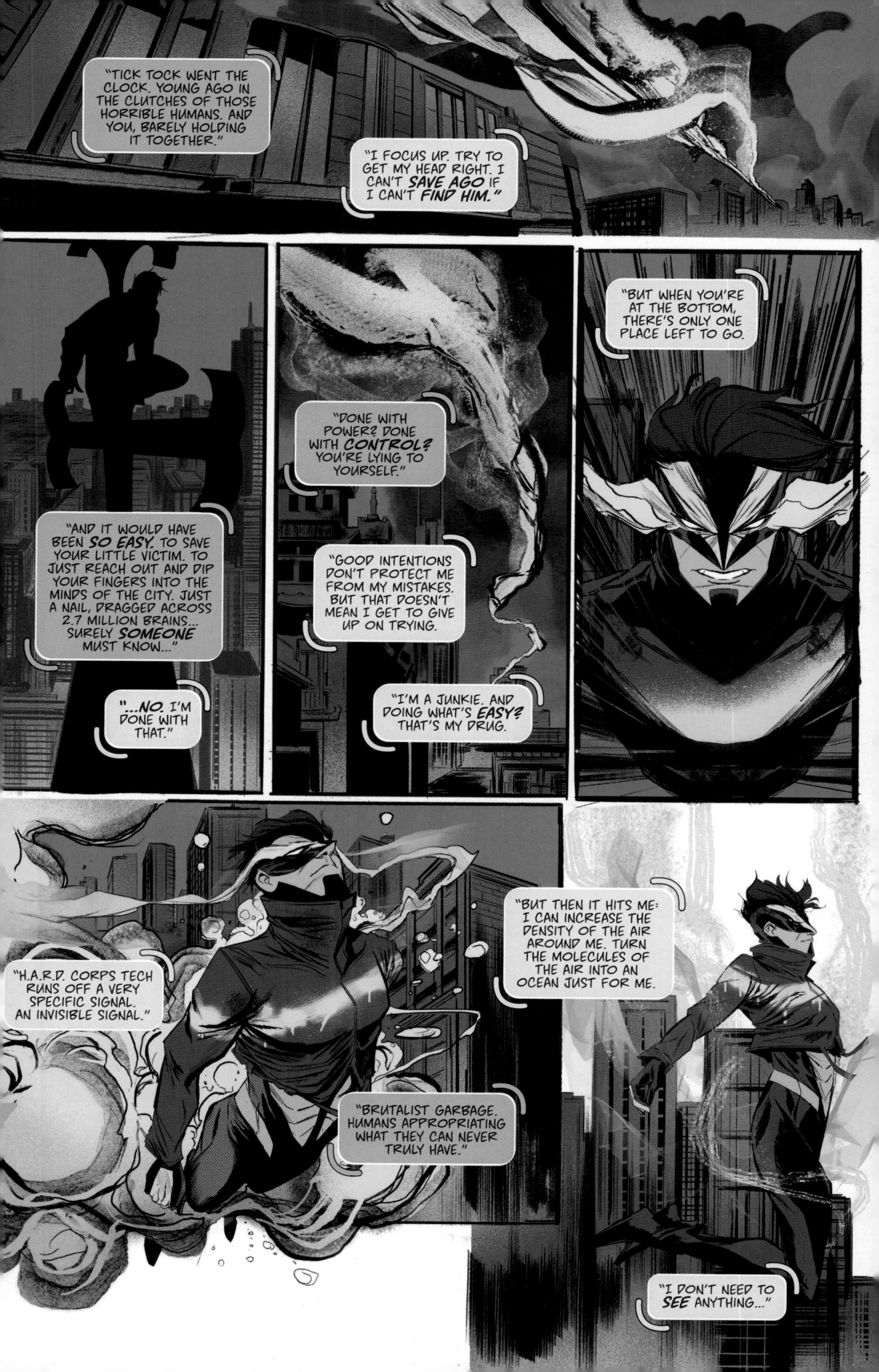
"TICK TOCK WENT THE CLOCK. YOUNG AGO IN THE CLUTCHES OF THOSE HORRIBLE HUMANS. AND YOU, BARELY HOLDING IT TOGETHER."
"I FOCUS UP. TRY TO GET MY HEAD RIGHT. I CAN'T SAVE AGO IF I CAN'T FIND HIM."
"AND IT WOULD HAVE BEEN SO EASY. TO SAVE YOUR LITTLE VICTIM. TO JUST REACH OUT AND DIP YOUR FINGERS INTO THE MINDS OF THE CITY. JUST A NAIL, DRAGGED ACROSS 2.7 MILLION BRAINS... SURELY SOMEONE MUST KNOW..."
"...NO. I'M DONE WITH THAT."
"DONE WITH POWER? DONE WITH CONTROL? YOU'RE LYING TO YOURSELF."
"GOOD INTENTIONS DON'T PROTECT ME FROM MY MISTAKES. BUT THAT DOESN'T MEAN I GET TO GIVE UP ON TRYING.
"I'M A JUNKIE. AND DOING WHAT'S EASY? THAT'S MY DRUG.
"BUT WHEN YOU'RE AT THE BOTTOM, THERE'S ONLY ONE PLACE LEFT TO GO.
"H.A.R.D. CORPS TECH RUNS OFF A VERY SPECIFIC SIGNAL. AN INVISIBLE SIGNAL."
"BRUTALIST GARBAGE. HUMANS APPROPRIATING WHAT THEY CAN NEVER TRULY HAVE."
"BUT THEN IT HITS ME: I CAN INCREASE THE DENSITY OF THE AIR AROUND ME. TURN THE MOLECULES OF THE AIR INTO AN OCEAN JUST FOR ME.
"I DON'T NEED TO SEE ANYTHING..."

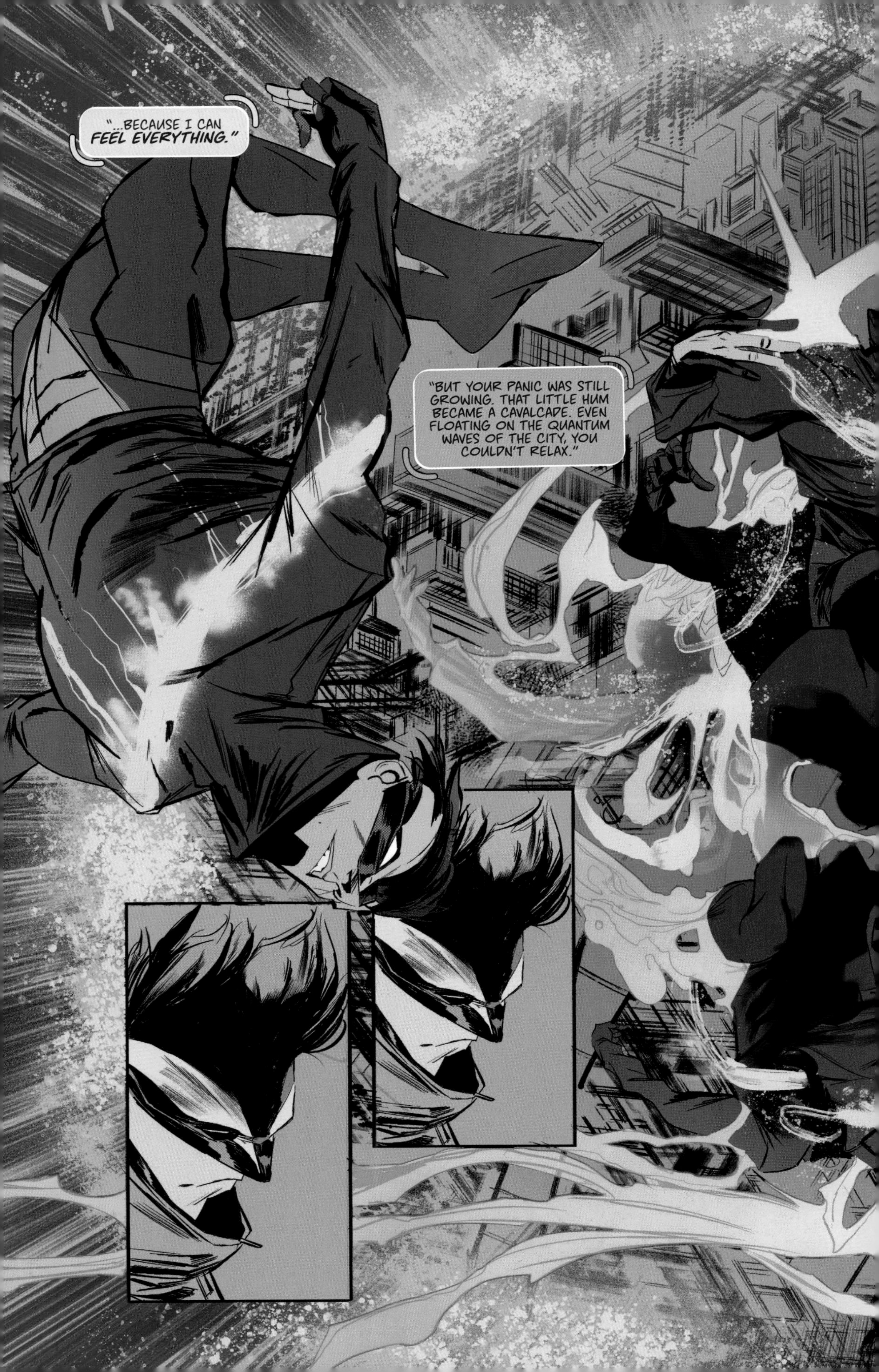
"...BECAUSE I CAN FEEL EVERYTHING."
"BUT YOUR PANIC WAS STILL GROWING. THAT LITTLE HUM BECAME A CAVALCADE. EVEN FLOATING ON THE QUANTUM WAVES OF THE CITY, YOU COULDN'T RELAX."

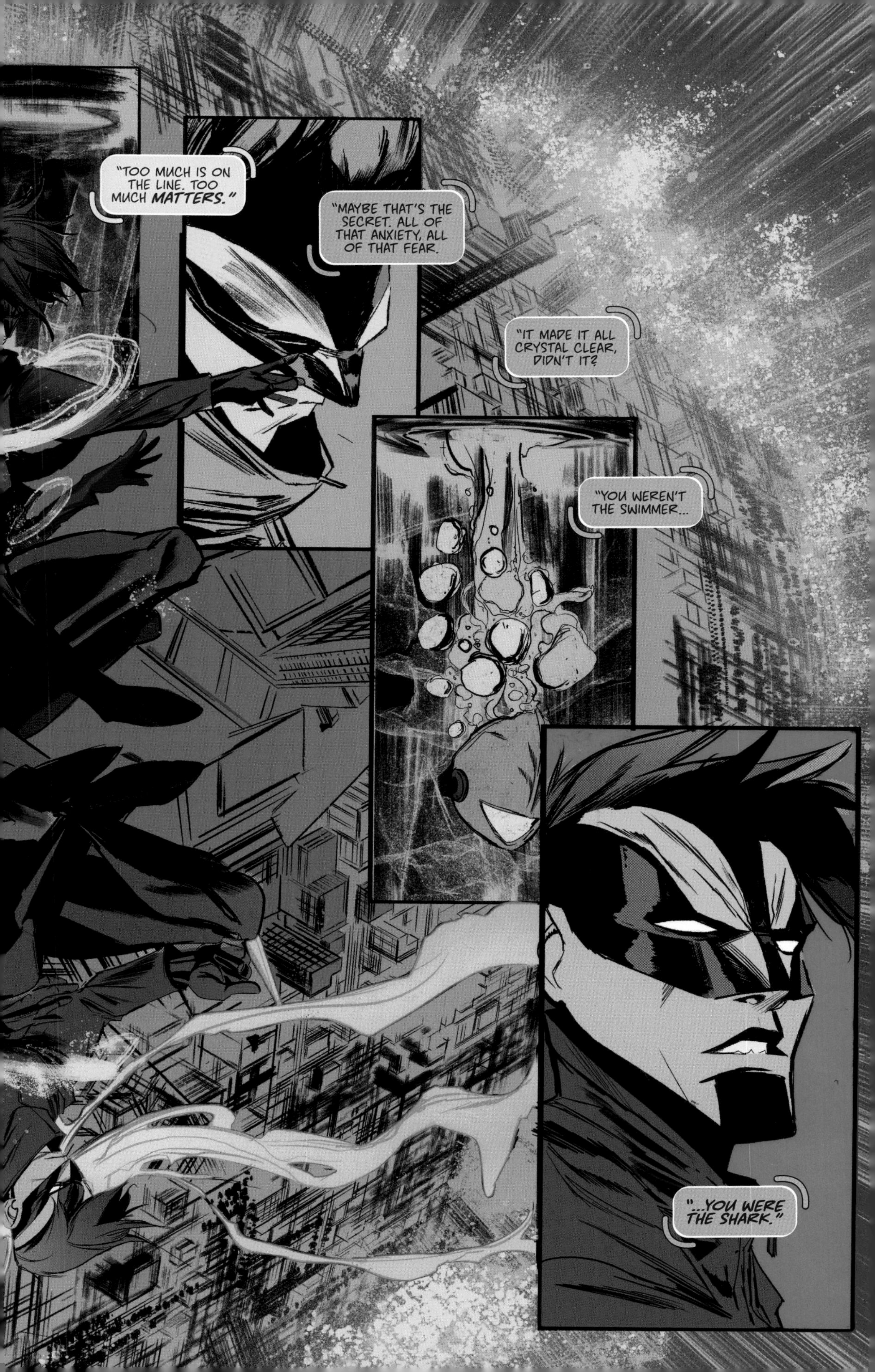
"TOO MUCH IS ON THE LINE. TOO MUCH MATTERS."
"MAYBE THAT'S THE SECRET. ALL OF THAT ANXIETY, ALL OF THAT FEAR.
"IT MADE IT ALL CRYSTAL CLEAR, DIDN'T IT?
"YOU WEREN'T THE SWIMMER...
"...YOU WERE THE SHARK."

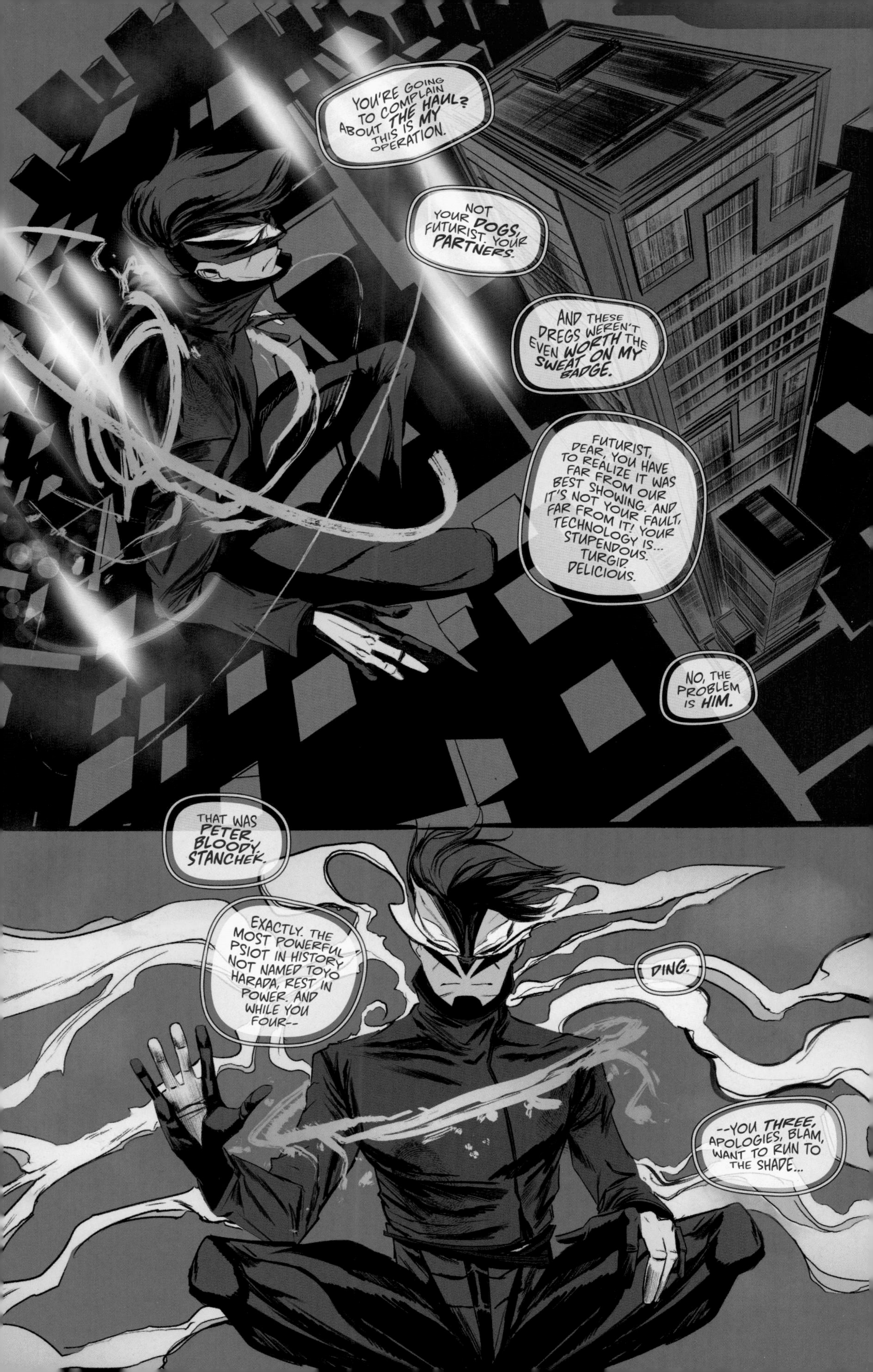
YOU'RE GOING TO COMPLAIN ABOUT THE HAUL? THIS IS MY OPERATION.
NOT YOUR DOGS, FUTURIST. YOUR PARTNERS.
AND THESE DREGS WEREN'T EVEN WORTH THE SWEAT ON MY BADGE.
FUTURIST, DEAR, YOU HAVE TO REALIZE IT WAS FAR FROM OUR BEST SHOWING. AND IT'S NOT YOUR FAULT, FAR FROM IT! YOUR TECHNOLOGY IS... STUPENDOUS. TURGID. DELICIOUS.
NO, THE PROBLEM IS HIM.
THAT WAS PETER. BLOODY. STANCHEK.
EXACTLY. THE MOST POWERFUL PSIOT IN HISTORY NOT NAMED TOYO HARADA, REST IN POWER. AND WHILE YOU FOUR--
DING.
--YOU THREE, APOLOGIES, BLAM, WANT TO RUN TO THE SHADE...

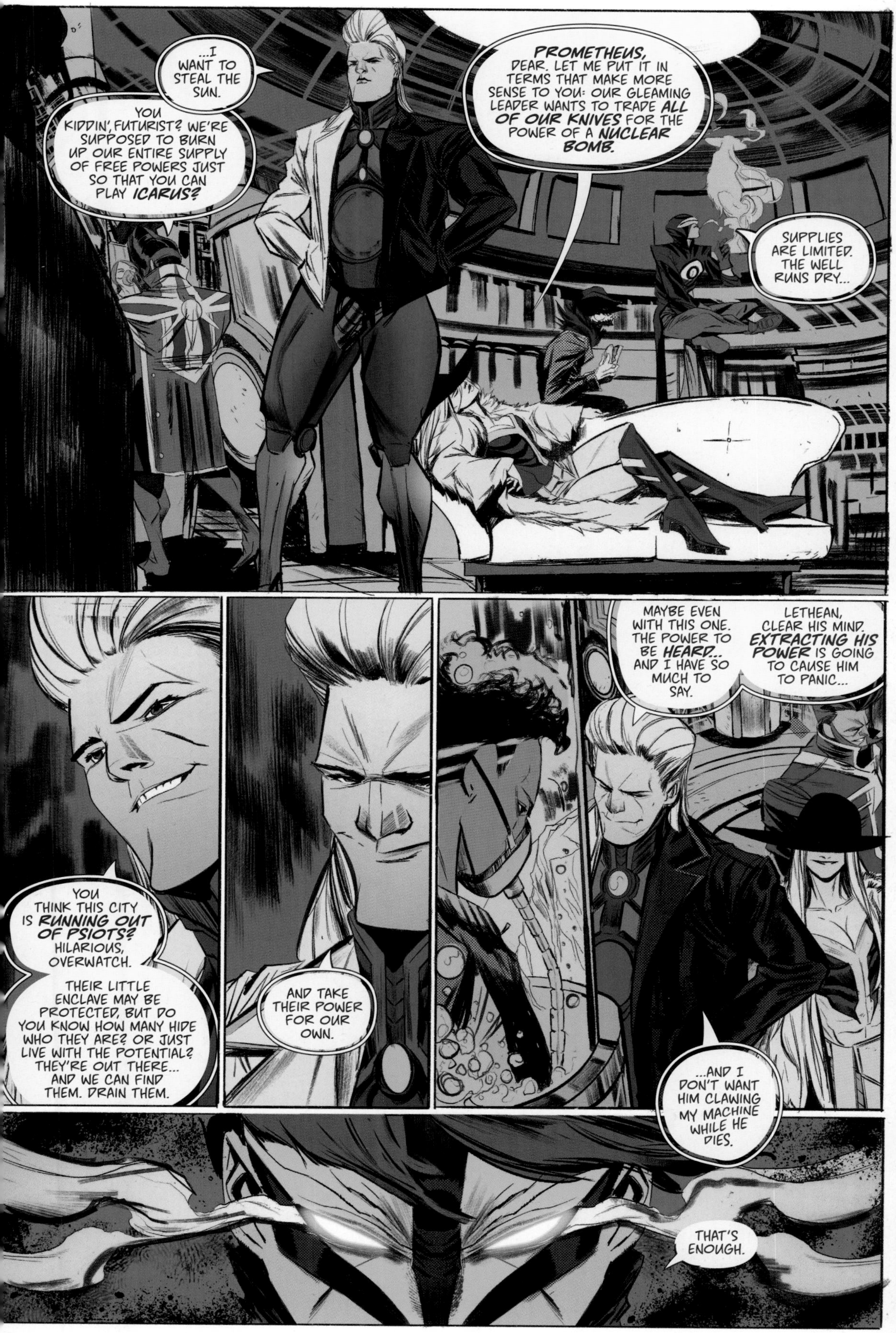
...I WANT TO STEAL THE SUN.
YOU KIDDIN', FUTURIST? WE'RE SUPPOSED TO BURN UP OUR ENTIRE SUPPLY OF FREE POWERS JUST SO THAT YOU CAN PLAY ICARUS?
PROMETHEUS, DEAR. LET ME PUT IT IN TERMS THAT MAKE MORE SENSE TO YOU: OUR GLEAMING LEADER WANTS TO TRADE ALL OF OUR KNIVES FOR THE POWER OF A NUCLEAR BOMB.
SUPPLIES ARE LIMITED. THE WELL RUNS DRY...
YOU THINK THIS CITY IS RUNNING OUT OF PSIOTS? HILARIOUS, OVERWATCH.
THEIR LITTLE ENCLAVE MAY BE PROTECTED, BUT DO YOU KNOW HOW MANY HIDE WHO THEY ARE? OR JUST LIVE WITH THE POTENTIAL? THEY'RE OUT THERE... AND WE CAN FIND THEM. DRAIN THEM.
AND TAKE THEIR POWER FOR OUR OWN.
MAYBE EVEN WITH THIS ONE. THE POWER TO BE HEARD... AND I HAVE SO MUCH TO SAY.
LETHEAN, CLEAR HIS MIND. EXTRACTING HIS POWER IS GOING TO CAUSE HIM TO PANIC...
...AND I DON'T WANT HIM CLAWING MY MACHINE WHILE HE DIES.
THAT'S ENOUGH.

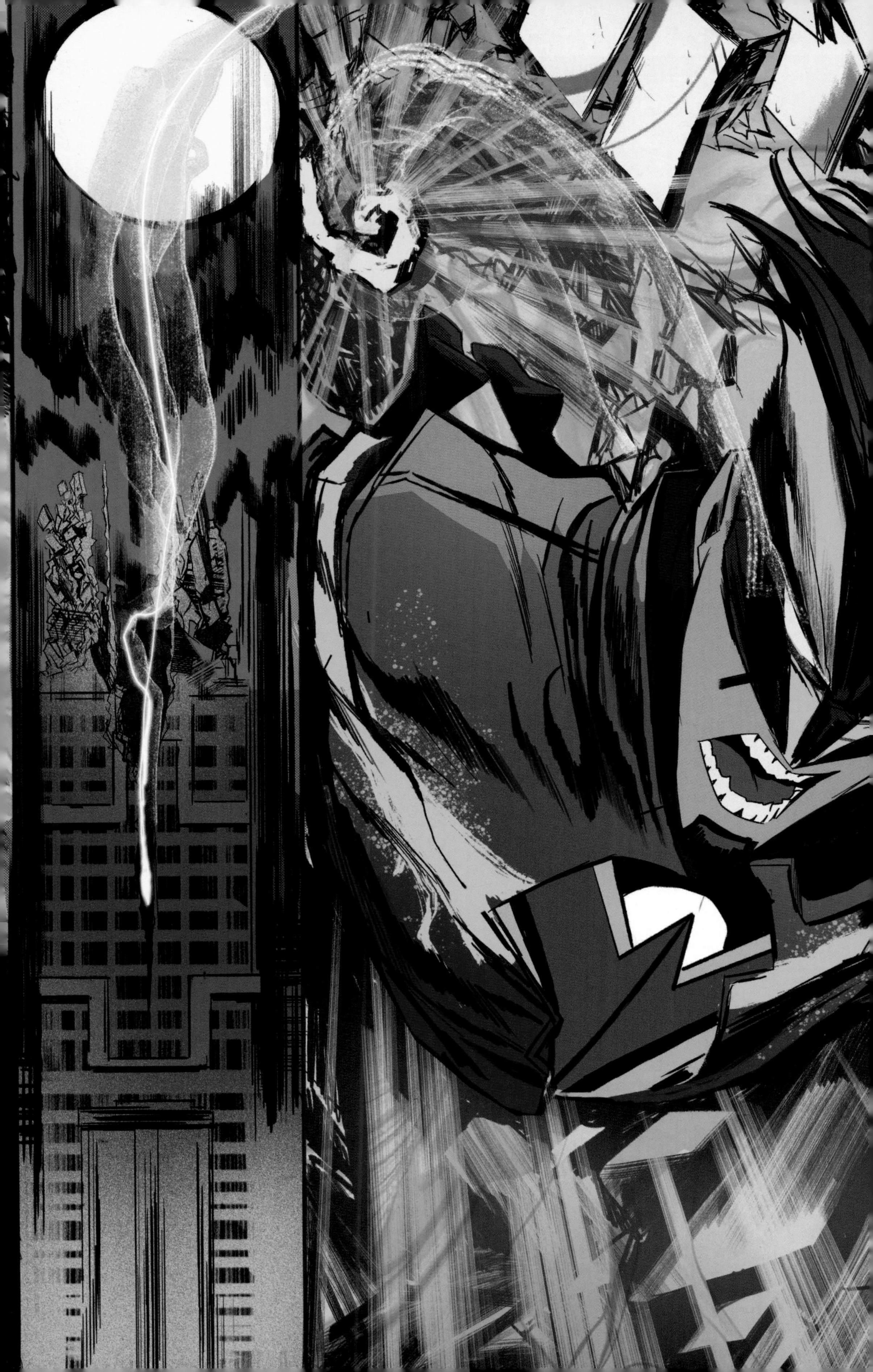

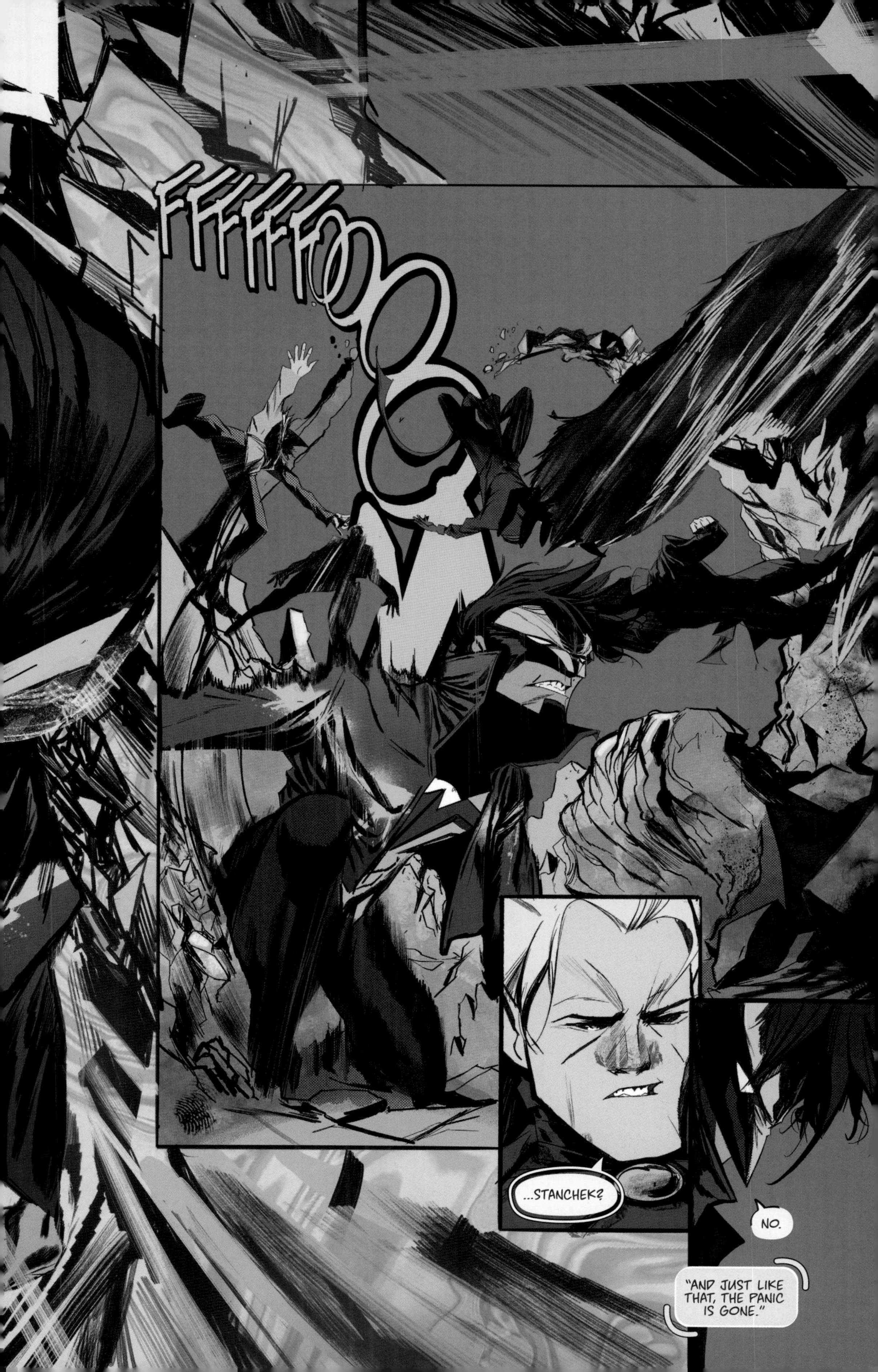
FFFFFOOO
...STANCHEK?
NO.
"AND JUST LIKE THAT, THE PANIC IS GONE."

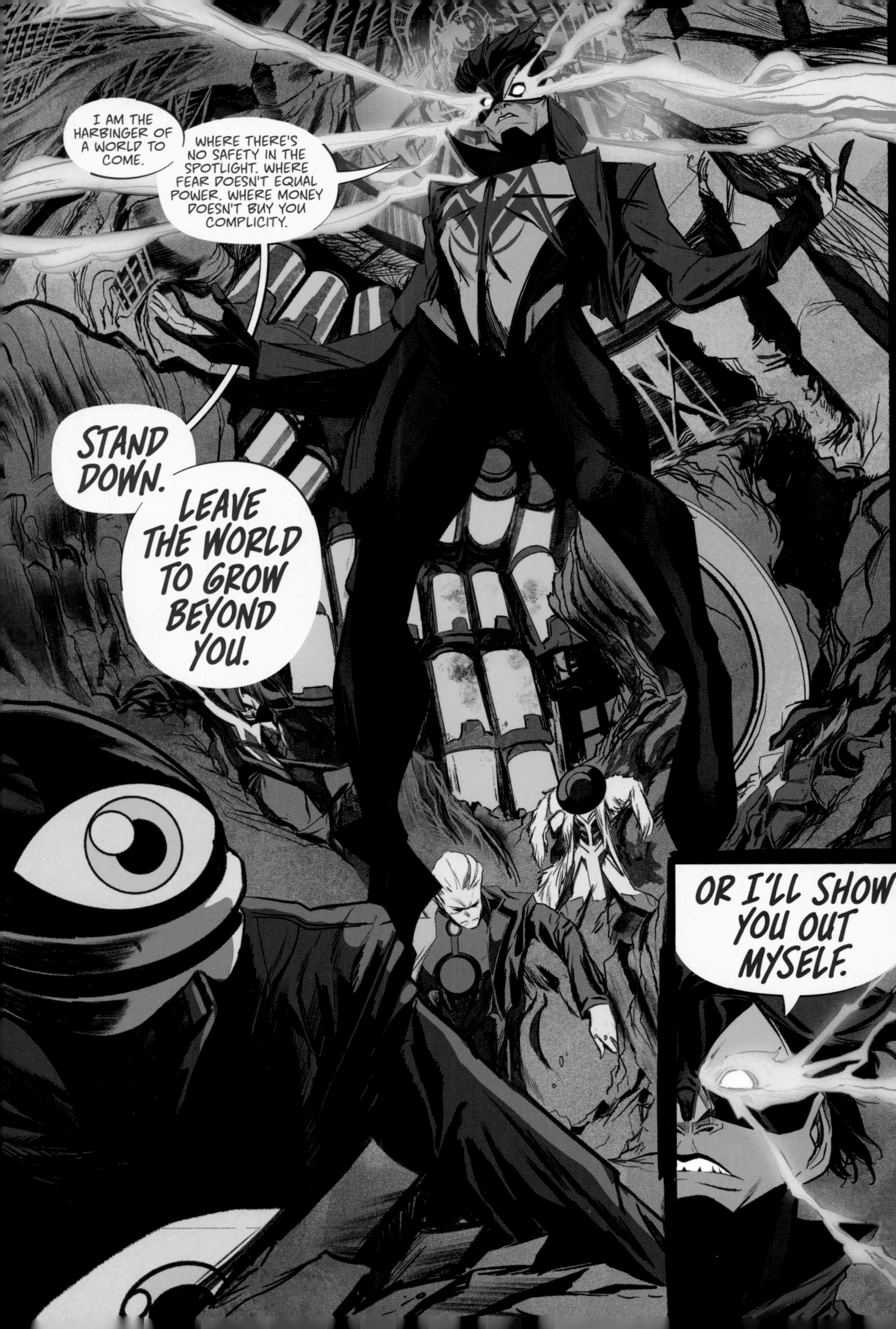
I AM THE HARBINGER OF A WORLD TO COME.
WHERE THERE'S NO SAFETY IN THE SPOTLIGHT. WHERE FEAR DOESN'T EQUAL POWER. WHERE MONEY DOESN'T BUY YOU COMPLICITY.
STAND DOWN.
LEAVE THE WORLD TO GROW BEYOND YOU.
OR I'LL SHOW YOU OUT MYSELF.

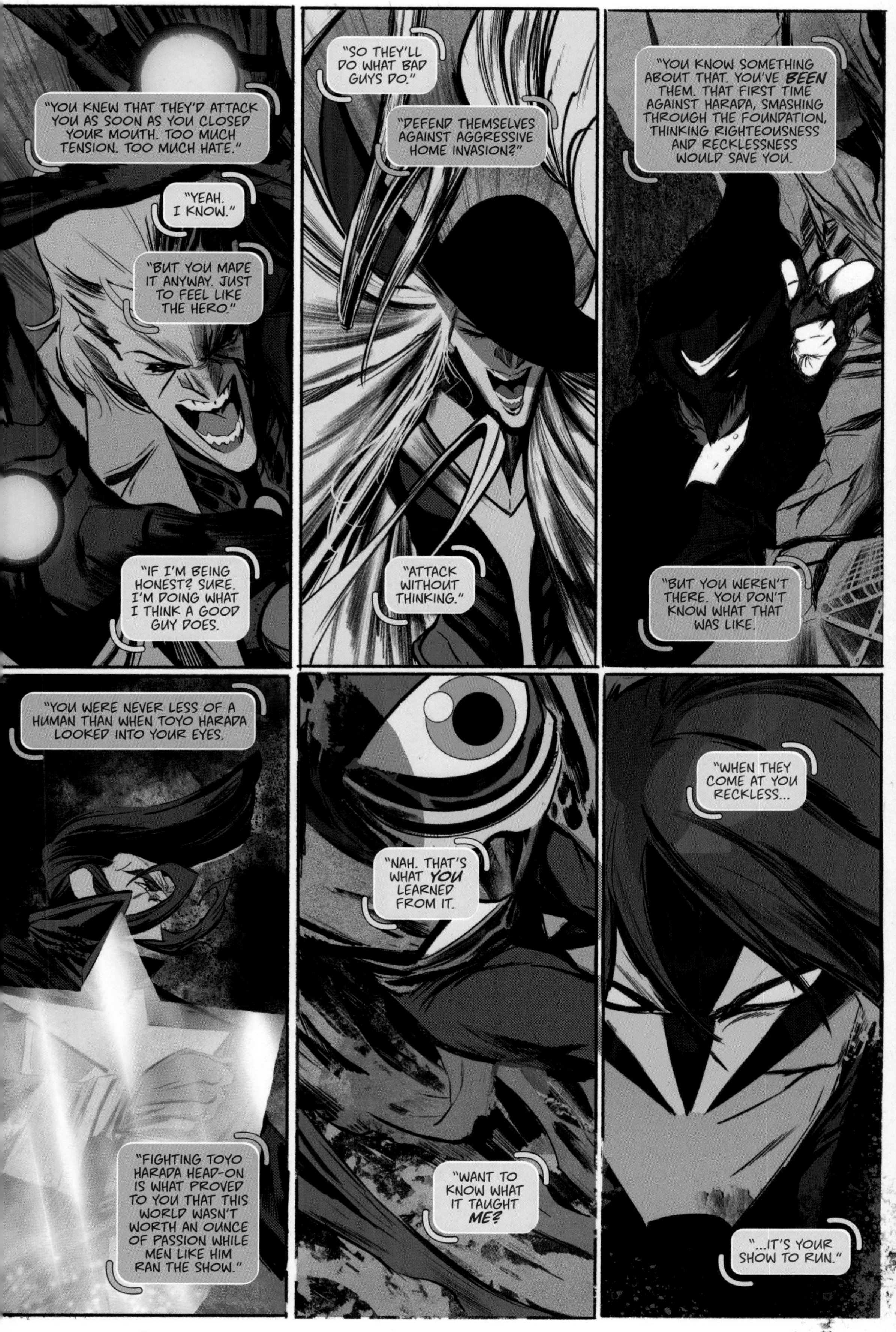
"YOU KNEW THAT THEY'D ATTACK YOU AS SOON AS YOU CLOSED YOUR MOUTH. TOO MUCH TENSION. TOO MUCH HATE."
"YEAH. I KNOW."
"BUT YOU MADE IT ANYWAY. JUST TO FEEL LIKE THE HERO."
"IF I'M BEING HONEST? SURE. I'M DOING WHAT I THINK A GOOD GUY DOES.
"SO THEY'LL DO WHAT BAD GUYS DO."
"DEFEND THEMSELVES AGAINST AGGRESSIVE HOME INVASION?"
"ATTACK WITHOUT THINKING."
"YOU KNOW SOMETHING ABOUT THAT. YOU'VE **BEEN** THEM. THAT FIRST TIME AGAINST HARADA, SMASHING THROUGH THE FOUNDATION, THINKING RIGHTEOUSNESS AND RECKLESSNESS WOULD SAVE YOU.
"BUT YOU WEREN'T THERE. YOU DON'T KNOW WHAT THAT WAS LIKE.
"YOU WERE NEVER LESS OF A HUMAN THAN WHEN TOYO HARADA LOOKED INTO YOUR EYES.
"FIGHTING TOYO HARADA HEAD-ON IS WHAT PROVED TO YOU THAT THIS WORLD WASN'T WORTH AN OUNCE OF PASSION WHILE MEN LIKE HIM RAN THE SHOW."
"NAH. THAT'S WHAT **YOU** LEARNED FROM IT.
"WANT TO KNOW WHAT IT TAUGHT **ME?**
"WHEN THEY COME AT YOU RECKLESS...
"...IT'S YOUR SHOW TO RUN."

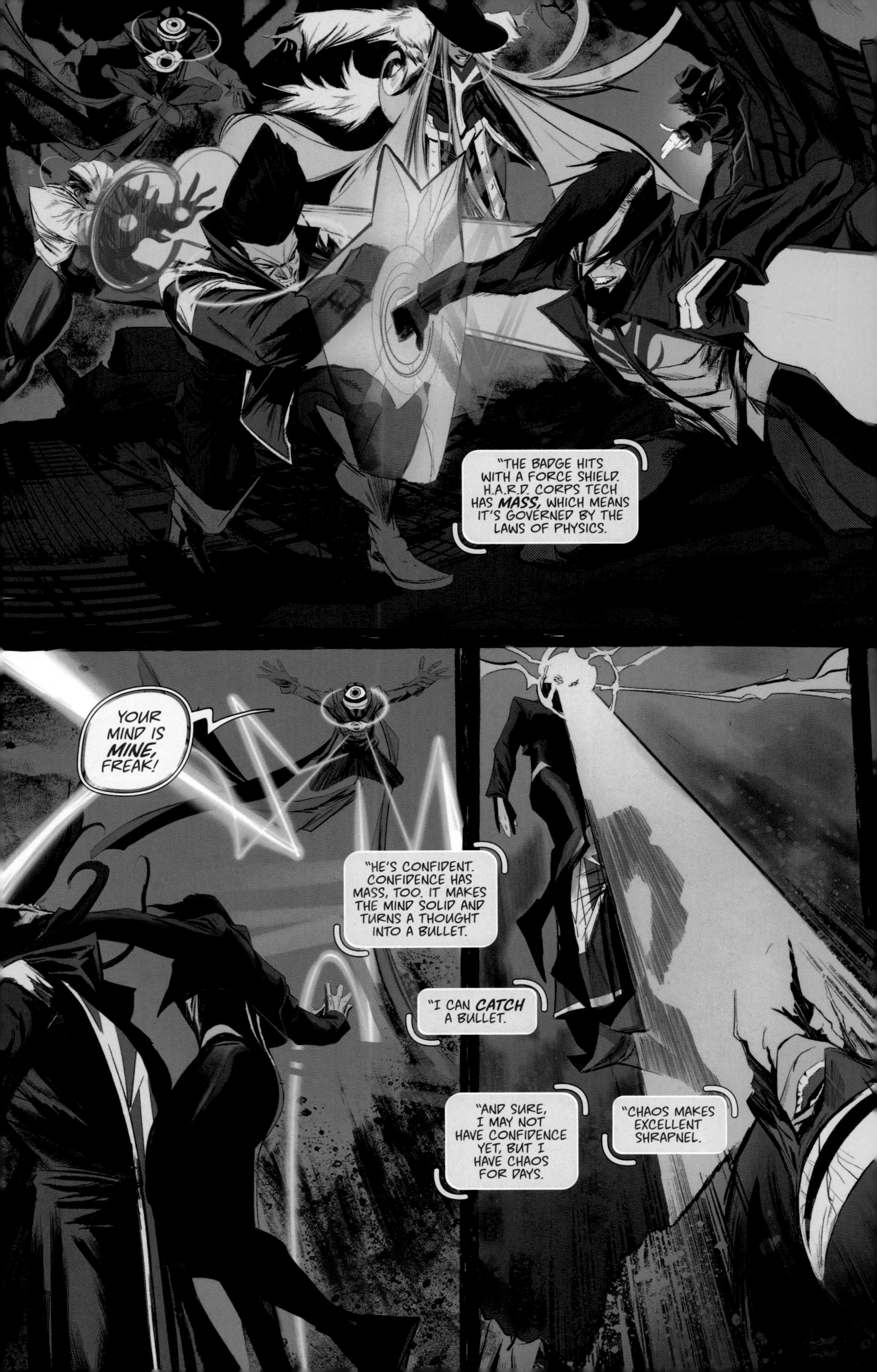
"THE BADGE HITS WITH A FORCE SHIELD. H.A.R.D. CORPS TECH HAS MASS, WHICH MEANS IT'S GOVERNED BY THE LAWS OF PHYSICS.
YOUR MIND IS MINE, FREAK!
"HE'S CONFIDENT. CONFIDENCE HAS MASS, TOO. IT MAKES THE MIND SOLID AND TURNS A THOUGHT INTO A BULLET.
"I CAN CATCH A BULLET.
"AND SURE, I MAY NOT HAVE CONFIDENCE YET, BUT I HAVE CHAOS FOR DAYS.
"CHAOS MAKES EXCELLENT SHRAPNEL.

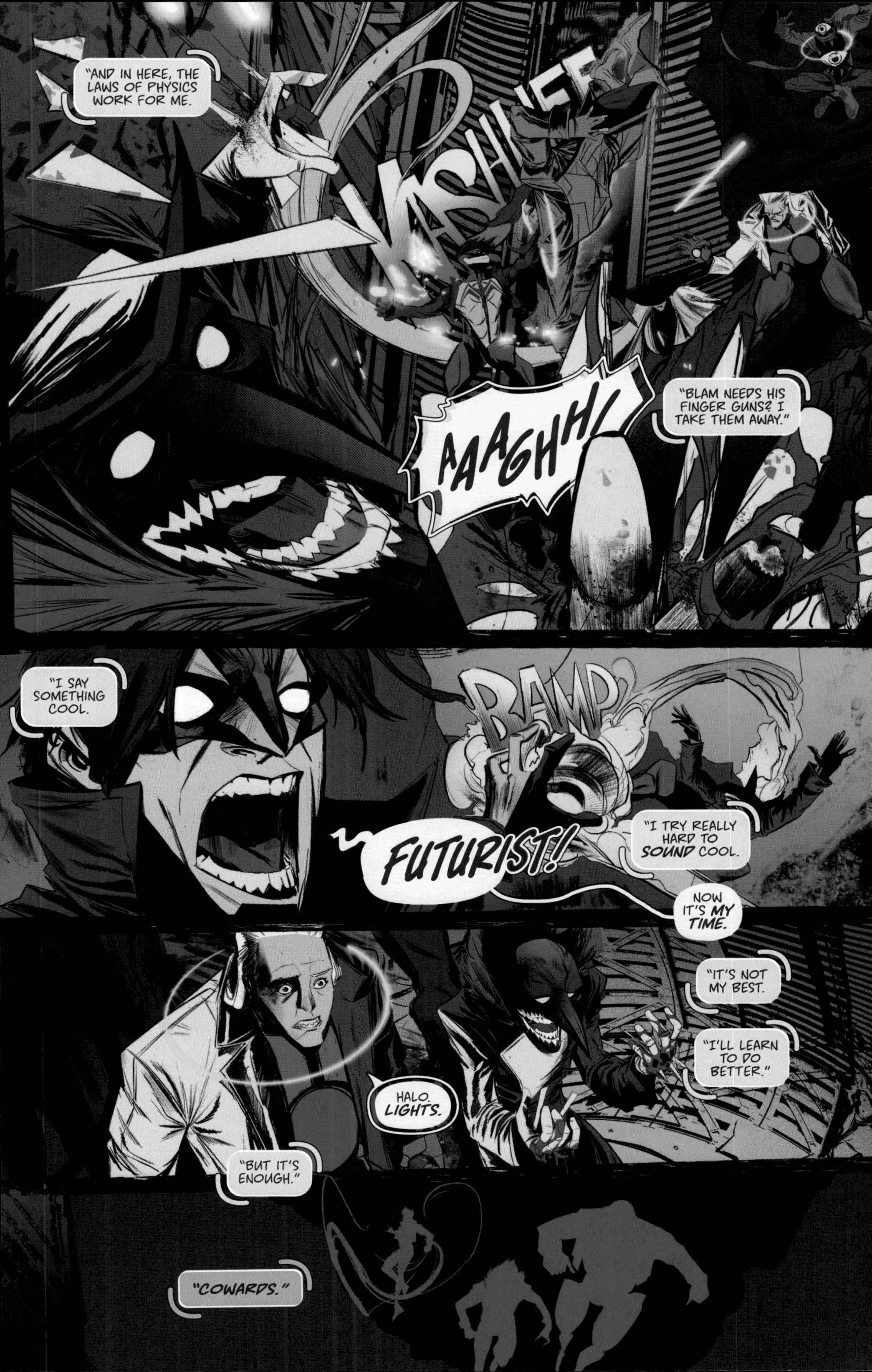
"AND IN HERE, THE LAWS OF PHYSICS WORK FOR ME.
VRSHH
"BLAM NEEDS HIS FINGER GUNS? I TAKE THEM AWAY."
AAAGHH!
"I SAY SOMETHING COOL.
BAMP
FUTURIST!
"I TRY REALLY HARD TO SOUND COOL.
NOW IT'S MY TIME.
"IT'S NOT MY BEST.
"I'LL LEARN TO DO BETTER."
HALO. LIGHTS.
"BUT IT'S ENOUGH."
"COWARDS."

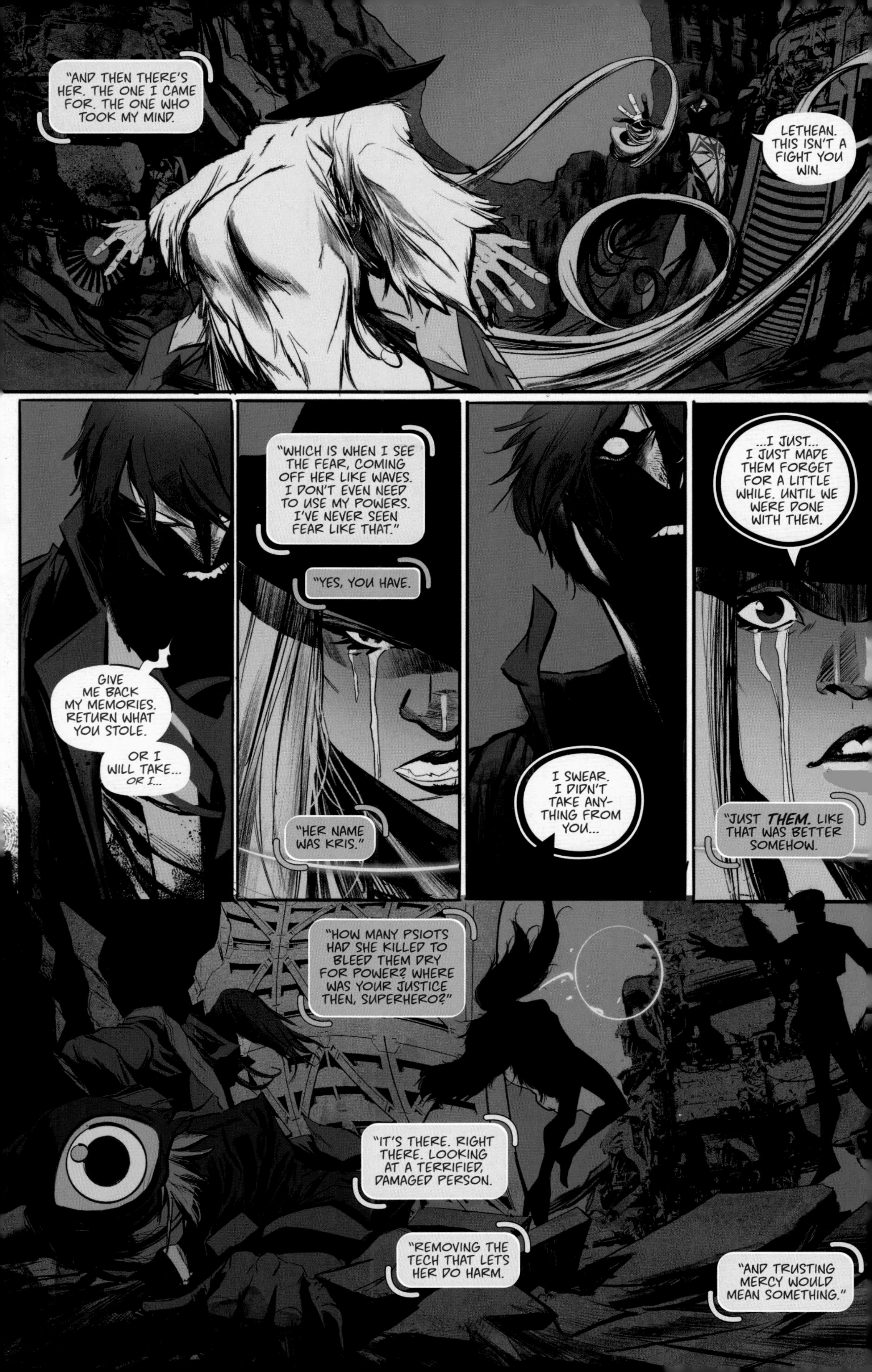
"AND THEN THERE'S HER. THE ONE I CAME FOR. THE ONE WHO TOOK MY MIND.
LETHEAN. THIS ISN'T A FIGHT YOU WIN.
GIVE ME BACK MY MEMORIES. RETURN WHAT YOU STOLE.
OR I WILL TAKE... OR I...
"WHICH IS WHEN I SEE THE FEAR, COMING OFF HER LIKE WAVES. I DON'T EVEN NEED TO USE MY POWERS. I'VE NEVER SEEN FEAR LIKE THAT."
"YES, YOU HAVE.
"HER NAME WAS KRIS."
I SWEAR. I DIDN'T TAKE ANYTHING FROM YOU...
...I JUST... I JUST MADE THEM FORGET FOR A LITTLE WHILE. UNTIL WE WERE DONE WITH THEM.
"JUST *THEM.* LIKE THAT WAS BETTER SOMEHOW.
"HOW MANY PSIOTS HAD SHE KILLED TO BLEED THEM DRY FOR POWER? WHERE WAS YOUR JUSTICE THEN, SUPERHERO?"
"IT'S THERE. RIGHT THERE. LOOKING AT A TERRIFIED, DAMAGED PERSON.
"REMOVING THE TECH THAT LETS HER DO HARM.
"AND TRUSTING MERCY WOULD MEAN SOMETHING."

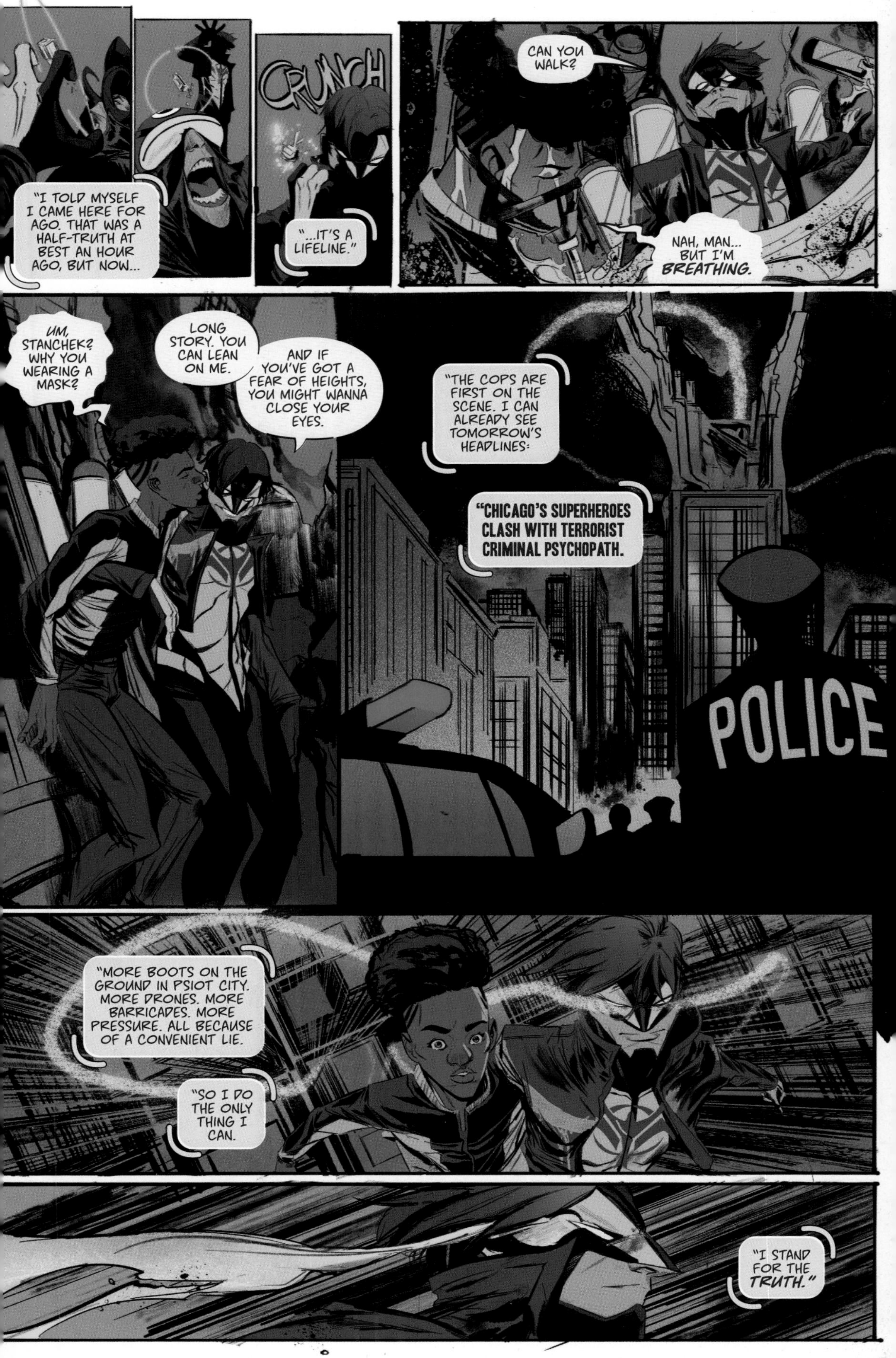
"I TOLD MYSELF I CAME HERE FOR AGO. THAT WAS A HALF-TRUTH AT BEST AN HOUR AGO, BUT NOW...
CRUNCH
"...IT'S A LIFELINE."
CAN YOU WALK?
NAH, MAN... BUT I'M *BREATHING.*
UM, STANCHEK? WHY YOU WEARING A MASK?
LONG STORY. YOU CAN LEAN ON ME.
AND IF YOU'VE GOT A FEAR OF HEIGHTS, YOU MIGHT WANNA CLOSE YOUR EYES.
"THE COPS ARE FIRST ON THE SCENE. I CAN ALREADY SEE TOMORROW'S HEADLINES:
"CHICAGO'S SUPERHEROES CLASH WITH TERRORIST CRIMINAL PSYCHOPATH.
POLICE
"MORE BOOTS ON THE GROUND IN PSIOT CITY. MORE DRONES. MORE BARRICADES. MORE PRESSURE. ALL BECAUSE OF A CONVENIENT LIE.
"SO I DO THE ONLY THING I CAN.
"I STAND FOR THE *TRUTH.*"

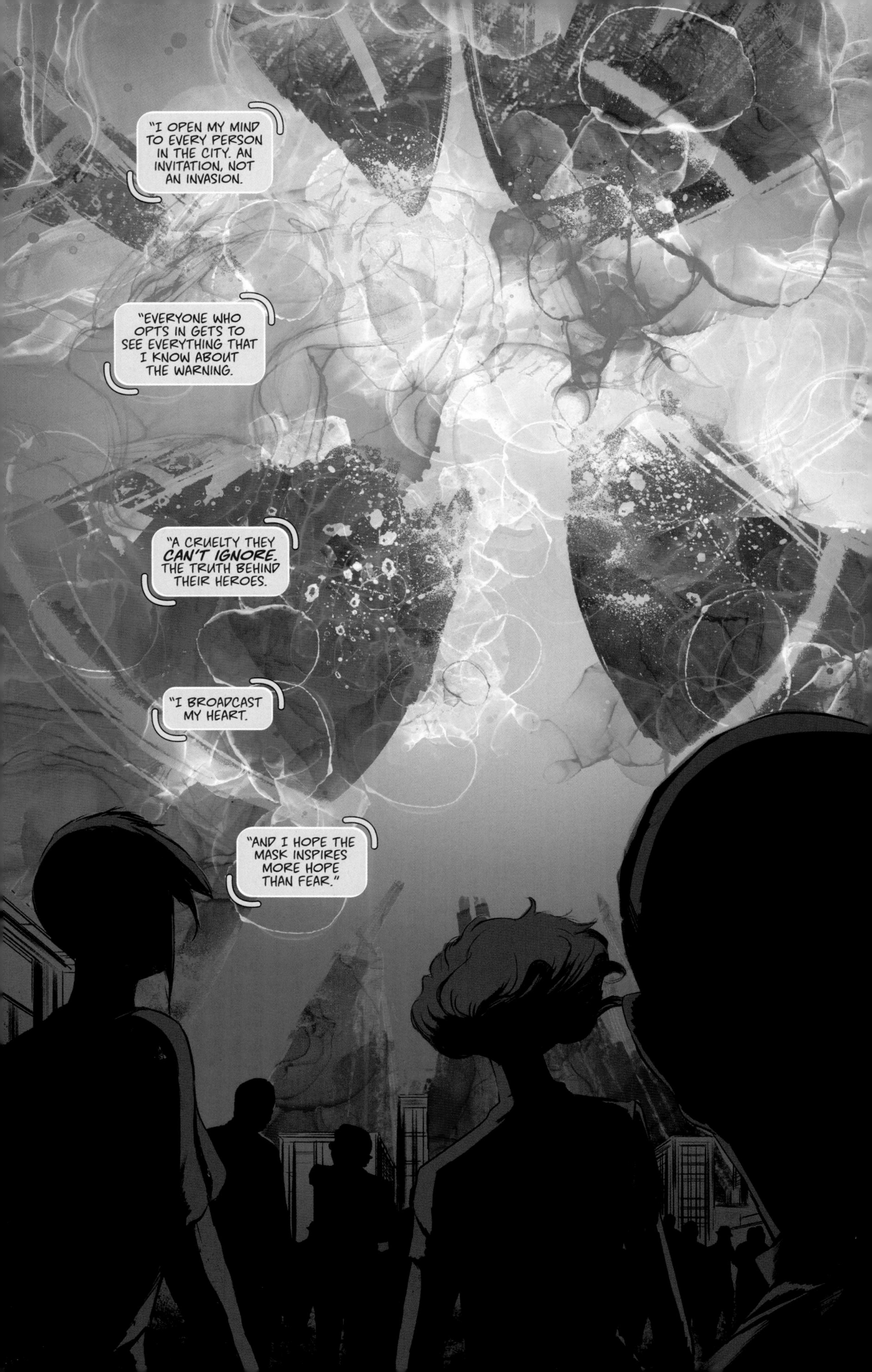
"I OPEN MY MIND TO EVERY PERSON IN THE CITY. AN INVITATION, NOT AN INVASION.
"EVERYONE WHO OPTS IN GETS TO SEE EVERYTHING THAT I KNOW ABOUT THE WARNING.
"A CRUELTY THEY **CAN'T IGNORE**. THE TRUTH BEHIND THEIR HEROES.
"I BROADCAST MY HEART.
"AND I HOPE THE MASK INSPIRES MORE HOPE THAN FEAR."

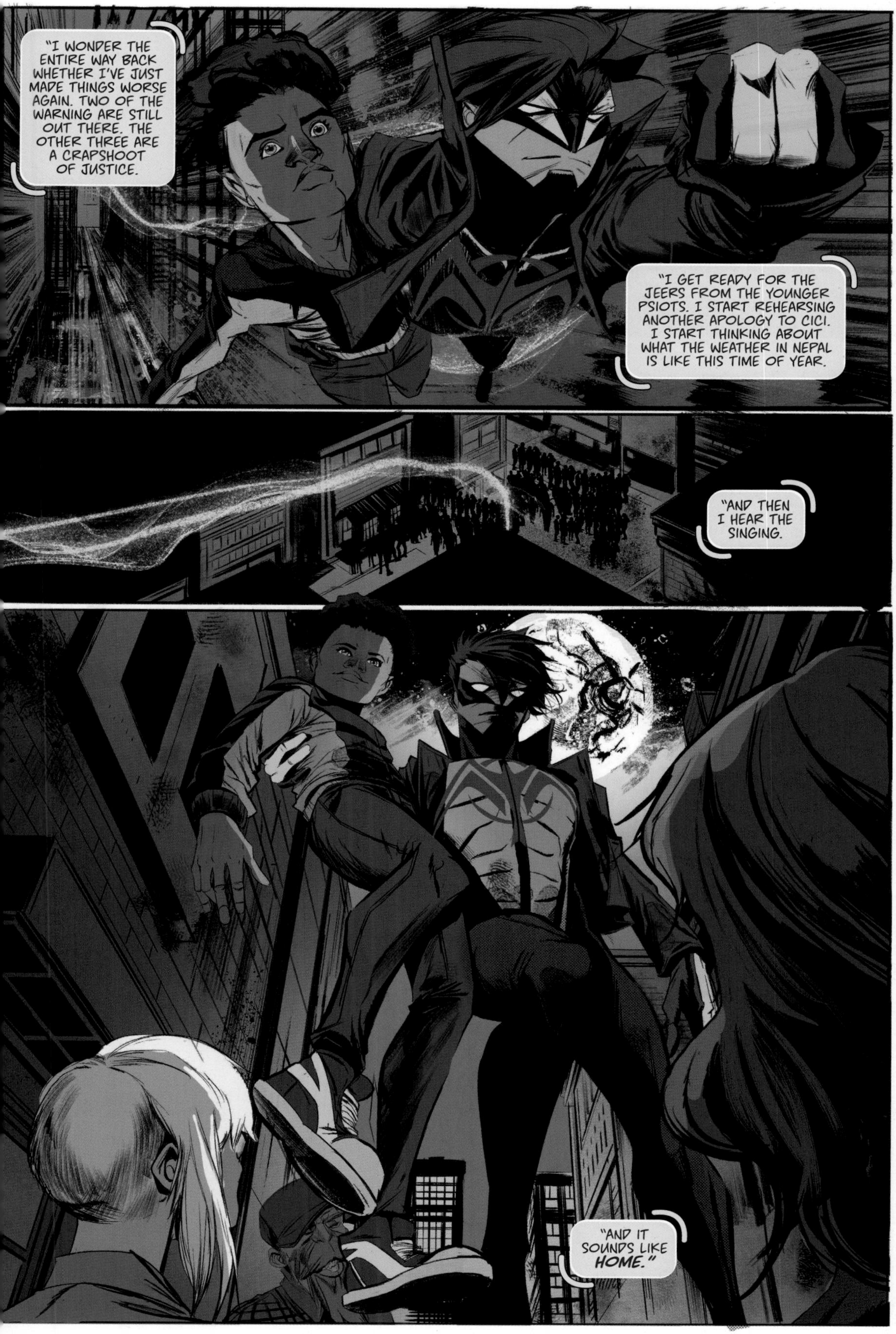
"I WONDER THE ENTIRE WAY BACK WHETHER I'VE JUST MADE THINGS WORSE AGAIN. TWO OF THE WARNING ARE STILL OUT THERE. THE OTHER THREE ARE A CRAPSHOOT OF JUSTICE.
"I GET READY FOR THE JEERS FROM THE YOUNGER PSIOTS. I START REHEARSING ANOTHER APOLOGY TO CICI. I START THINKING ABOUT WHAT THE WEATHER IN NEPAL IS LIKE THIS TIME OF YEAR.
"AND THEN I HEAR THE SINGING.
"AND IT SOUNDS LIKE *HOME.*"

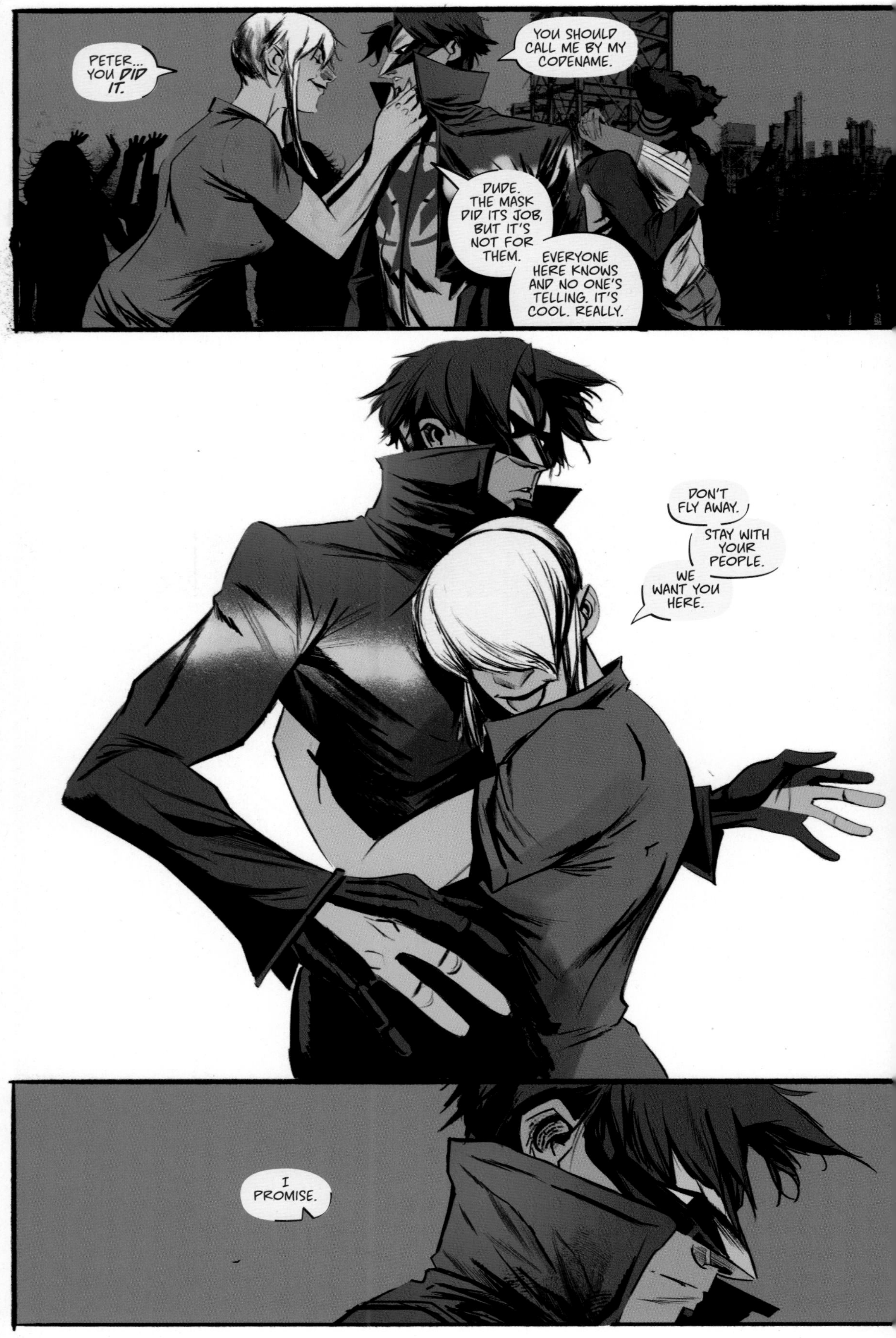
PETER... YOU DID IT.
YOU SHOULD CALL ME BY MY CODENAME.
DUDE. THE MASK DID ITS JOB, BUT IT'S NOT FOR THEM.
EVERYONE HERE KNOWS AND NO ONE'S TELLING. IT'S COOL. REALLY.
DON'T FLY AWAY.
STAY WITH YOUR PEOPLE.
WE WANT YOU HERE.
I PROMISE.

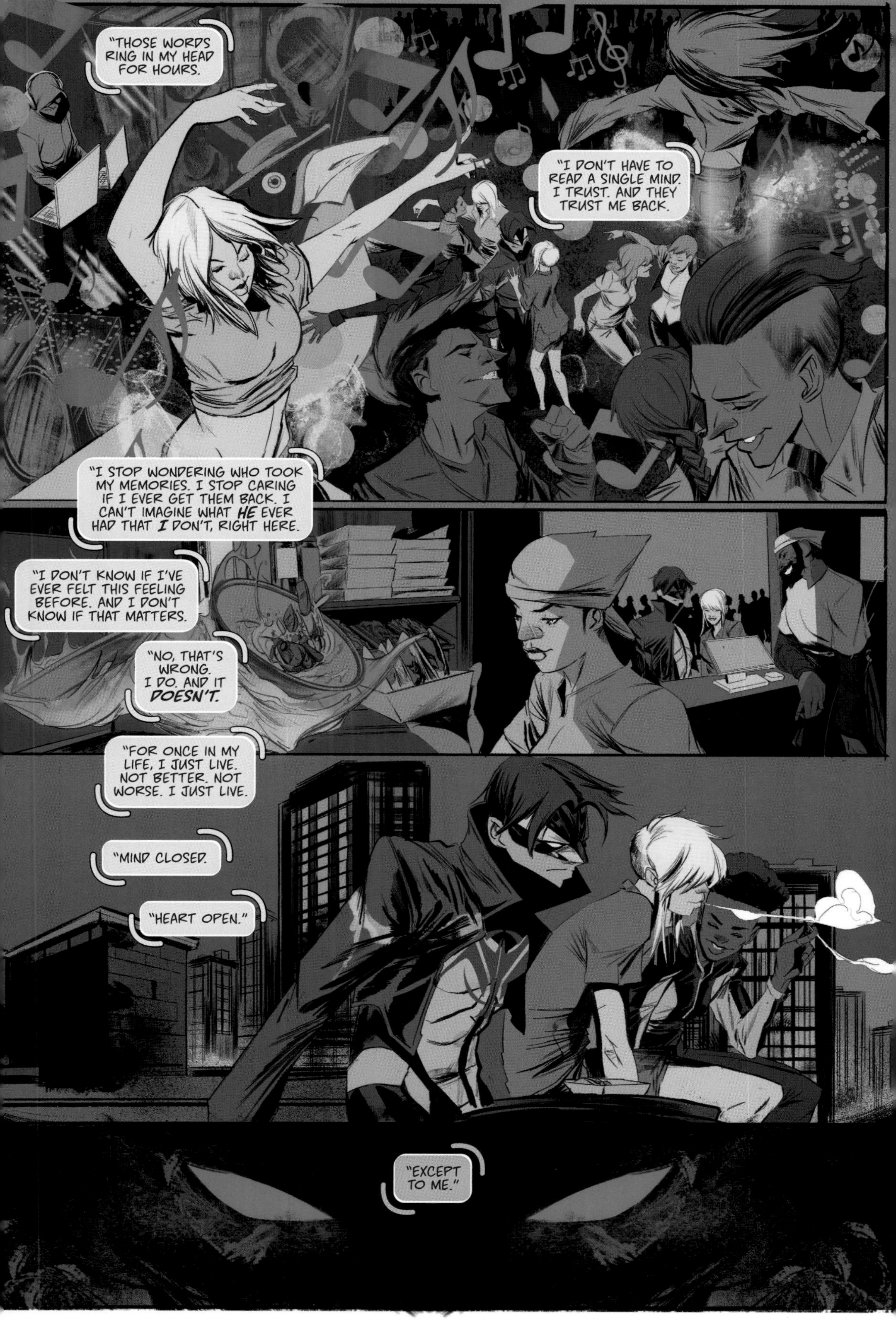
"THOSE WORDS RING IN MY HEAD FOR HOURS.
"I DON'T HAVE TO READ A SINGLE MIND. I TRUST. AND THEY TRUST ME BACK.
"I STOP WONDERING WHO TOOK MY MEMORIES. I STOP CARING IF I EVER GET THEM BACK. I CAN'T IMAGINE WHAT HE EVER HAD THAT I DON'T, RIGHT HERE.
"I DON'T KNOW IF I'VE EVER FELT THIS FEELING BEFORE. AND I DON'T KNOW IF THAT MATTERS.
"NO, THAT'S WRONG. I DO. AND IT DOESN'T.
"FOR ONCE IN MY LIFE, I JUST LIVE. NOT BETTER. NOT WORSE. I JUST LIVE.
"MIND CLOSED.
"HEART OPEN."
"EXCEPT TO ME."

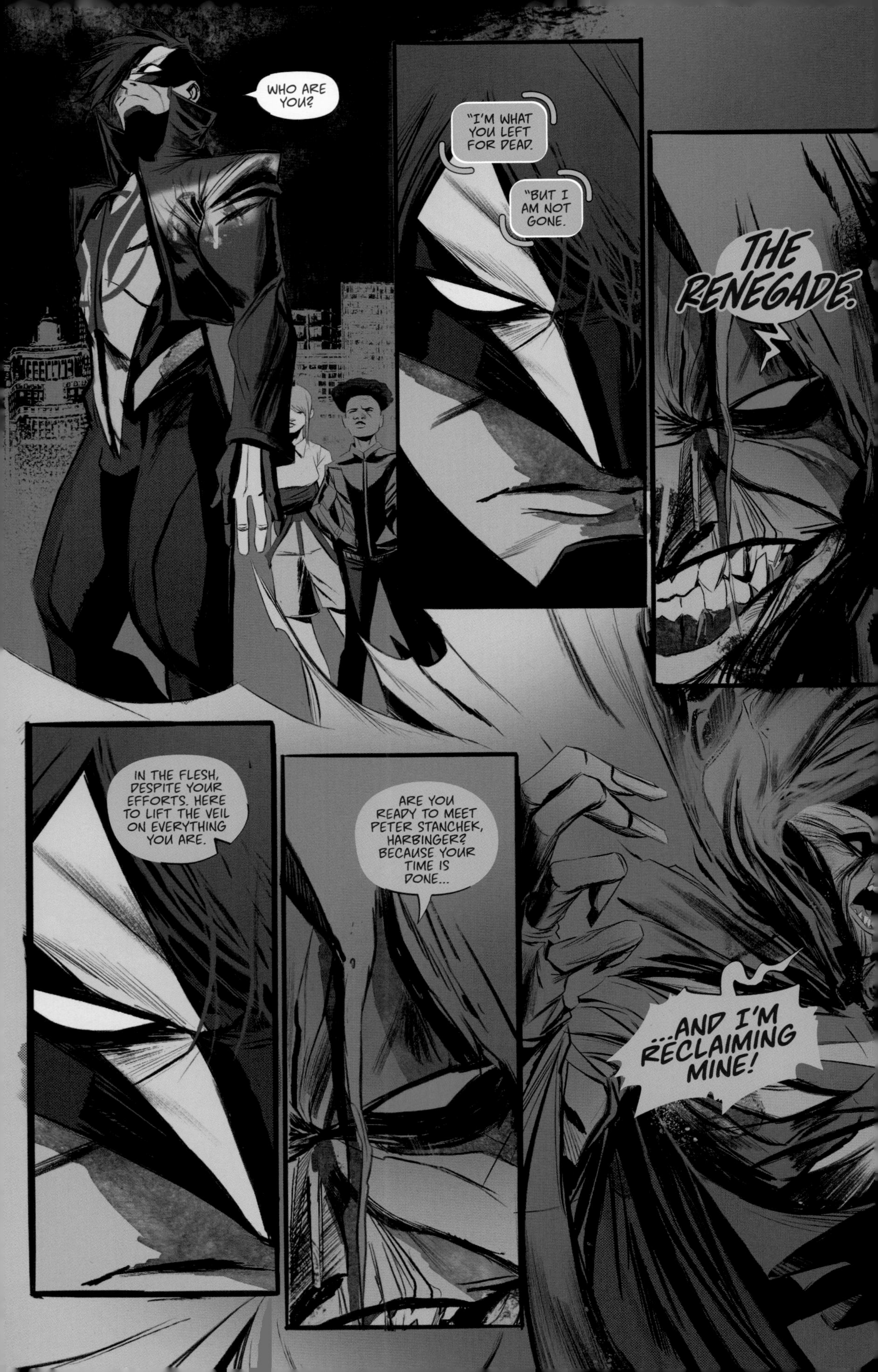
WHO ARE YOU?
"I'M WHAT YOU LEFT FOR DEAD.
"BUT I AM NOT GONE.
THE RENEGADE.
IN THE FLESH, DESPITE YOUR EFFORTS. HERE TO LIFT THE VEIL ON EVERYTHING YOU ARE.
ARE YOU READY TO MEET PETER STANCHEK, HARBINGER? BECAUSE YOUR TIME IS DONE...
...AND I'M RECLAIMING MINE!

COLLIN KELLY | JACKSON LANZING | ROBBI RODRIGUEZ | RICO RENZI | HASSAN OTSMANE-ELHAOU
4
THE HARBINGER®
LIANT

"Be Better: Finale"

THE HARBINGER #4

WORDS: Collin Kelly and Jackson Lanzing
ART: Robbi Rodriguez
COLORS: Rico Renzi
LETTERS: Hassan Otsmane-Elhaou
COVER ART: Robbi Rodriguez
ASSISTANT EDITOR: Audrey Meeker
SENIOR EDITORS: Lysa Hawkins and Heather Antos

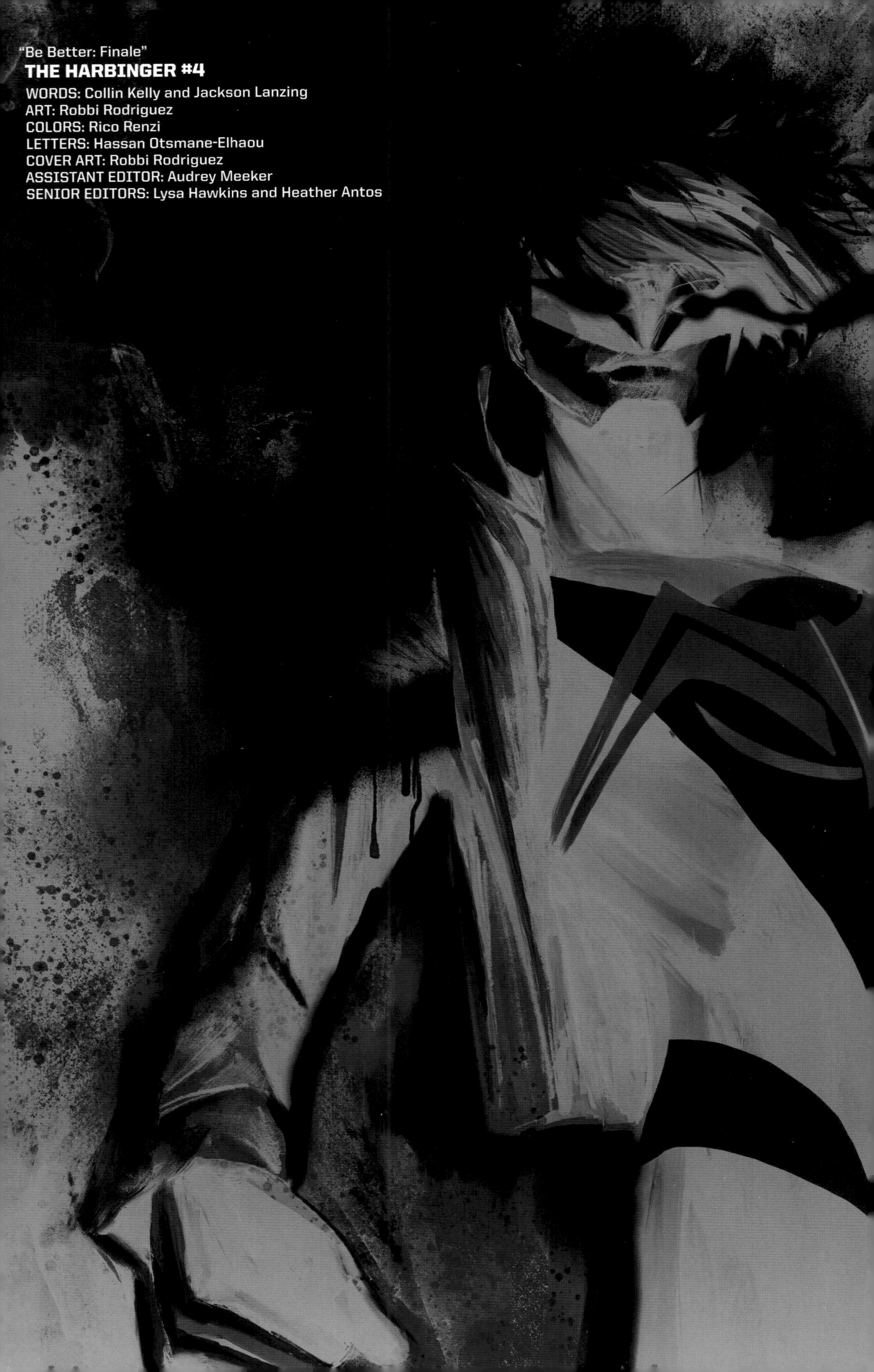

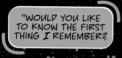
"WOULD YOU LIKE TO KNOW THE FIRST THING *I* REMEMBER?

"BESIDES THE STARS?

"IT WAS THE ABSOLUTE CERTAINTY THAT I COULD *NEVER* REACH THEM.

"NO MEMORIES. NO IDEA HOW I GOT THERE. A FRESH START.

"EXCEPT IT TOOK LESS THAN A MINUTE FOR THE SHAKES TO KICK IN.

"FOR THE *WANTING* TO START. FOR THE FIX TO SETTLE IN MY MIND.

"I WANTED A HIT BEFORE I EVEN NOTICED THE STENCH. BEFORE I EVEN KNEW WHAT THE FIX WAS.

"THE FIX.

"*A* FIX.

"*ANY* FIX.

"TO STOP THE HUM.

"BUT THE THOUGHTS. THE ENDLESS DRONING THOUGHTS OF EVERY *NOBODY* ON THE PLANET. THEY NEVER STOP. MAYBE THEY DO FOR *YOU*, CHOSEN ONE THAT YOU ARE.

"BUT FOR ME, THE HUM JUST GOT LOUDER. SHARPENED ITSELF AGAINST MY PARIETAL LIKE A BOWIE KNIFE AGAINST A WHETSTONE OF FLESH.

"MY FEET WERE WEAK. MY POWER WAS DIMINISHED. I BARELY KNEW MY OWN NAME.

"BUT THE HUM KNEW ME.

"EVERY MIND THIS SIDE OF LAKE MICHIGAN REACHED INTO MINE..."

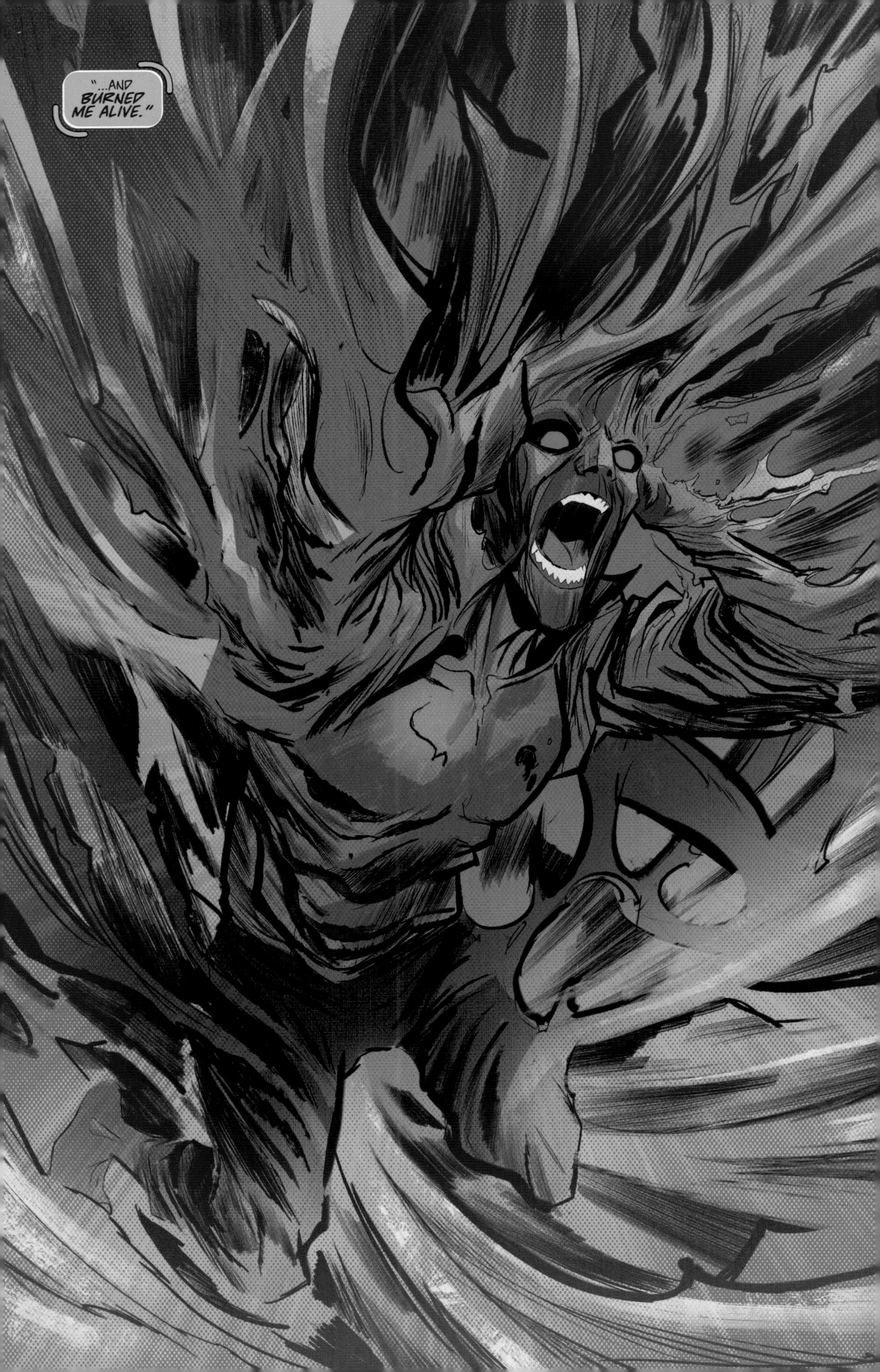
"...AND BURNED ME ALIVE."

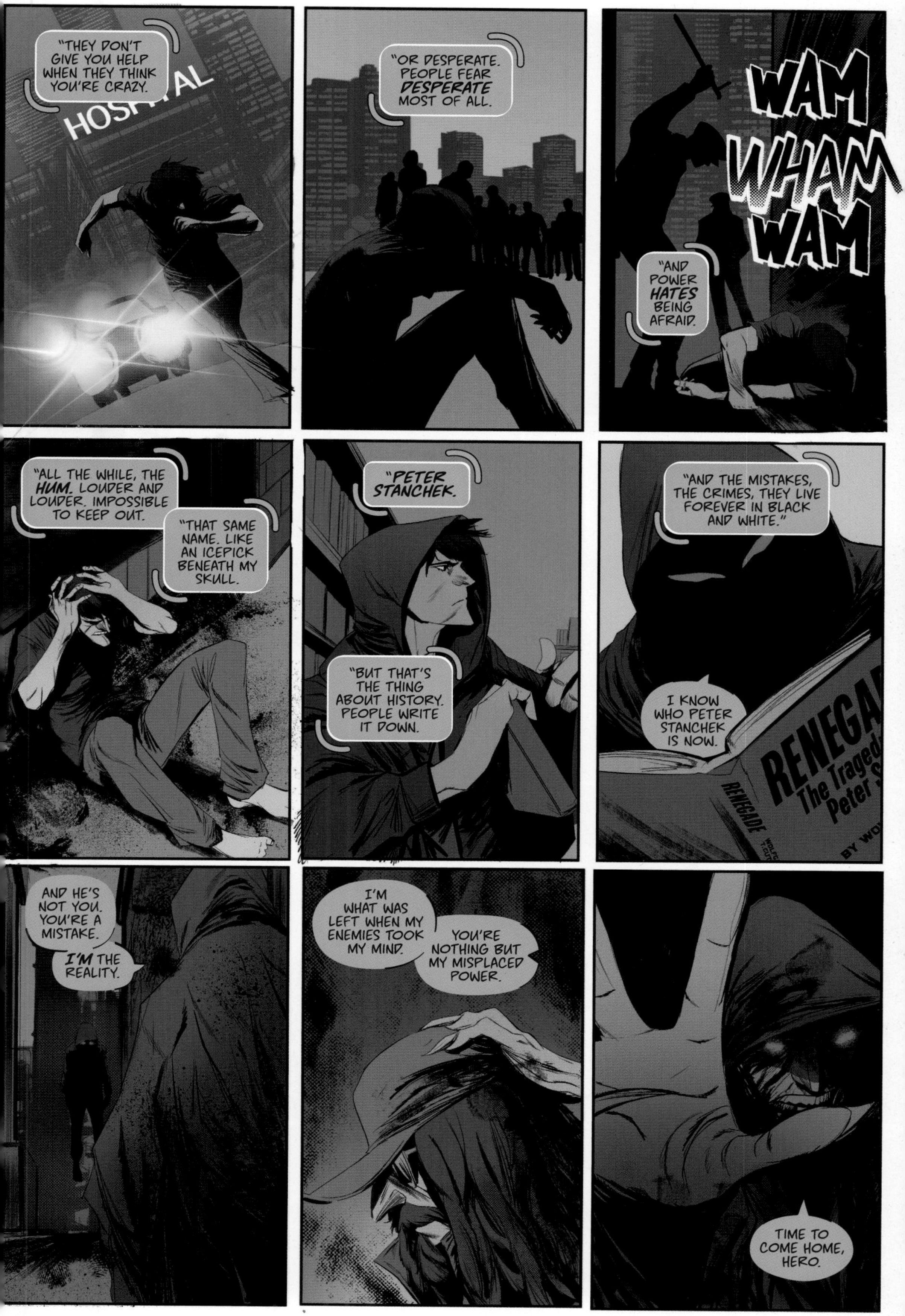
HOSPITAL
"THEY DON'T GIVE YOU HELP WHEN THEY THINK YOU'RE CRAZY.
"OR DESPERATE. PEOPLE FEAR **DESPERATE** MOST OF ALL.
WAM
WHAM
WAM
"AND POWER **HATES** BEING AFRAID.
"ALL THE WHILE, THE **HUM.** LOUDER AND LOUDER. IMPOSSIBLE TO KEEP OUT.
"THAT SAME NAME. LIKE AN ICEPICK BENEATH MY SKULL.
"**PETER STANCHEK.**
"BUT THAT'S THE THING ABOUT HISTORY. PEOPLE WRITE IT DOWN.
"AND THE MISTAKES, THE CRIMES, THEY LIVE FOREVER IN BLACK AND WHITE."
I KNOW WHO PETER STANCHEK IS NOW.
RENEGA
The Traged
Peter S
RENEGADE
AND HE'S NOT YOU. YOU'RE A MISTAKE.
I'M THE REALITY.
I'M WHAT WAS LEFT WHEN MY ENEMIES TOOK MY MIND.
YOU'RE NOTHING BUT MY MISPLACED POWER.
TIME TO COME HOME, HERO.

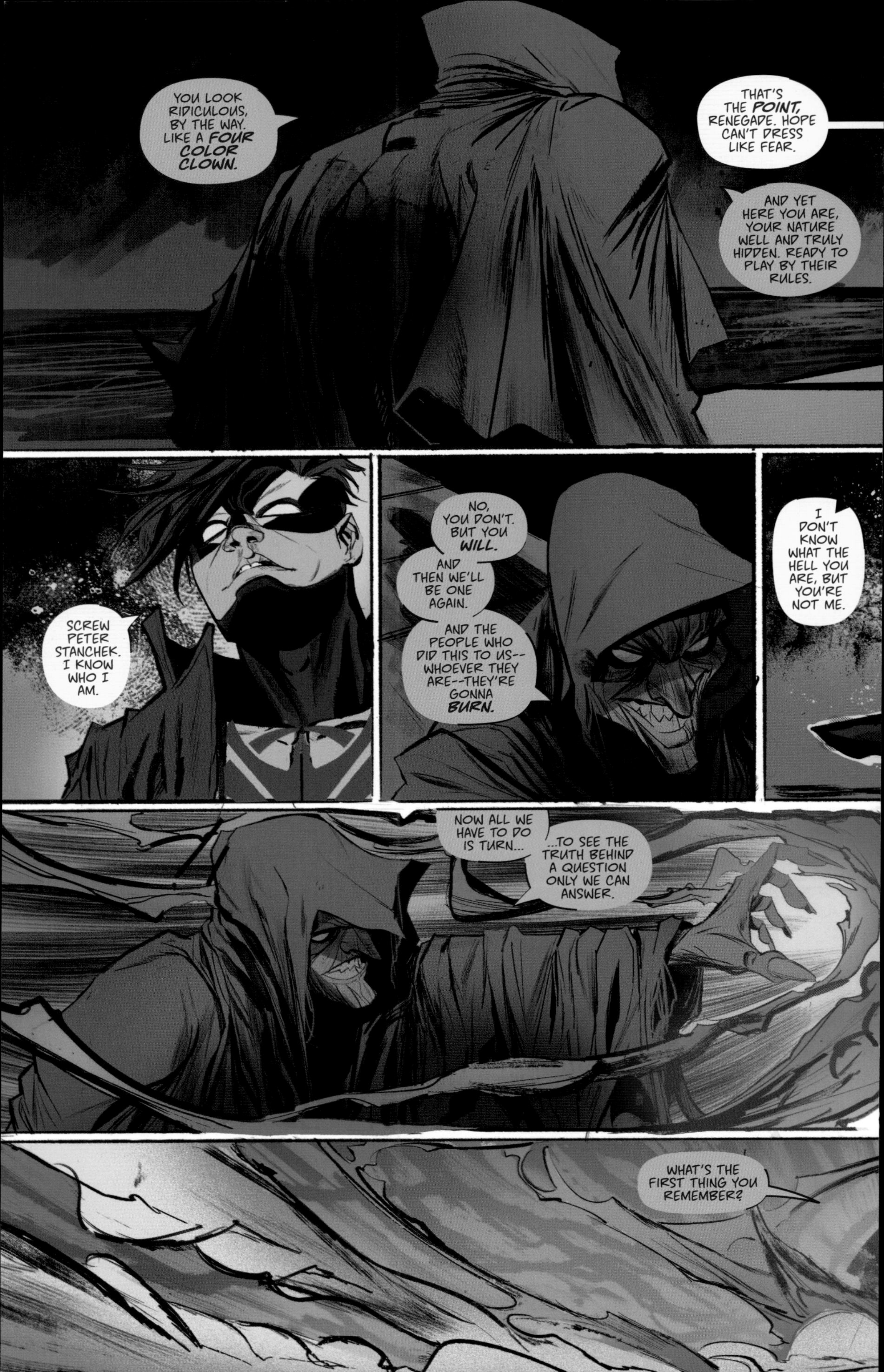
YOU LOOK RIDICULOUS, BY THE WAY. LIKE A FOUR COLOR CLOWN.
THAT'S THE POINT, RENEGADE. HOPE CAN'T DRESS LIKE FEAR.
AND YET HERE YOU ARE, YOUR NATURE WELL AND TRULY HIDDEN. READY TO PLAY BY THEIR RULES.
SCREW PETER STANCHEK. I KNOW WHO I AM.
NO, YOU DON'T. BUT YOU WILL.
AND THEN WE'LL BE ONE AGAIN.
AND THE PEOPLE WHO DID THIS TO US--WHOEVER THEY ARE--THEY'RE GONNA BURN.
I DON'T KNOW WHAT THE HELL YOU ARE, BUT YOU'RE NOT ME.
NOW ALL WE HAVE TO DO IS TURN...
...TO SEE THE TRUTH BEHIND A QUESTION ONLY WE CAN ANSWER.
WHAT'S THE FIRST THING YOU REMEMBER?

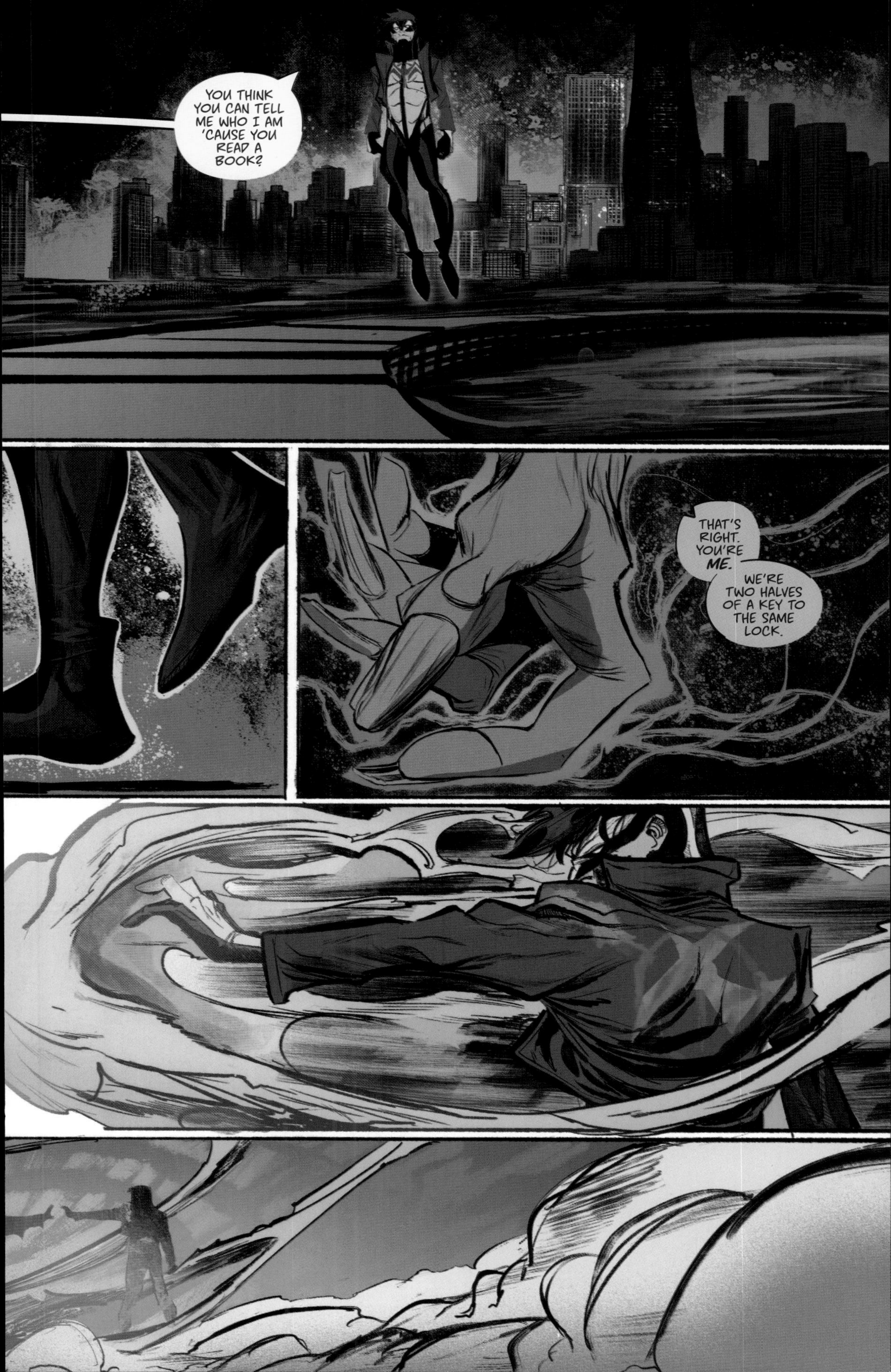
YOU THINK YOU CAN TELL ME WHO I AM 'CAUSE YOU READ A BOOK?
THAT'S RIGHT. YOU'RE ME.
WE'RE TWO HALVES OF A KEY TO THE SAME LOCK.

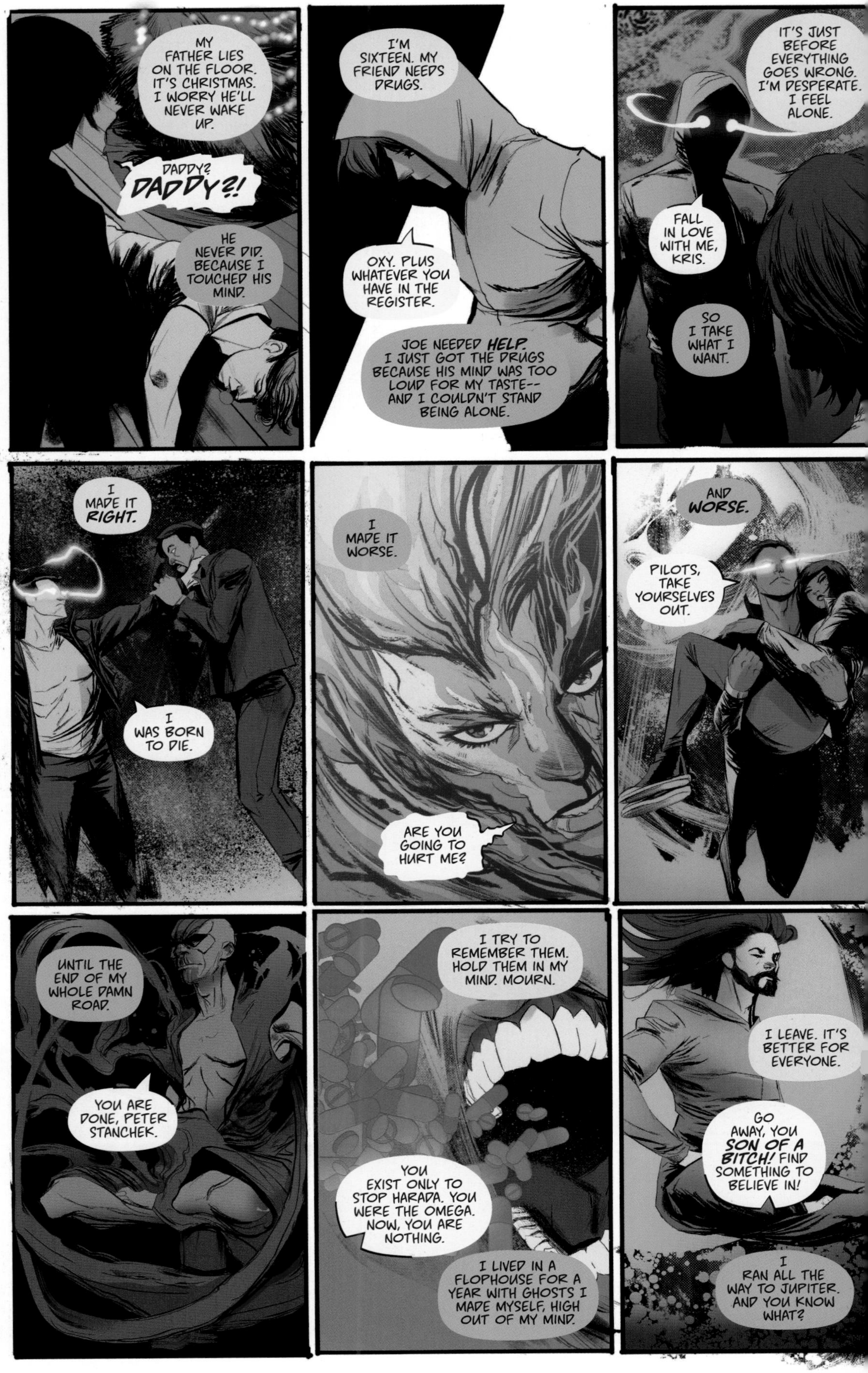
MY FATHER LIES ON THE FLOOR. IT'S CHRISTMAS. I WORRY HE'LL NEVER WAKE UP.
DADDY? DADDY?!
HE NEVER DID. BECAUSE I TOUCHED HIS MIND.
I'M SIXTEEN. MY FRIEND NEEDS DRUGS.
OXY. PLUS WHATEVER YOU HAVE IN THE REGISTER.
JOE NEEDED HELP. I JUST GOT THE DRUGS BECAUSE HIS MIND WAS TOO LOUD FOR MY TASTE-- AND I COULDN'T STAND BEING ALONE.
IT'S JUST BEFORE EVERYTHING GOES WRONG. I'M DESPERATE. I FEEL ALONE.
FALL IN LOVE WITH ME, KRIS.
SO I TAKE WHAT I WANT.
I MADE IT RIGHT.
I WAS BORN TO DIE.
I MADE IT WORSE.
ARE YOU GOING TO HURT ME?
AND WORSE.
PILOTS, TAKE YOURSELVES OUT.
UNTIL THE END OF MY WHOLE DAMN ROAD.
YOU ARE DONE, PETER STANCHEK.
I TRY TO REMEMBER THEM. HOLD THEM IN MY MIND. MOURN.
YOU EXIST ONLY TO STOP HARADA. YOU WERE THE OMEGA. NOW, YOU ARE NOTHING.
I LIVED IN A FLOPHOUSE FOR A YEAR WITH GHOSTS I MADE MYSELF, HIGH OUT OF MY MIND.
I LEAVE. IT'S BETTER FOR EVERYONE.
GO AWAY, YOU SON OF A BITCH! FIND SOMETHING TO BELIEVE IN!
I RAN ALL THE WAY TO JUPITER. AND YOU KNOW WHAT?

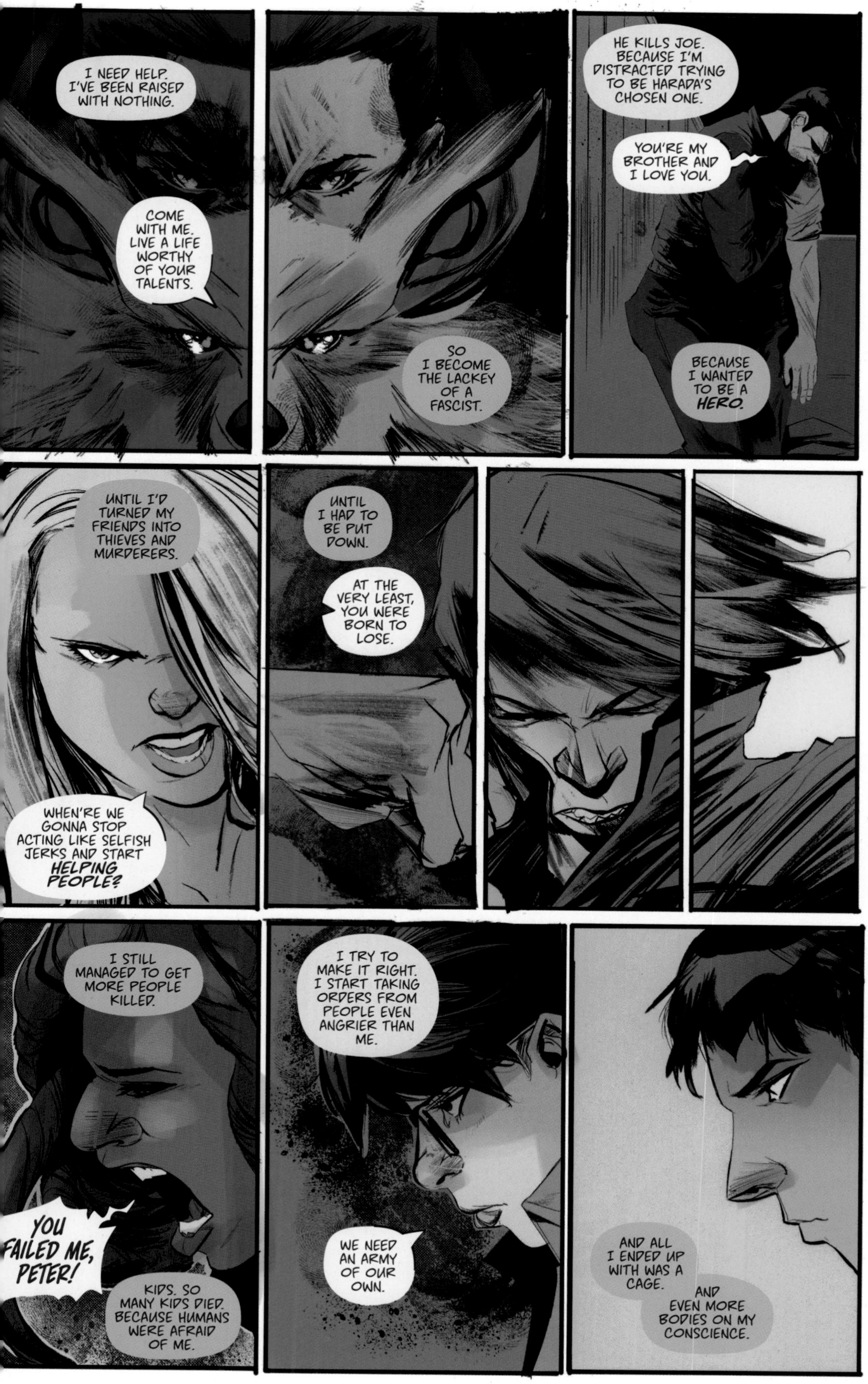
I NEED HELP. I'VE BEEN RAISED WITH NOTHING.
COME WITH ME. LIVE A LIFE WORTHY OF YOUR TALENTS.
SO I BECOME THE LACKEY OF A FASCIST.
HE KILLS JOE. BECAUSE I'M DISTRACTED TRYING TO BE HARADA'S CHOSEN ONE.
YOU'RE MY BROTHER AND I LOVE YOU.
BECAUSE I WANTED TO BE A HERO.
UNTIL I'D TURNED MY FRIENDS INTO THIEVES AND MURDERERS.
WHEN'RE WE GONNA STOP ACTING LIKE SELFISH JERKS AND START HELPING PEOPLE?
UNTIL I HAD TO BE PUT DOWN.
AT THE VERY LEAST, YOU WERE BORN TO LOSE.
I STILL MANAGED TO GET MORE PEOPLE KILLED.
YOU FAILED ME, PETER!
KIDS. SO MANY KIDS DIED. BECAUSE HUMANS WERE AFRAID OF ME.
I TRY TO MAKE IT RIGHT. I START TAKING ORDERS FROM PEOPLE EVEN ANGRIER THAN ME.
WE NEED AN ARMY OF OUR OWN.
AND ALL I ENDED UP WITH WAS A CAGE.
AND EVEN MORE BODIES ON MY CONSCIENCE.

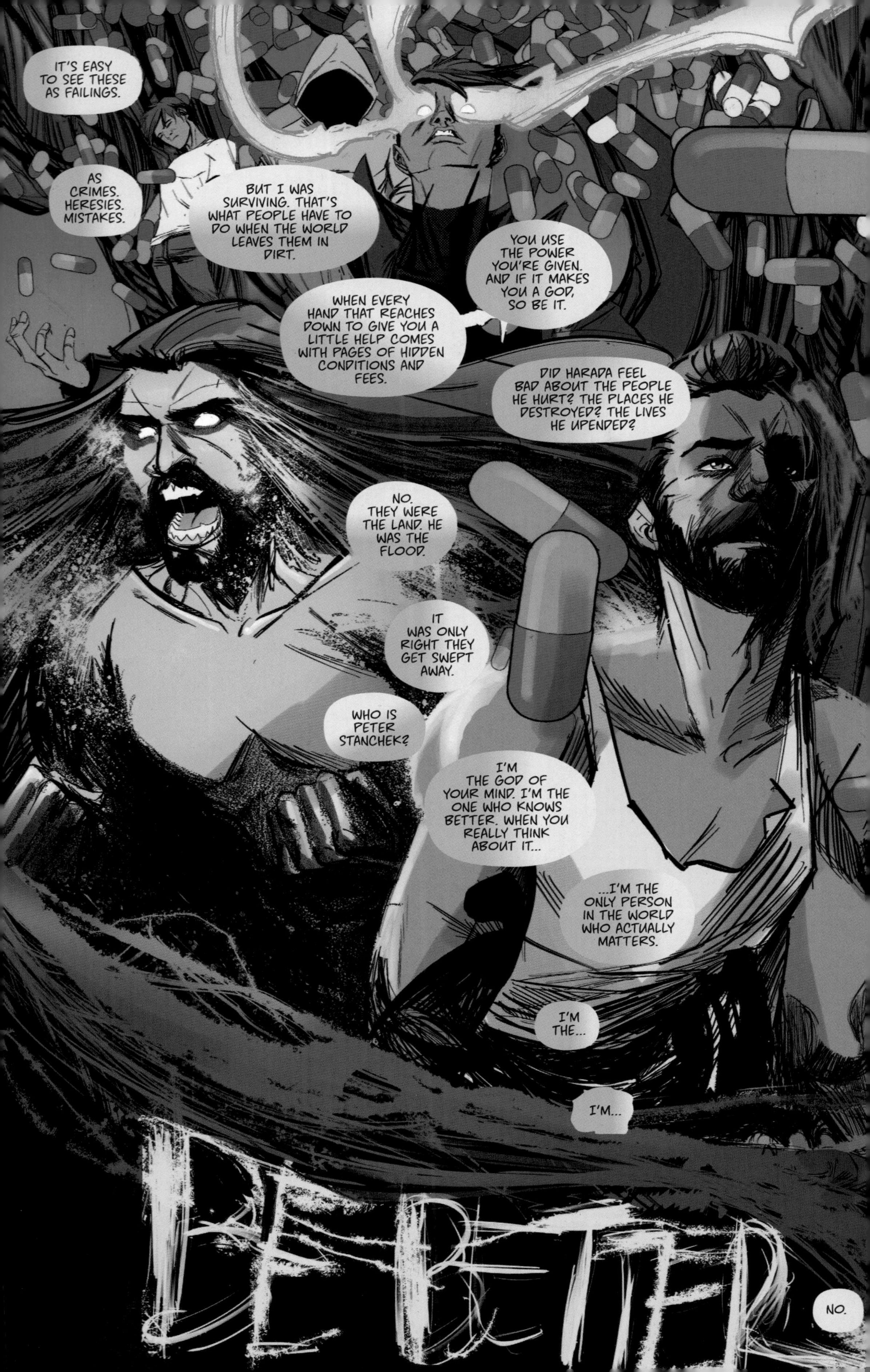
IT'S EASY TO SEE THESE AS FAILINGS.
AS CRIMES. HERESIES. MISTAKES.
BUT I WAS SURVIVING. THAT'S WHAT PEOPLE HAVE TO DO WHEN THE WORLD LEAVES THEM IN DIRT.
WHEN EVERY HAND THAT REACHES DOWN TO GIVE YOU A LITTLE HELP COMES WITH PAGES OF HIDDEN CONDITIONS AND FEES.
YOU USE THE POWER YOU'RE GIVEN. AND IF IT MAKES YOU A GOD, SO BE IT.
DID HARADA FEEL BAD ABOUT THE PEOPLE HE HURT? THE PLACES HE DESTROYED? THE LIVES HE UPENDED?
NO. THEY WERE THE LAND. HE WAS THE FLOOD.
IT WAS ONLY RIGHT THEY GET SWEPT AWAY.
WHO IS PETER STANCHEK?
I'M THE GOD OF YOUR MIND. I'M THE ONE WHO KNOWS BETTER. WHEN YOU REALLY THINK ABOUT IT...
...I'M THE ONLY PERSON IN THE WORLD WHO ACTUALLY MATTERS.
I'M THE...
I'M...
BE BETTER
NO.

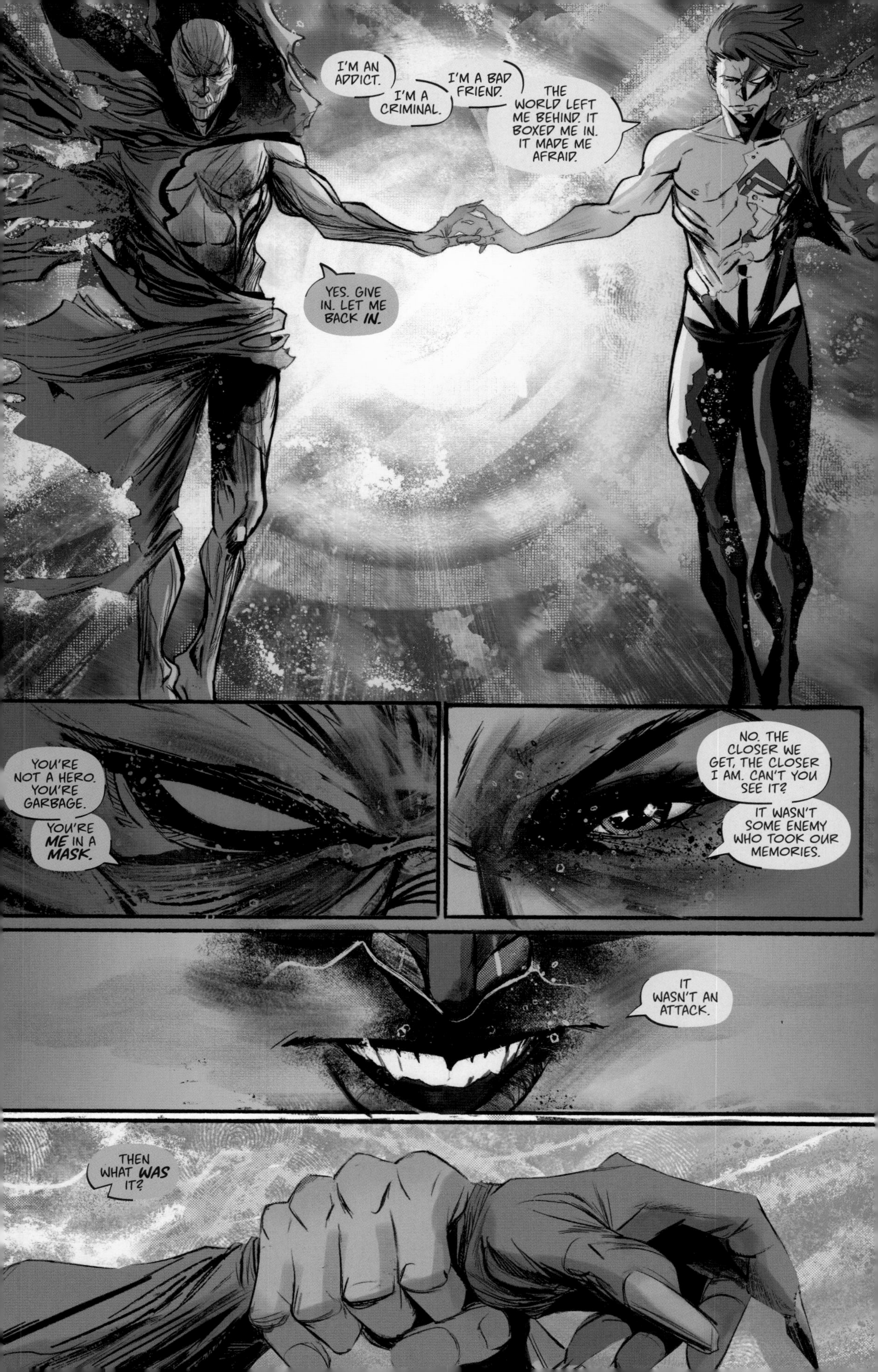
I'M AN ADDICT.
I'M A CRIMINAL.
I'M A BAD FRIEND.
THE WORLD LEFT ME BEHIND. IT BOXED ME IN. IT MADE ME AFRAID.
YES. GIVE IN. LET ME BACK IN.
YOU'RE NOT A HERO. YOU'RE GARBAGE.
YOU'RE ME IN A MASK.
NO. THE CLOSER WE GET, THE CLOSER I AM. CAN'T YOU SEE IT?
IT WASN'T SOME ENEMY WHO TOOK OUR MEMORIES.
IT WASN'T AN ATTACK.
THEN WHAT WAS IT?

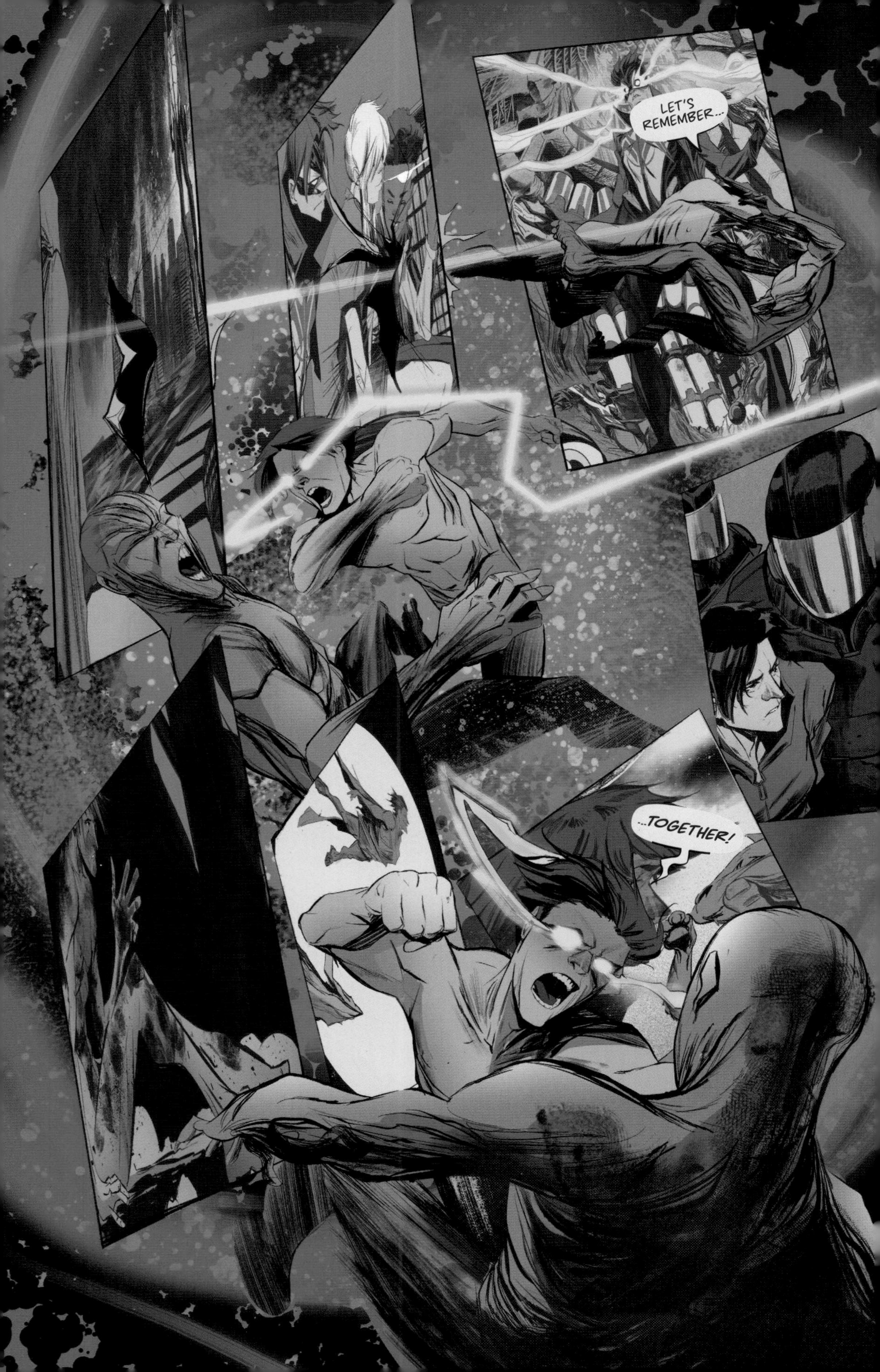
LET'S REMEMBER...
...TOGETHER!

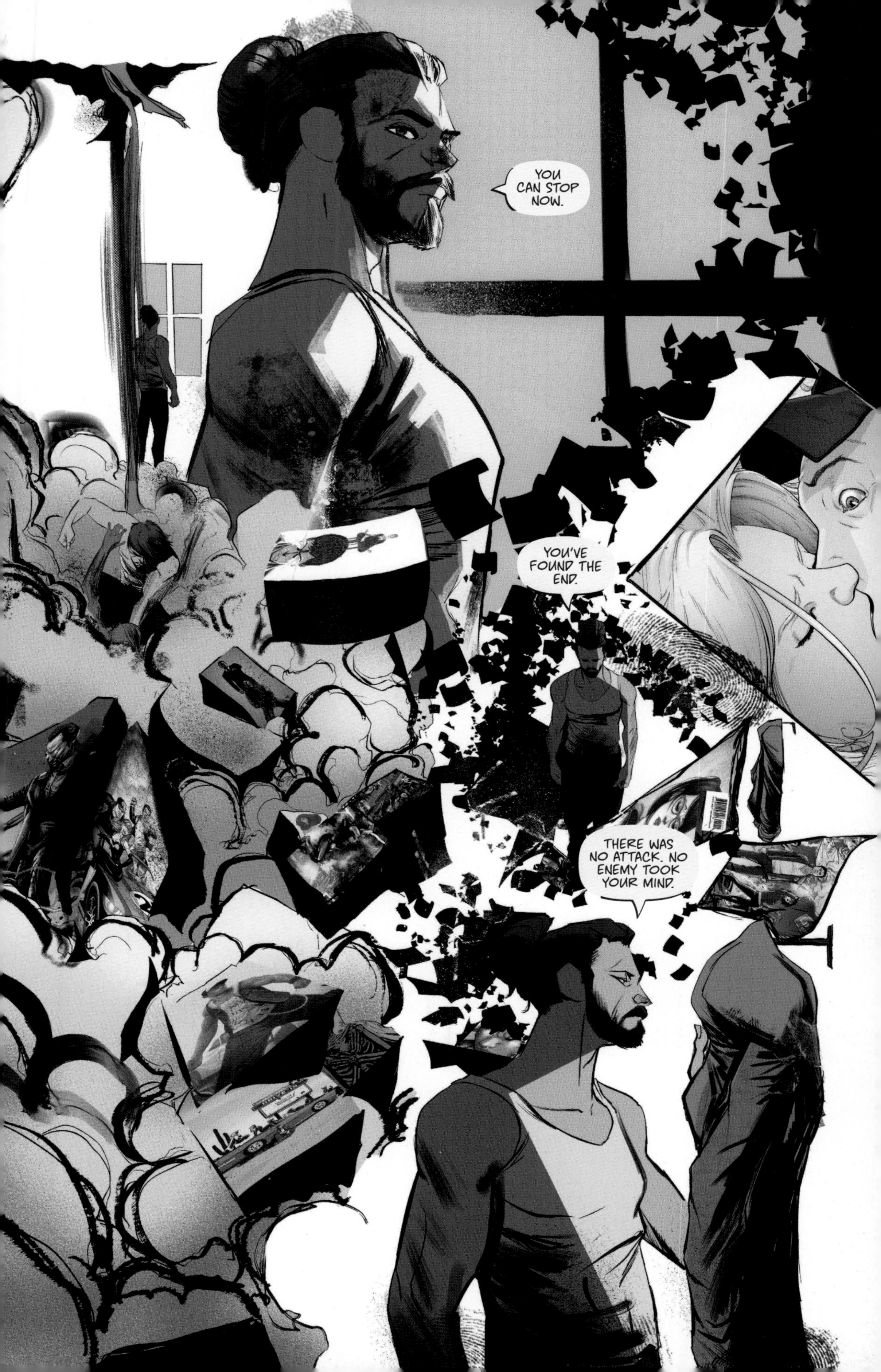

YOU CAN STOP NOW.
YOU'VE FOUND THE END.
THERE WAS NO ATTACK. NO ENEMY TOOK YOUR MIND.

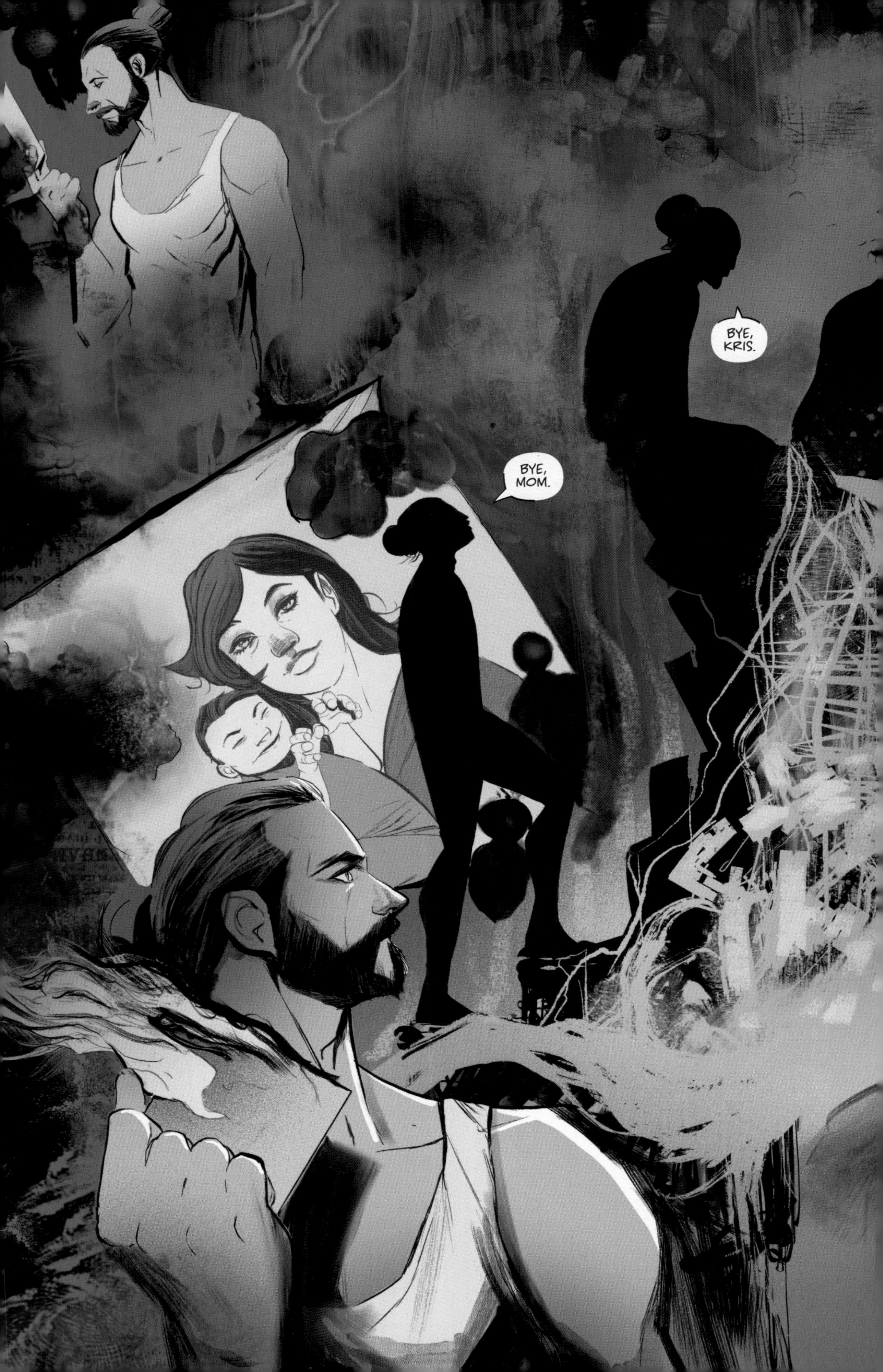
BYE, KRIS.
BYE, MOM.

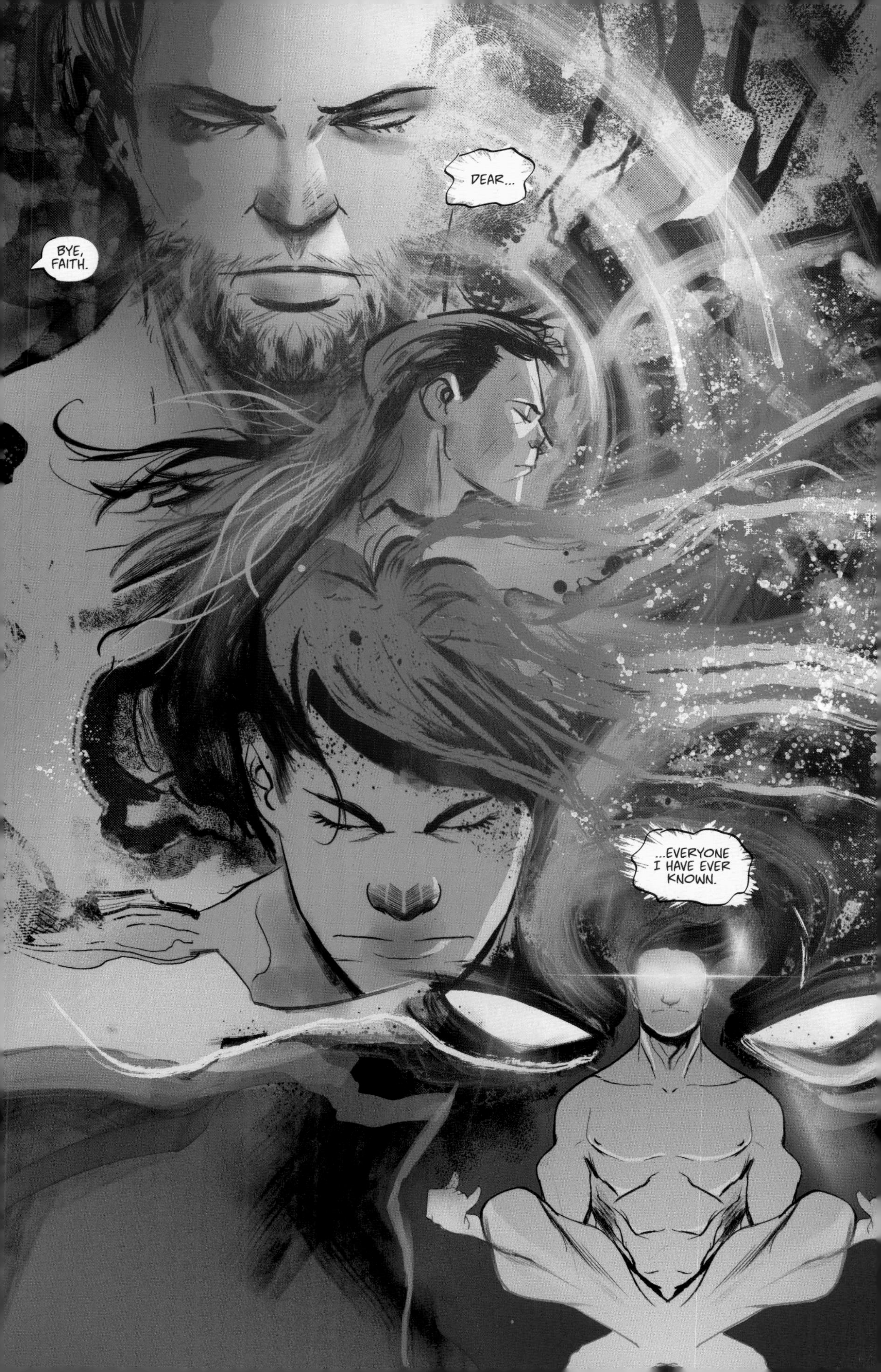
DEAR...
BYE, FAITH.
...EVERYONE I HAVE EVER KNOWN.

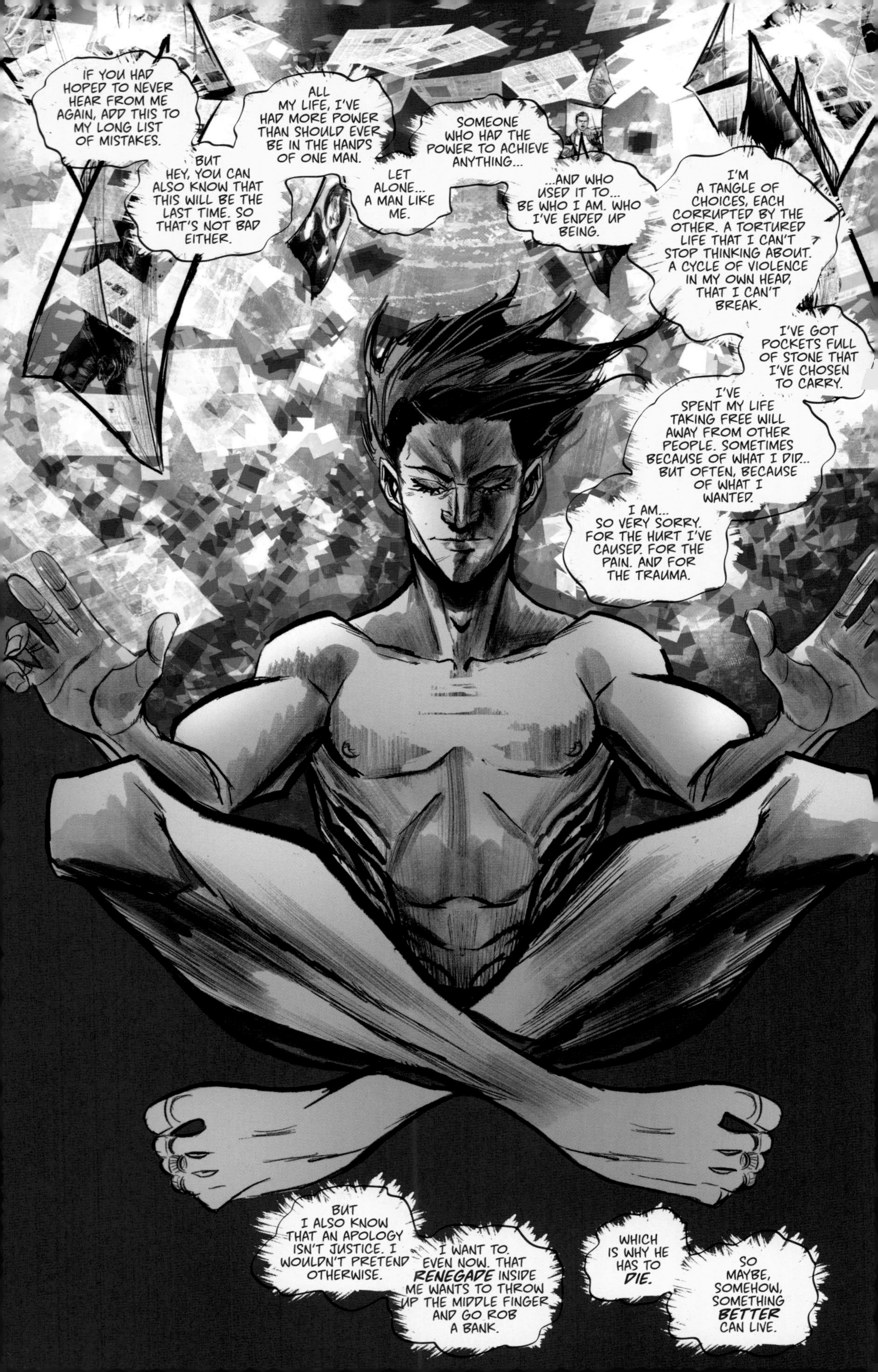
IF YOU HAD HOPED TO NEVER HEAR FROM ME AGAIN, ADD THIS TO MY LONG LIST OF MISTAKES.
BUT HEY, YOU CAN ALSO KNOW THAT THIS WILL BE THE LAST TIME. SO THAT'S NOT BAD EITHER.
ALL MY LIFE, I'VE HAD MORE POWER THAN SHOULD EVER BE IN THE HANDS OF ONE MAN.
LET ALONE... A MAN LIKE ME.
SOMEONE WHO HAD THE POWER TO ACHIEVE ANYTHING...
...AND WHO USED IT TO... BE WHO I AM. WHO I'VE ENDED UP BEING.
I'M A TANGLE OF CHOICES, EACH CORRUPTED BY THE OTHER. A TORTURED LIFE THAT I CAN'T STOP THINKING ABOUT. A CYCLE OF VIOLENCE IN MY OWN HEAD, THAT I CAN'T BREAK.
I'VE GOT POCKETS FULL OF STONE THAT I'VE CHOSEN TO CARRY.
I'VE SPENT MY LIFE TAKING FREE WILL AWAY FROM OTHER PEOPLE. SOMETIMES BECAUSE OF WHAT I DID... BUT OFTEN, BECAUSE OF WHAT I WANTED.
I AM... SO VERY SORRY. FOR THE HURT I'VE CAUSED. FOR THE PAIN. AND FOR THE TRAUMA.
BUT I ALSO KNOW THAT AN APOLOGY ISN'T JUSTICE. I WOULDN'T PRETEND OTHERWISE.
I WANT TO. EVEN NOW. THAT RENEGADE INSIDE ME WANTS TO THROW UP THE MIDDLE FINGER AND GO ROB A BANK.
WHICH IS WHY HE HAS TO DIE.
SO MAYBE, SOMEHOW, SOMETHING BETTER CAN LIVE.

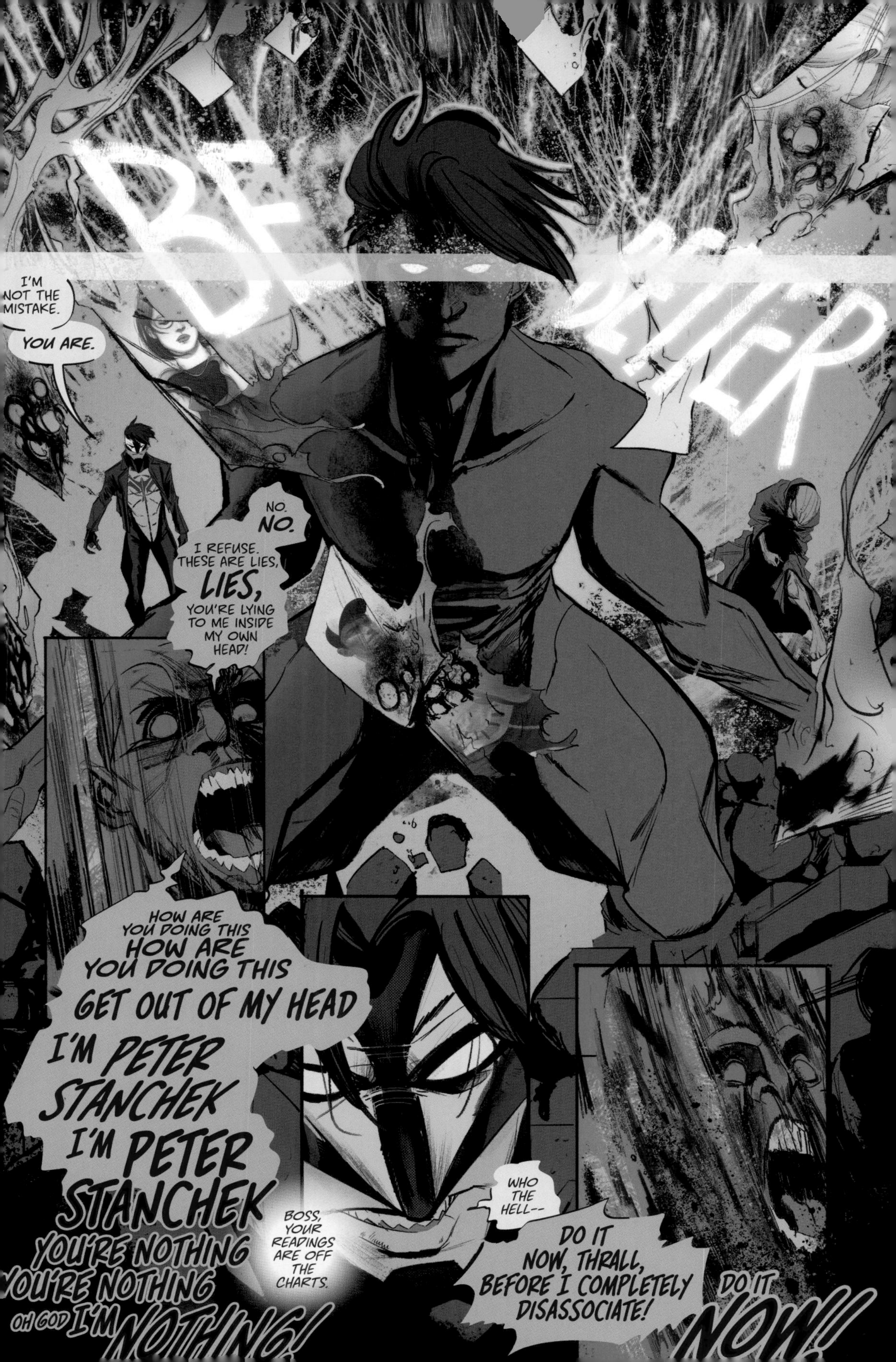

BE BETTER
I'M NOT THE MISTAKE.
YOU ARE.
NO. NO.
I REFUSE. THESE ARE LIES, LIES, YOU'RE LYING TO ME INSIDE MY OWN HEAD!
HOW ARE YOU DOING THIS HOW ARE YOU DOING THIS GET OUT OF MY HEAD I'M PETER STANCHEK I'M PETER STANCHEK YOU'RE NOTHING YOU'RE NOTHING OH GOD I'M NOTHING!
BOSS, YOUR READINGS ARE OFF THE CHARTS.
WHO THE HELL--
DO IT NOW, THRALL, BEFORE I COMPLETELY DISASSOCIATE!
DO IT NOW!!

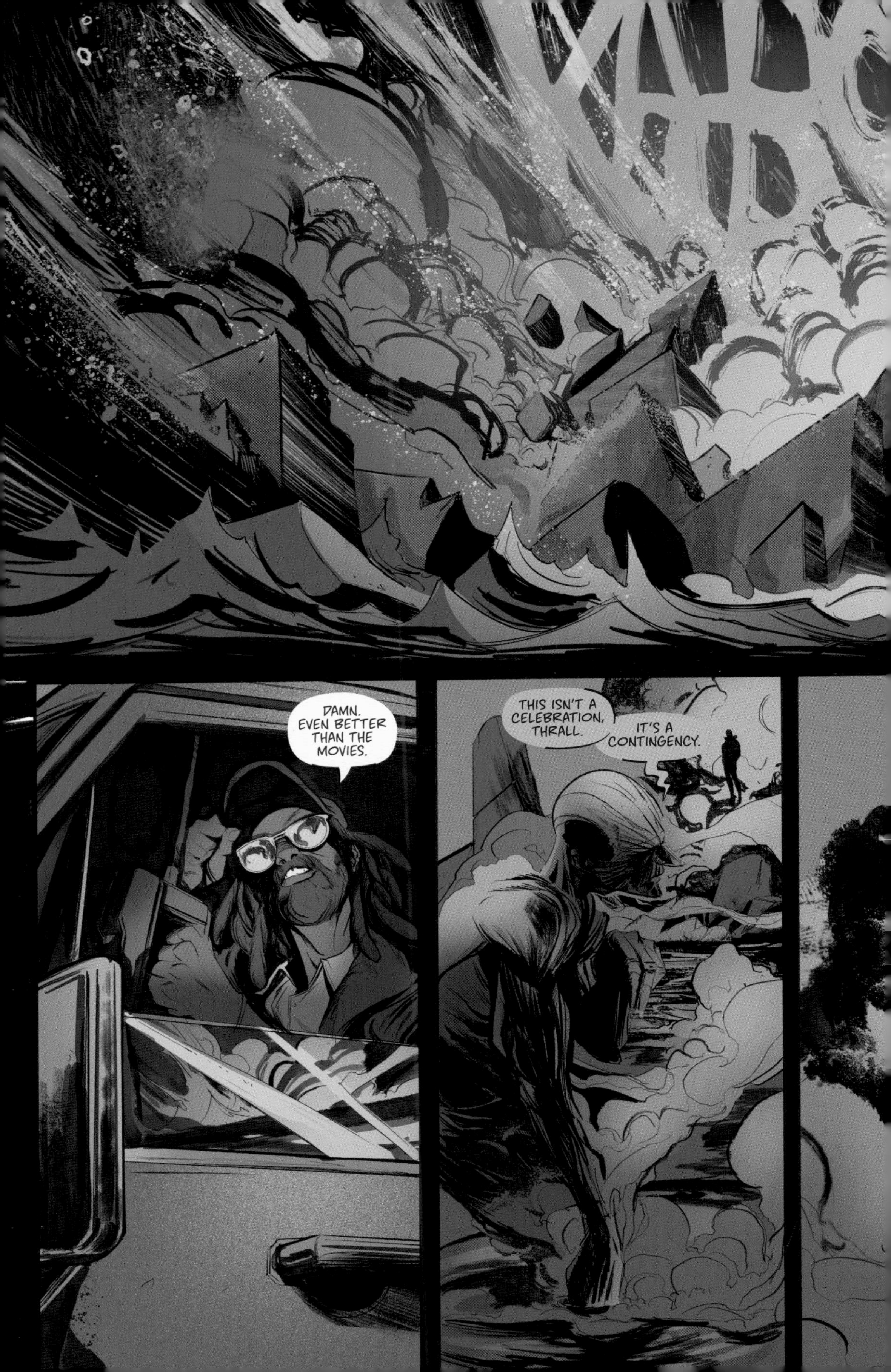
DAMN. EVEN BETTER THAN THE MOVIES.
THIS ISN'T A CELEBRATION, THRALL.
IT'S A CONTINGENCY.

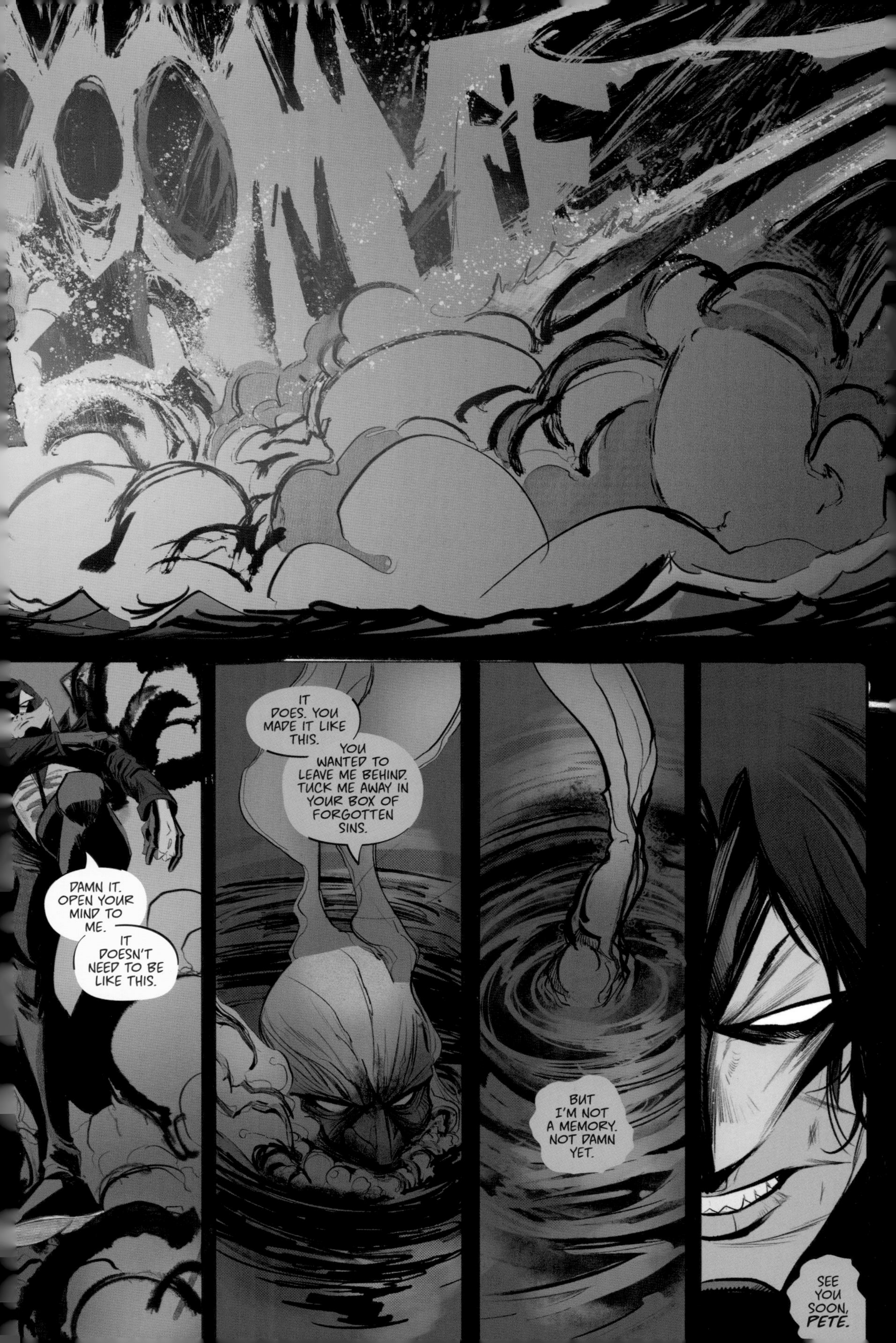
DAMN IT. OPEN YOUR MIND TO ME.
IT DOESN'T NEED TO BE LIKE THIS.
IT DOES. YOU MADE IT LIKE THIS.
YOU WANTED TO LEAVE ME BEHIND. TUCK ME AWAY IN YOUR BOX OF FORGOTTEN SINS.
BUT I'M NOT A MEMORY. NOT DAMN YET.
SEE YOU SOON, PETE.

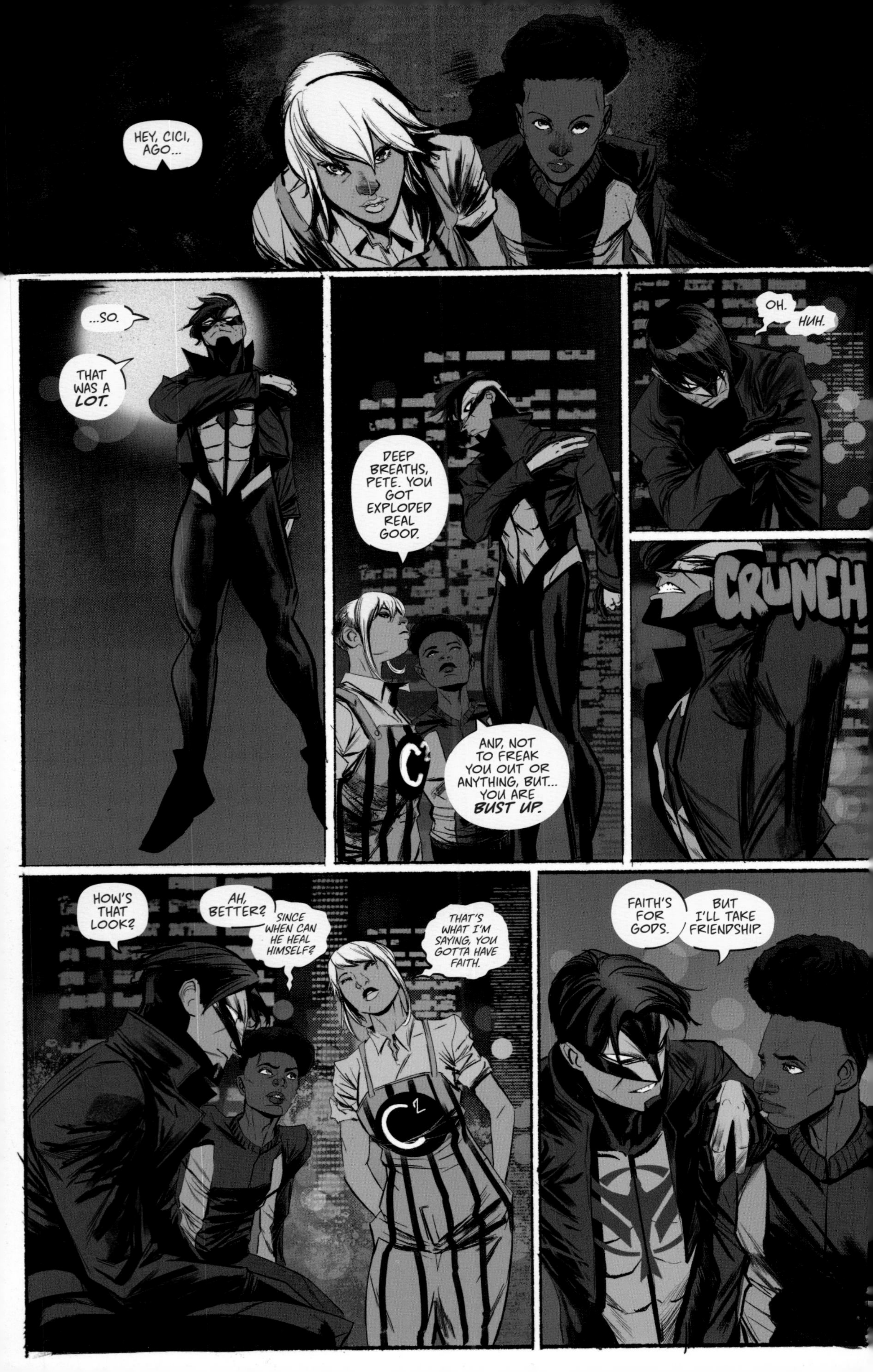
HEY, CICI, AGO...
...SO.
THAT WAS A LOT.
DEEP BREATHS, PETE. YOU GOT EXPLODED REAL GOOD.
AND, NOT TO FREAK YOU OUT OR ANYTHING, BUT... YOU ARE BUST UP.
OH.
HUH.
CRUNCH
HOW'S THAT LOOK?
AH, BETTER?
SINCE WHEN CAN HE HEAL HIMSELF?
THAT'S WHAT I'M SAYING, YOU GOTTA HAVE FAITH.
FAITH'S FOR GODS.
BUT I'LL TAKE FRIENDSHIP.

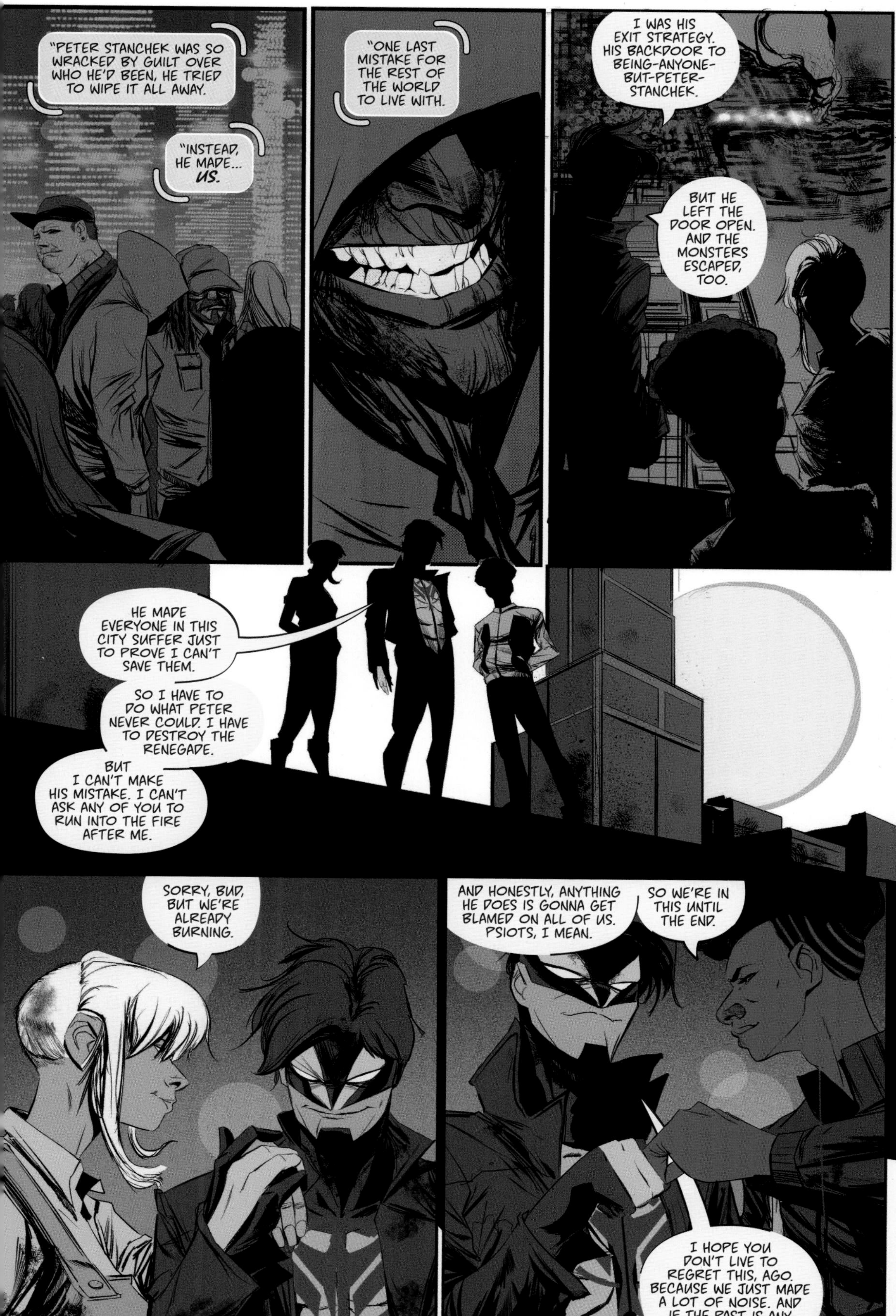
"PETER STANCHEK WAS SO WRACKED BY GUILT OVER WHO HE'D BEEN, HE TRIED TO WIPE IT ALL AWAY.
"INSTEAD, HE MADE... *US.*
"ONE LAST MISTAKE FOR THE REST OF THE WORLD TO LIVE WITH.
I WAS HIS EXIT STRATEGY. HIS BACKDOOR TO BEING-ANYONE-BUT-PETER-STANCHEK.
BUT HE LEFT THE DOOR OPEN. AND THE MONSTERS ESCAPED, TOO.
HE MADE EVERYONE IN THIS CITY SUFFER JUST TO PROVE I CAN'T SAVE THEM.
SO I HAVE TO DO WHAT PETER NEVER COULD. I HAVE TO DESTROY THE RENEGADE.
BUT I CAN'T MAKE HIS MISTAKE. I CAN'T ASK ANY OF YOU TO RUN INTO THE FIRE AFTER ME.
SORRY, BUD, BUT WE'RE ALREADY BURNING.
AND HONESTLY, ANYTHING HE DOES IS GONNA GET BLAMED ON ALL OF US. PSIOTS, I MEAN.
SO WE'RE IN THIS UNTIL THE END.
I HOPE YOU DON'T LIVE TO REGRET THIS, AGO. BECAUSE WE JUST MADE A LOT OF NOISE. AND IF THE PAST IS ANY INDICATION...

"...THEY WILL SEND EVERYTHING THEY'VE GOT.
"THEY'LL CREATE WEAPONS JUST TO END US.
"THEY'LL HAVE THE MONEY. THE POWER. THE PROTECTION. AND THE IMMUNITY.
"AND THEY WON'T STOP UNTIL EVERY PSIOT IN CHICAGO PAYS FOR MY MISTAKES.
"WE CAN'T PLAY NICE.
WE CAN'T BE MODEL CITIZENS. WE CAN'T BE RENEGADES. WE CAN'T BE INSURGENTS.
THAT'S THE ONE THING PETER STANCHEK GOT RIGHT, AGO.
THEN WHAT THE HELL ARE WE SUPPOSED TO BE?
WE CAN BE BETTER.
NEXT:
BOOK TWO

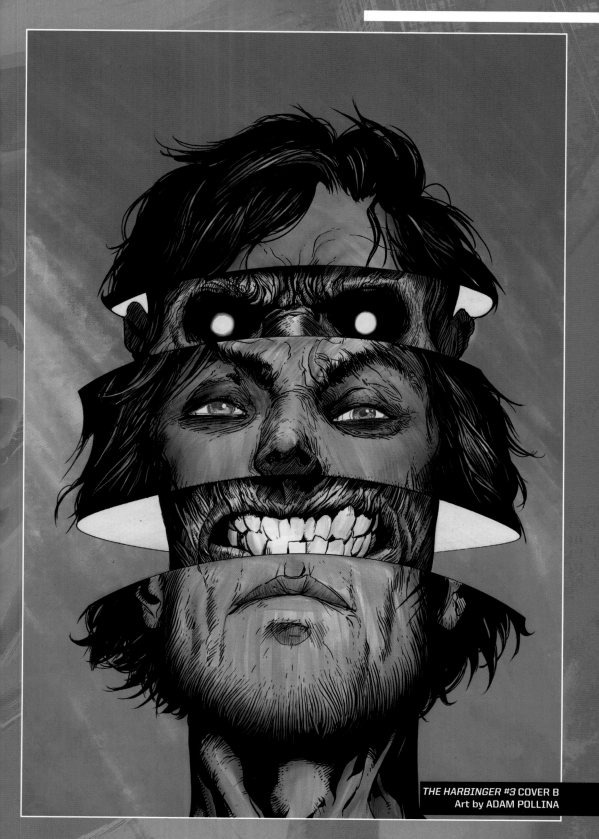

THE HARBINGER #3 COVER B
Art by ADAM POLLINA

P.R.S. FILES - REPORT #0041

TOYO HARADA

Toyo Harada, C.E.O. of Harada Global Conglomerates and the most powerful telepath in the world, has a vision for a perfect future. Behind the scenes, he assembled a private army in the form of the Harbinger Foundation, a secret academy built to activate and train young super humans called "psiots" that, like himself, exhibit an array of a extraordinary abilities. He utilized his powers and many resources to weave a secret web of manipulation throughout the world that was later exposed by the Renegades.

Powers: Near-limitless telekinesis and telepathy. Harada also possesses a high level of intellect and resourcefulness.

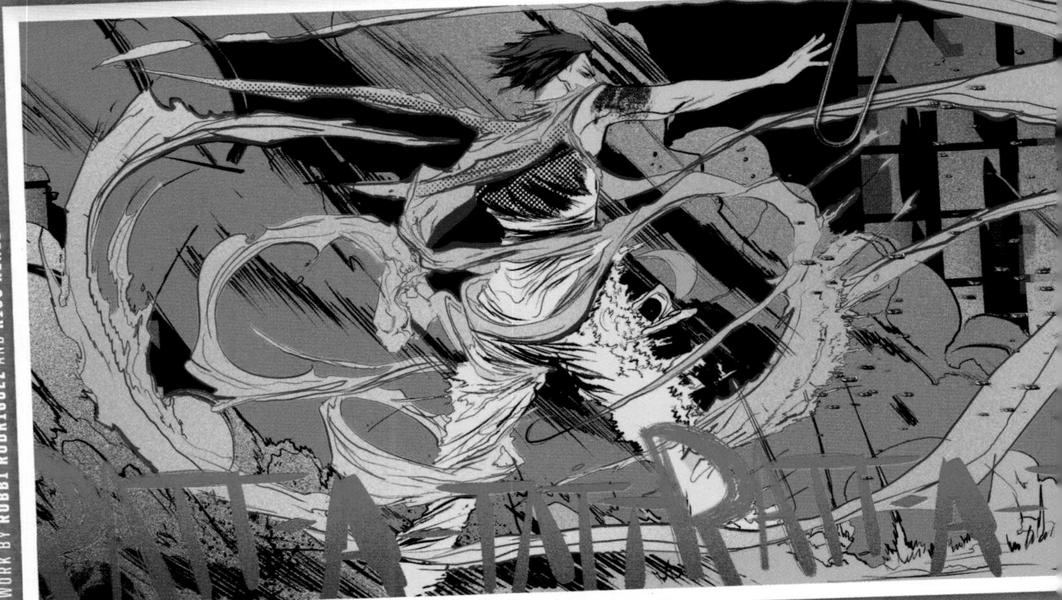

ARTWORK BY ROBBI RODRIGUEZ AND RICO RENZI

Originally presented in *THE HARBINGER PREORDER EDITION #1*

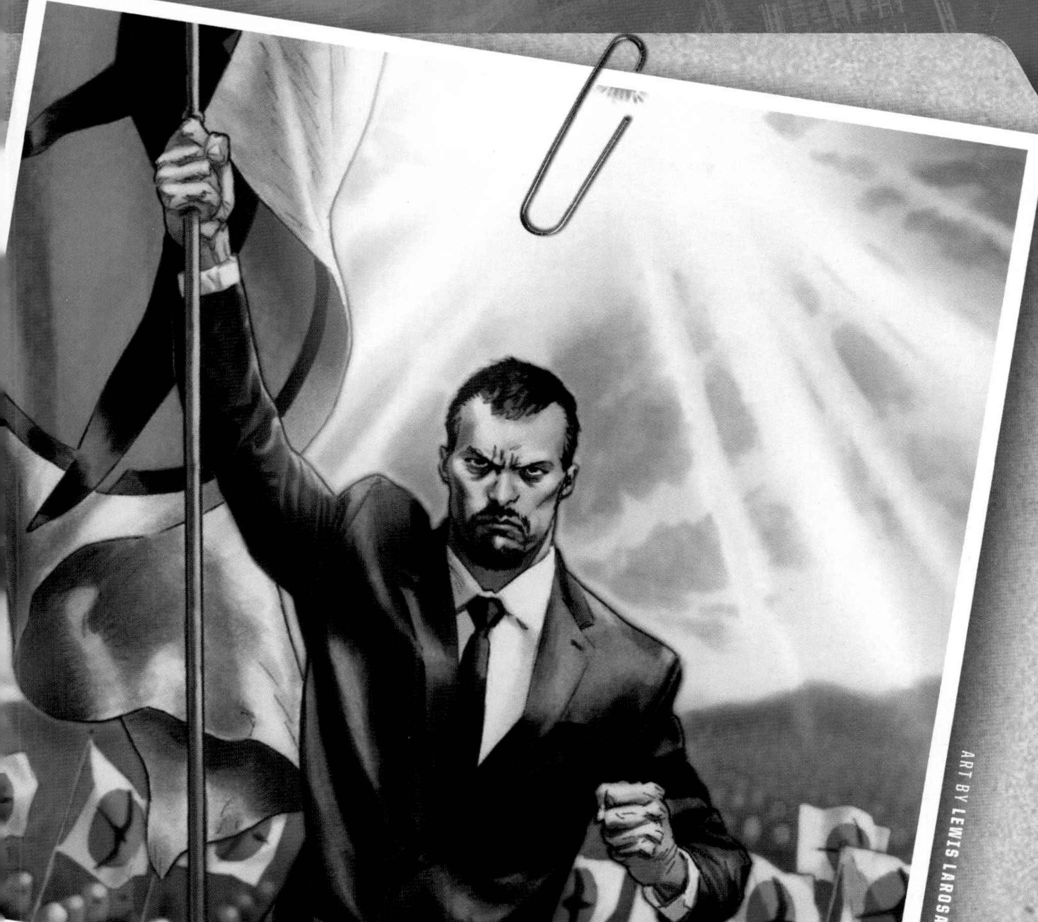

ART BY LEWIS LAROSA AND BRIAN REBER

PETER STANCHEK

Peter Stanchek is an alcoholic and drug addict that possesses extraordinary powers. Stanchek was previously one of Harada's students at the Harbinger Foundation, but after a failed attempt of manipulation that resulted in the death of Peter's best friend, Joe, Peter turned on Harada and assembled his own team of ragtag psiots called the Renegades. This team worked to take down Harada and eventually exposed his plans of domination to the world.

Powers: Telekinesis, telepathy, and many more untapped abilities.

P.R.S. FILES - REPORT #0156

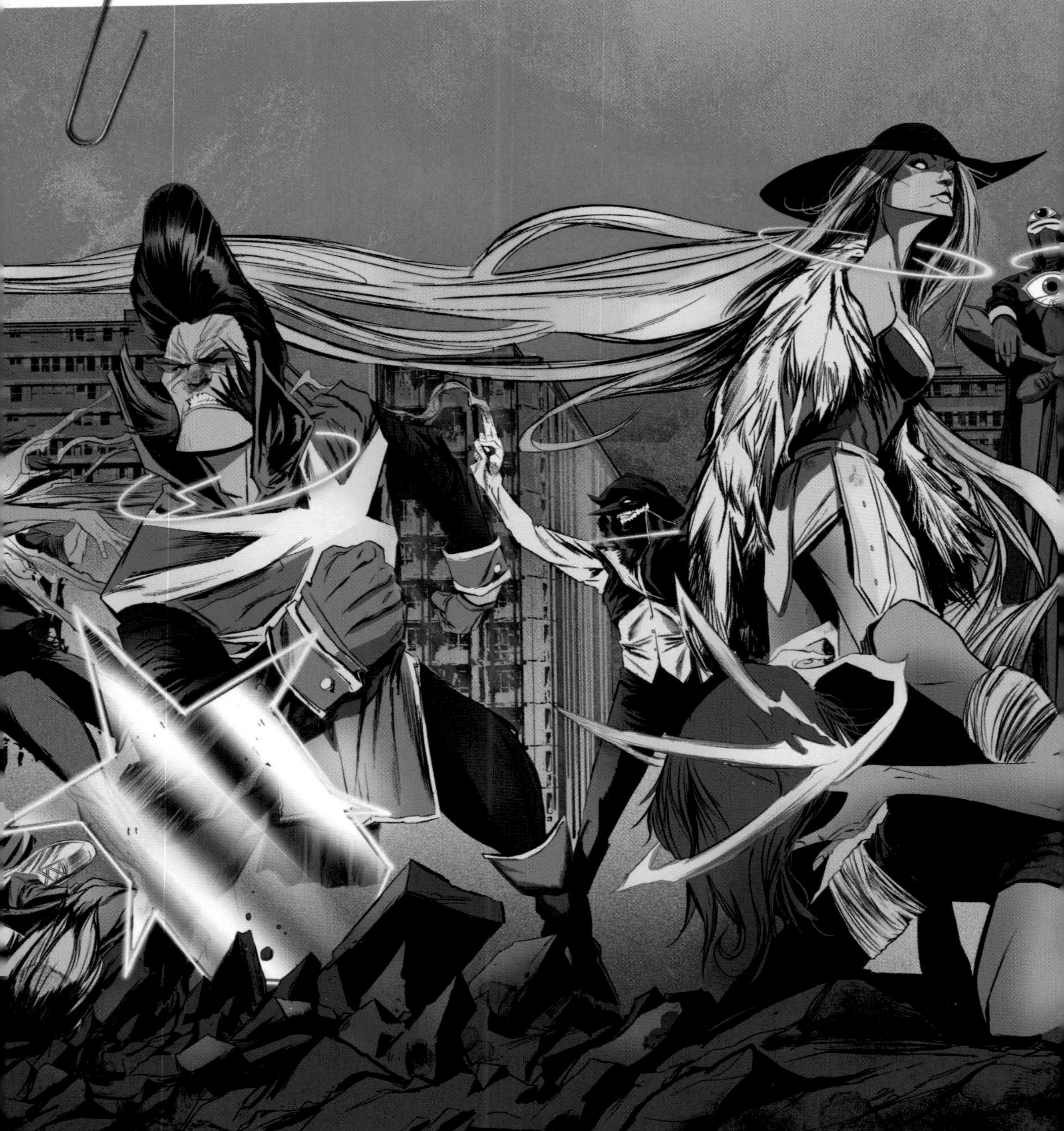

ARTWORK BY **ROBBI RODRIGUEZ** AND **RICO RENZI**

THE WARNING:

A group of vigilante "heroes" that utilize H.A.R.D. Corps technology to capture and exploit psiots. The world sees them as heroes, but they only cause fear and destruction for the inhabitants of Psiot City.

THE BADGE is a Chicago cop, who watched one too many criminals walk free...at least, that's what he tells himself when he screams "Law and Order" and cracks psiot skulls. With bulletproof skin and a telekinetic riot shield, for him the line between psiot, criminal and immigrant is virtually non-existent.

BLAM only speaks to trigger his powers, "Eye," "Arm," and "Blam." He's an incredibly deadly marksman with a suite of powers exclusively designed to kill. Dressed in all-black, a threatening presence despite his odd name, Blam is the Rorschach of the crew, an off-putting element in an already off-putting force.

A Greek heiress turning to vengeance for the rise of Harada's psiot empire and the fall of her family's fortune, the mythically inspired LETHEAN has a suite of powers that reflect the gods of her homeland, including the power to wipe her target's memory.

OVERWATCH dominates the mind of any target he sees, turning them into private puppets, utterly unconcerned with the damage he leaves behind. A coward at his core, Overwatch's secret is that he fears psiots. When Harada's Eggbreakers came for his psiot brother at their home in Somalia, the family rose up and were slaughtered for their defiance.

FUTURIST is a billionaire with a god complex. A man devoted to increasing his own abilities, his suite of abilities were almost exclusively purchased from the disbanded remnants of the H.A.R.D. Corps. At his core, he believes himself to be the next Harada.

Originally presented in *THE HARBINGER PREORDER EDITION #2*

CHARACTER DESCRIPTION: **CICI**

Cici is a stylish, Asian-American woman that's currently living in Psiot City as an unactivated psiot. Cici's personal look is wild and chic, with ever-changing bleach blonde hair and structured clothes that she makes herself.

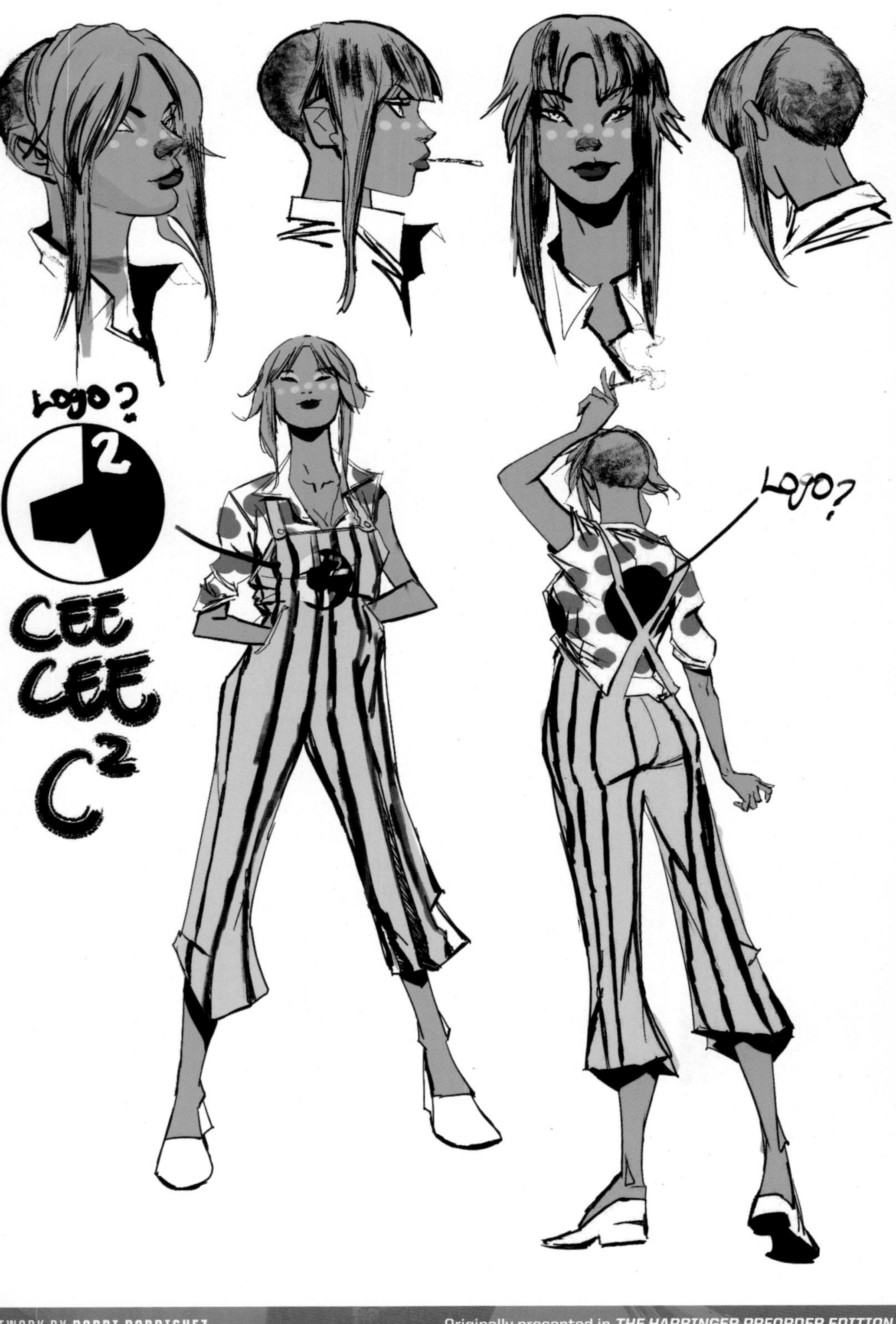

LOGO?
2
CEE
CEE
C²
LOGO?

Young Ago is a Black, stylish, good-looking teenager with amazing sneakers. This young psiot is the voice of Psiot City and a friend and foil to Peter as The Harbinger rises. His powers make him an antenna–whatever he says, people listen. Young Ago is at the the very beginning of his journey and showcases his fearless and radical nature by standing up to those who bully the inhabitants of Psiot City.

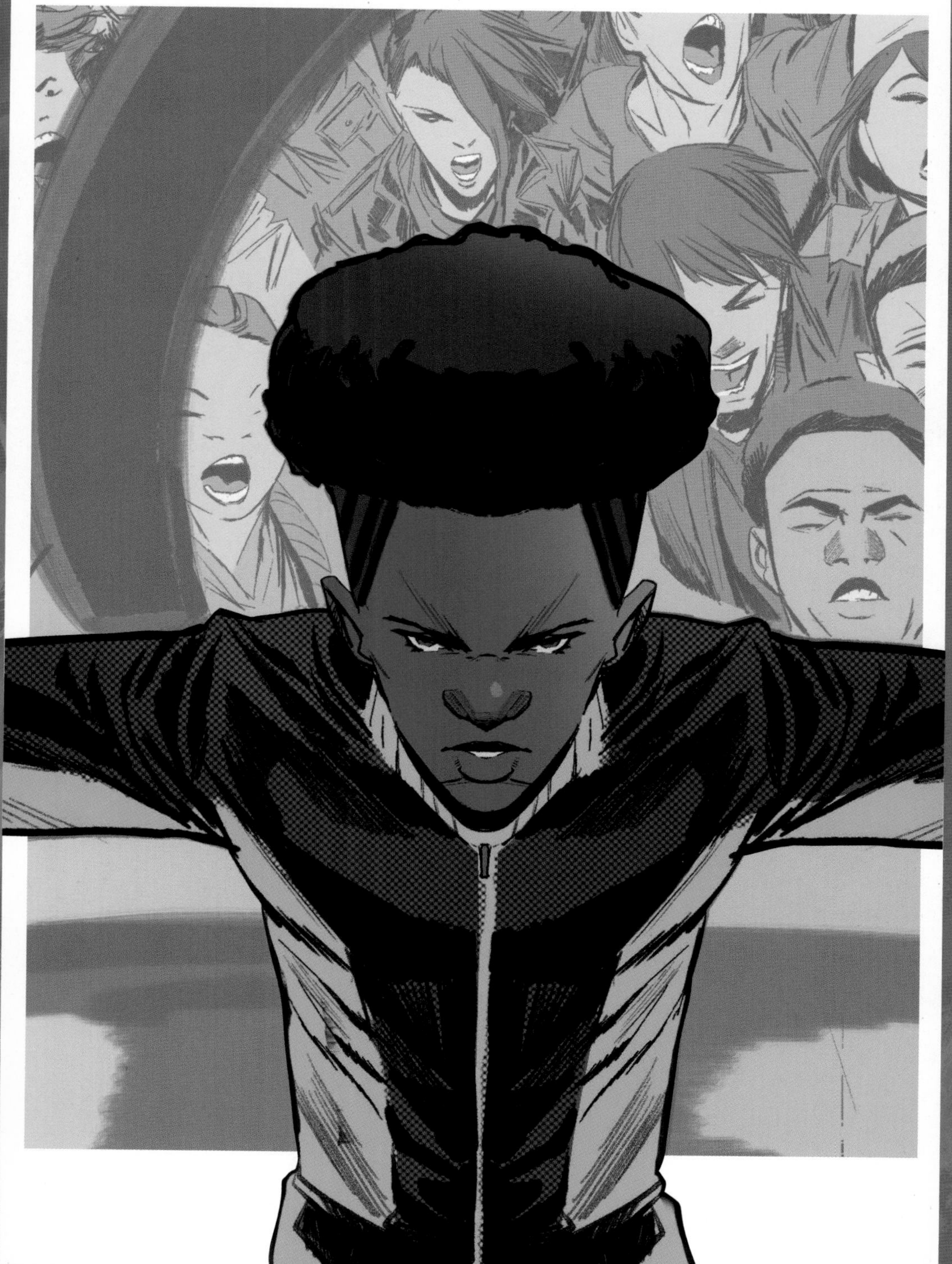

ARTWORK BY **ROBBI RODRIGUEZ** AND **RICO RENZI**

Originally presented in ***THE HARBINGER PREORDER EDITION #2***

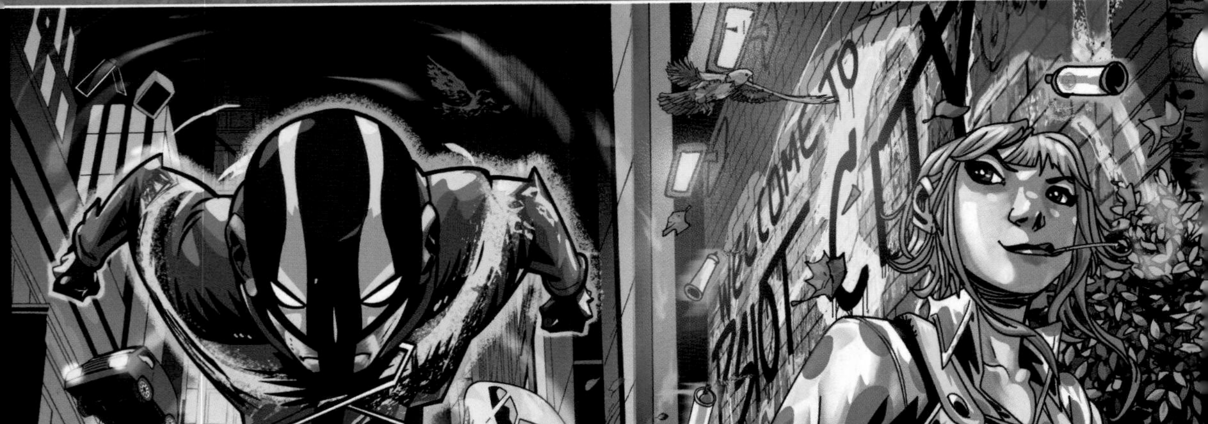
WELCOME TO
PSIOT

THE HARBINGER #1-4 INTERLOCKING PREORDER EDITION COVERS
Art by DAMION SCOTT

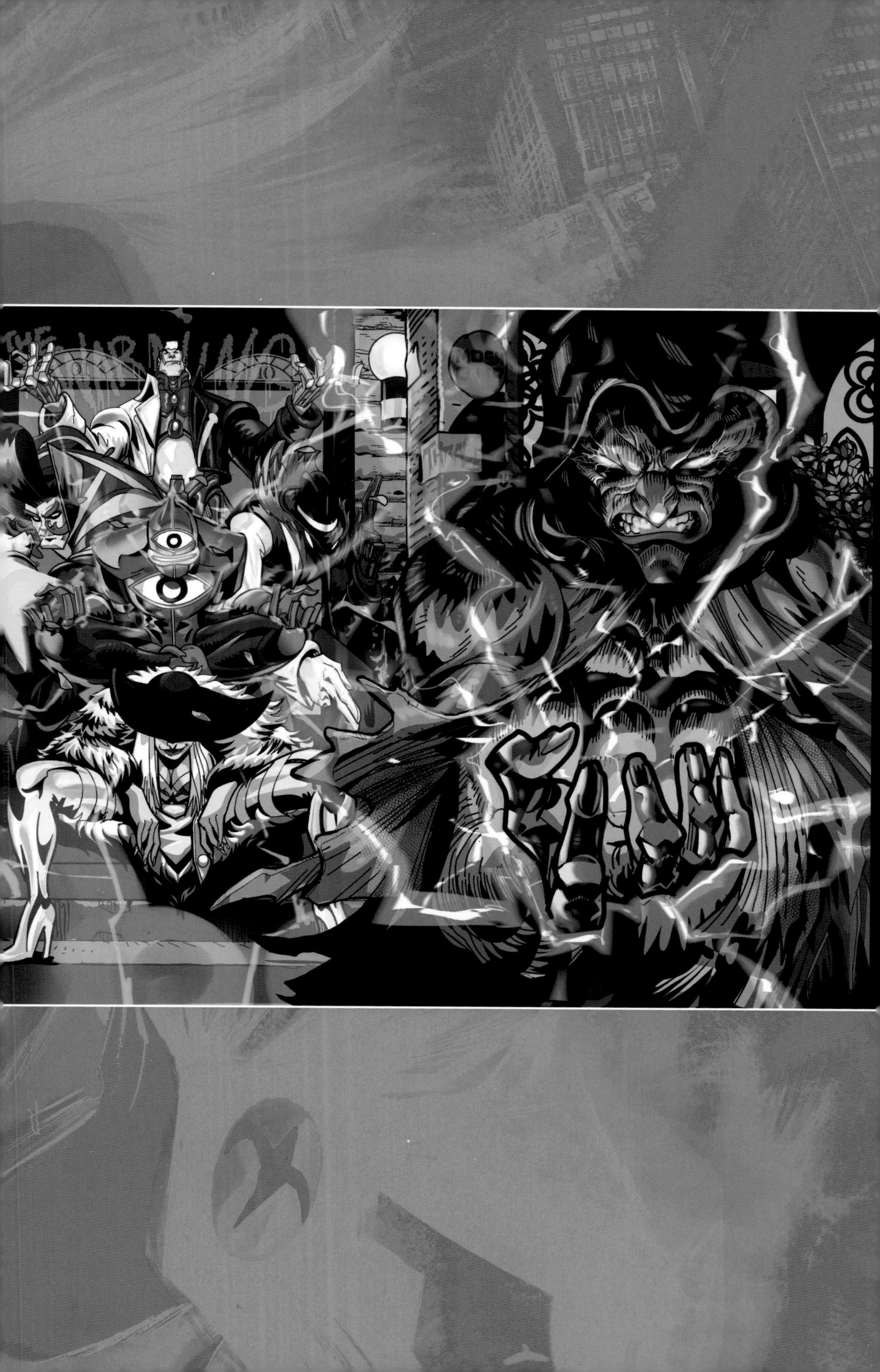

THE HARBINGER #2 COVER B
Art by NIK VIRELLA

THE HARBINGER #4 COVER B
Art by CLAUDIA IANNICELLO

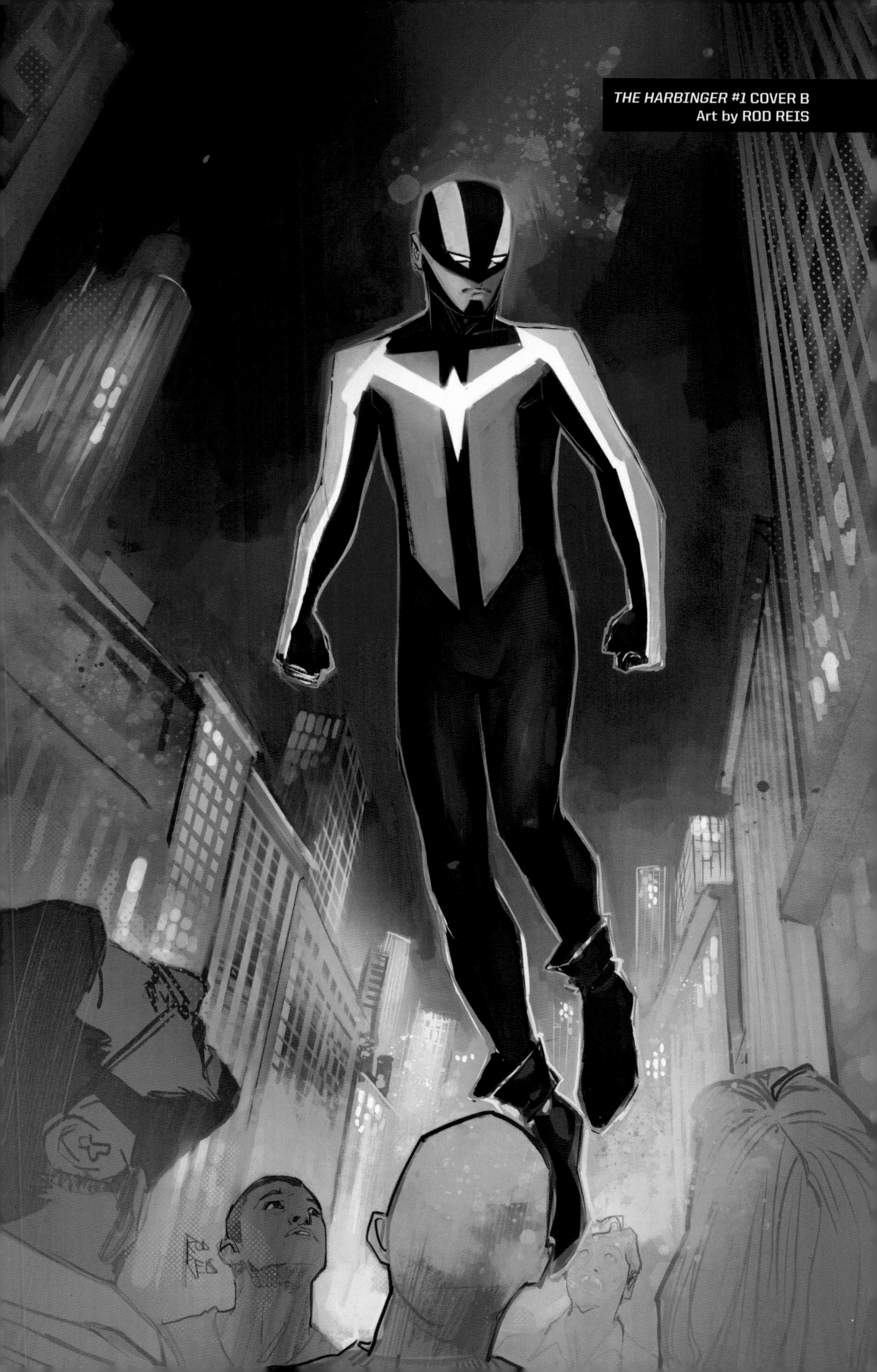

THE HARBINGER #1 COVER B
Art by ROD REIS

THE HARBINGER #1, pages 8, 9, and (facing) 10
Art by ROBBI RODRIGUEZ

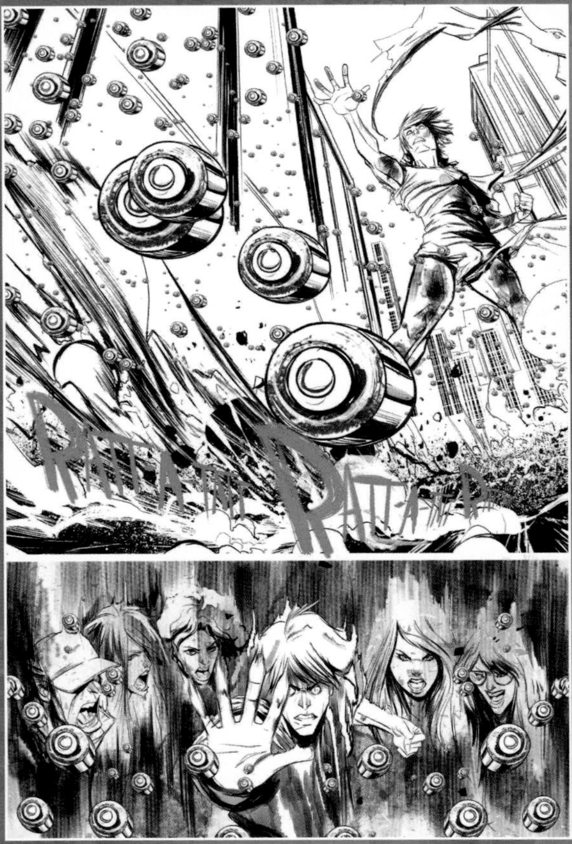

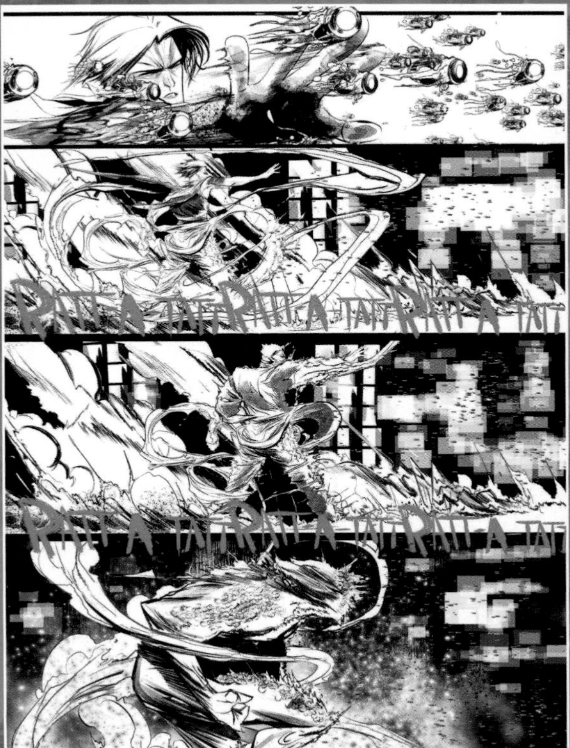
RATT A TATT RATT A TATT RATT A TATT
RATT A TATT RATT A TATT RATT A TATT

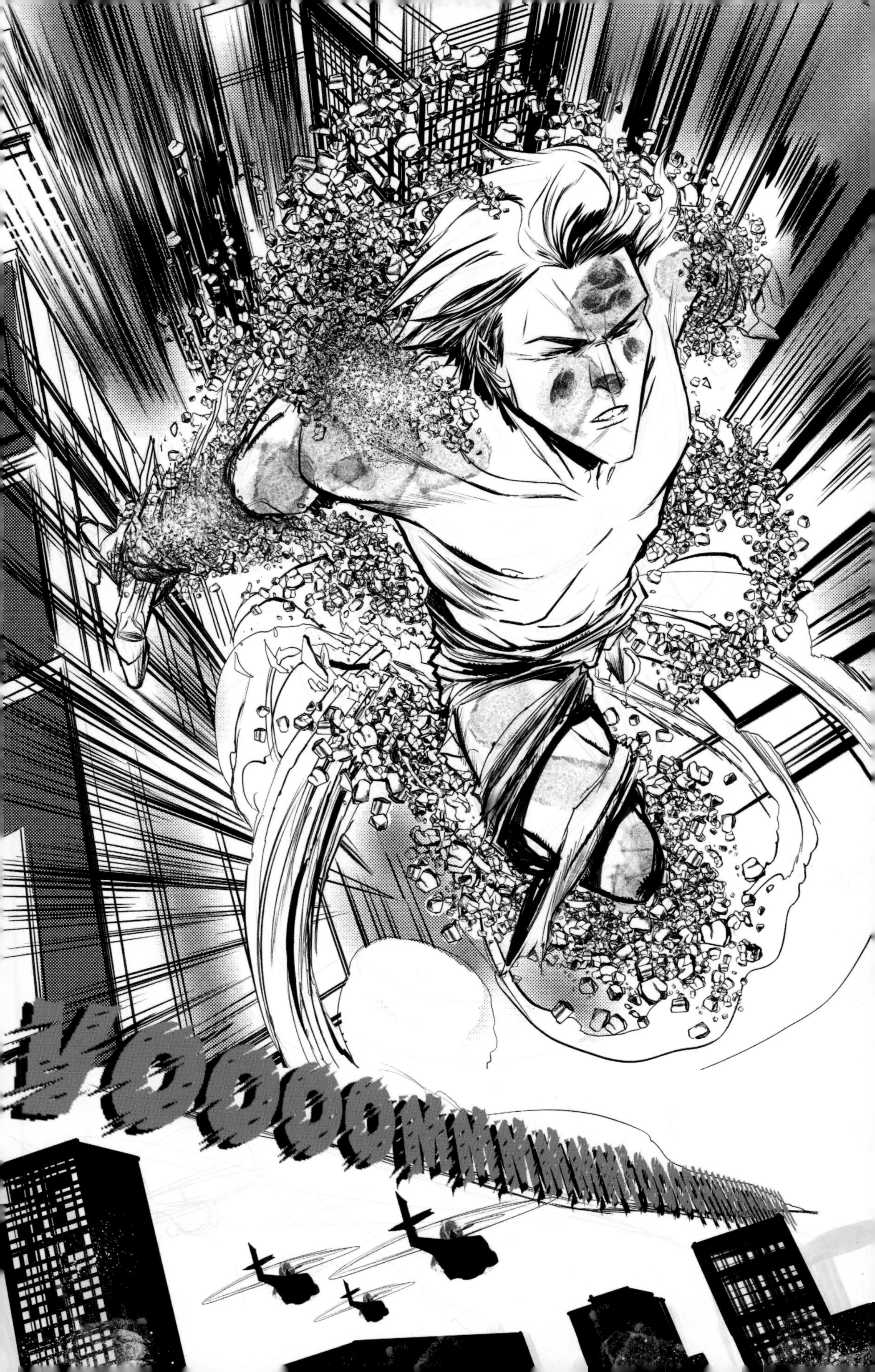
VOOOOOMMMMMM

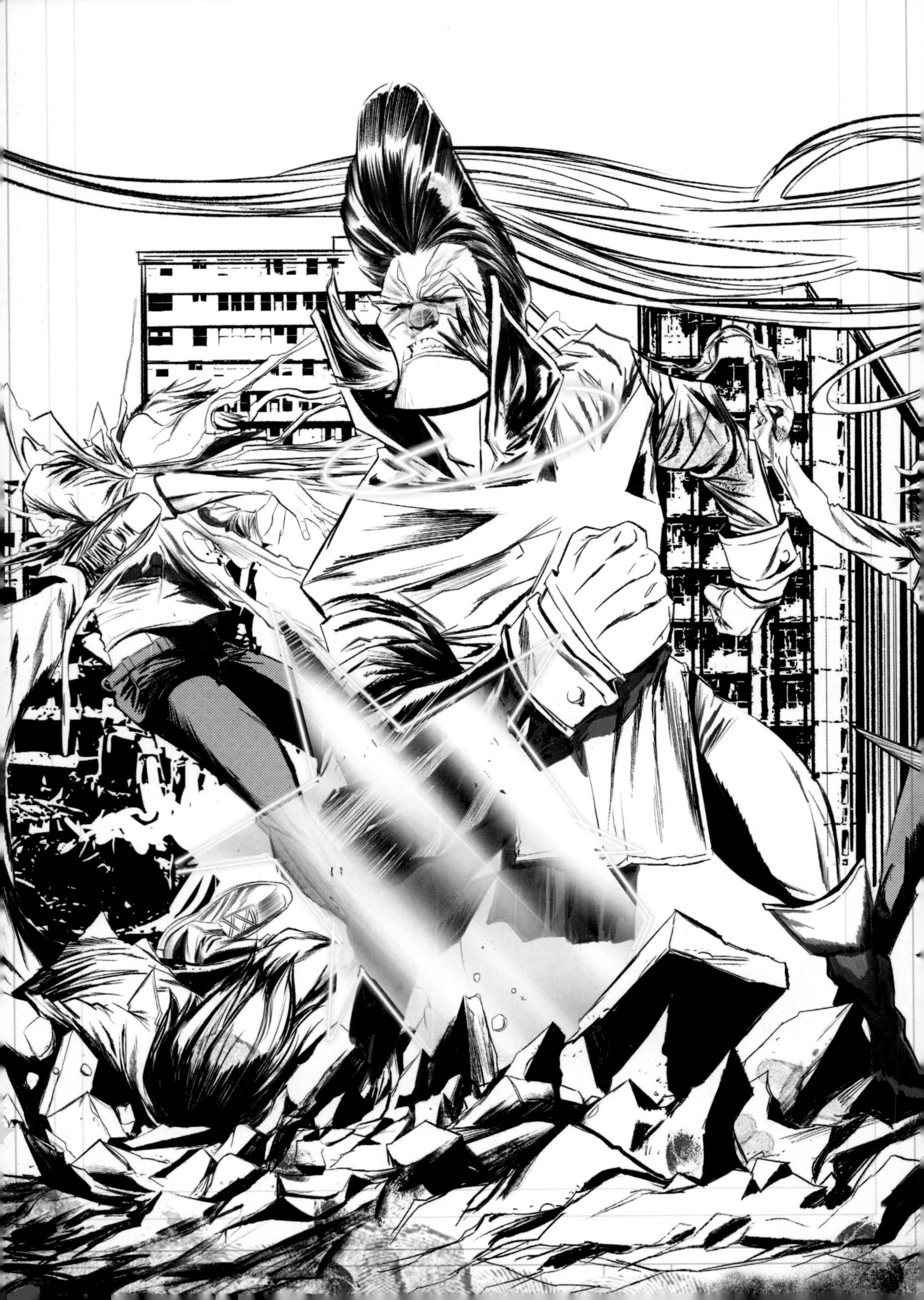

THE HARBINGER #3, pages 12-13
Art by ROBBI RODRIGUEZ

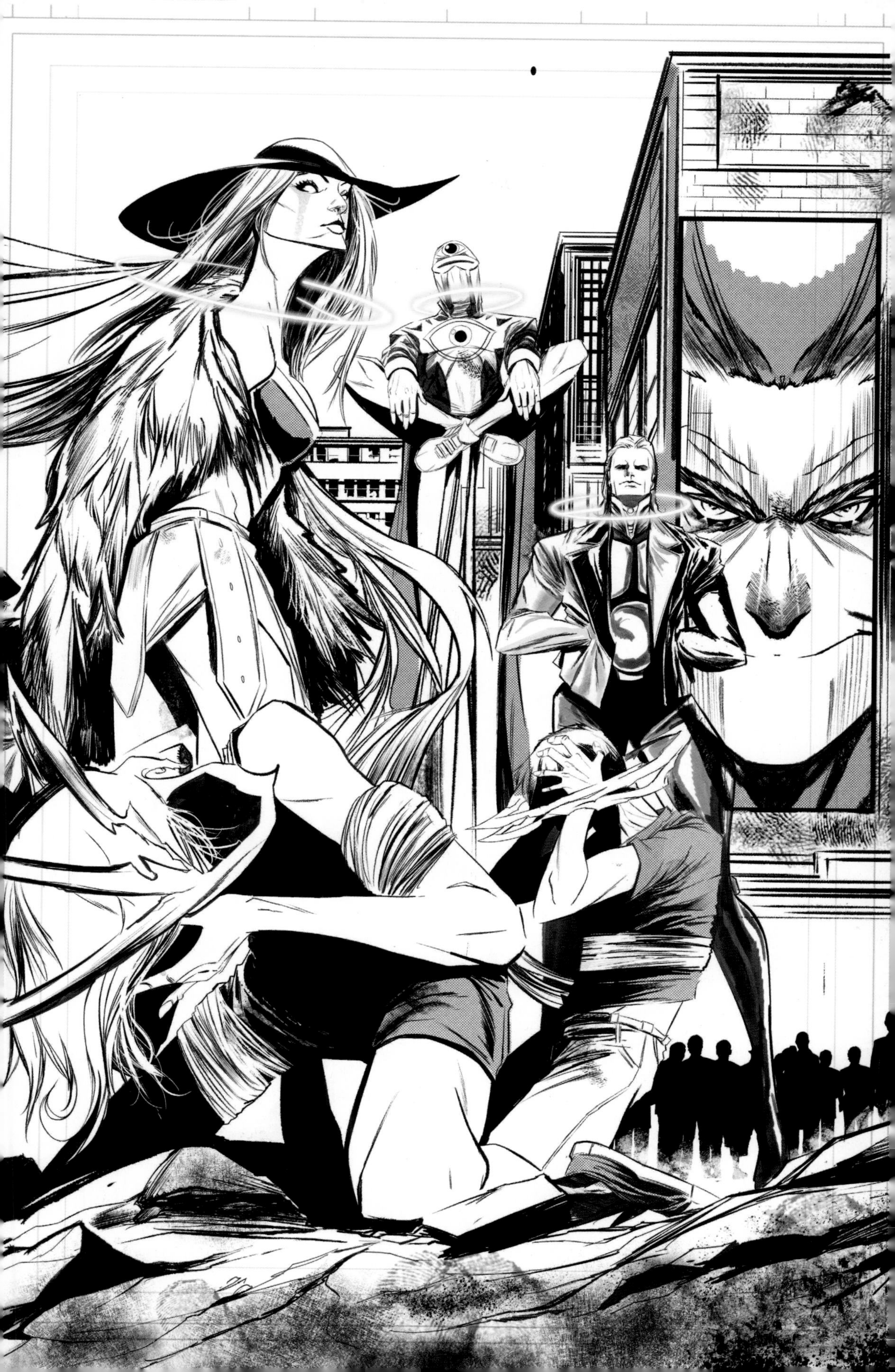

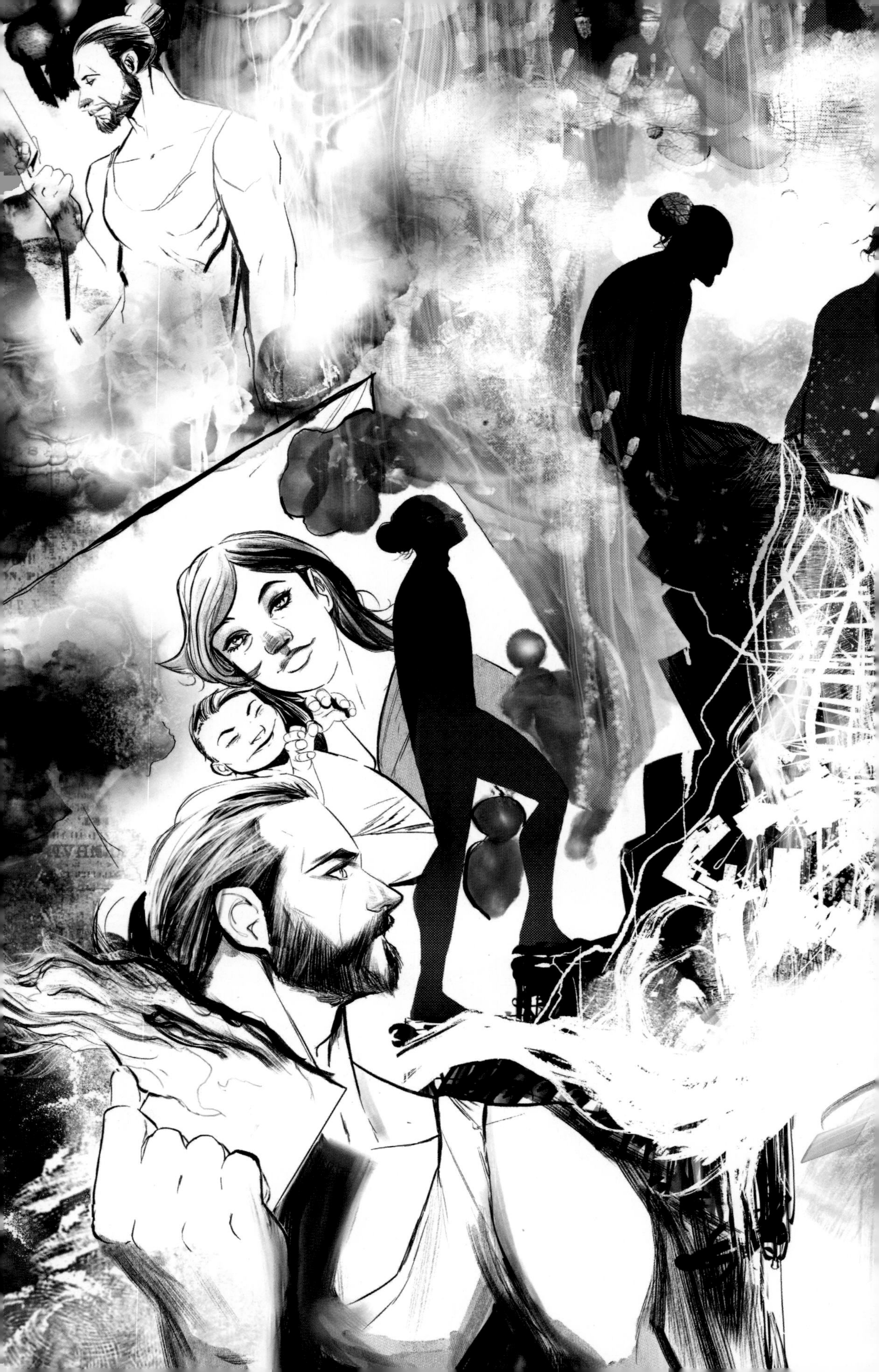

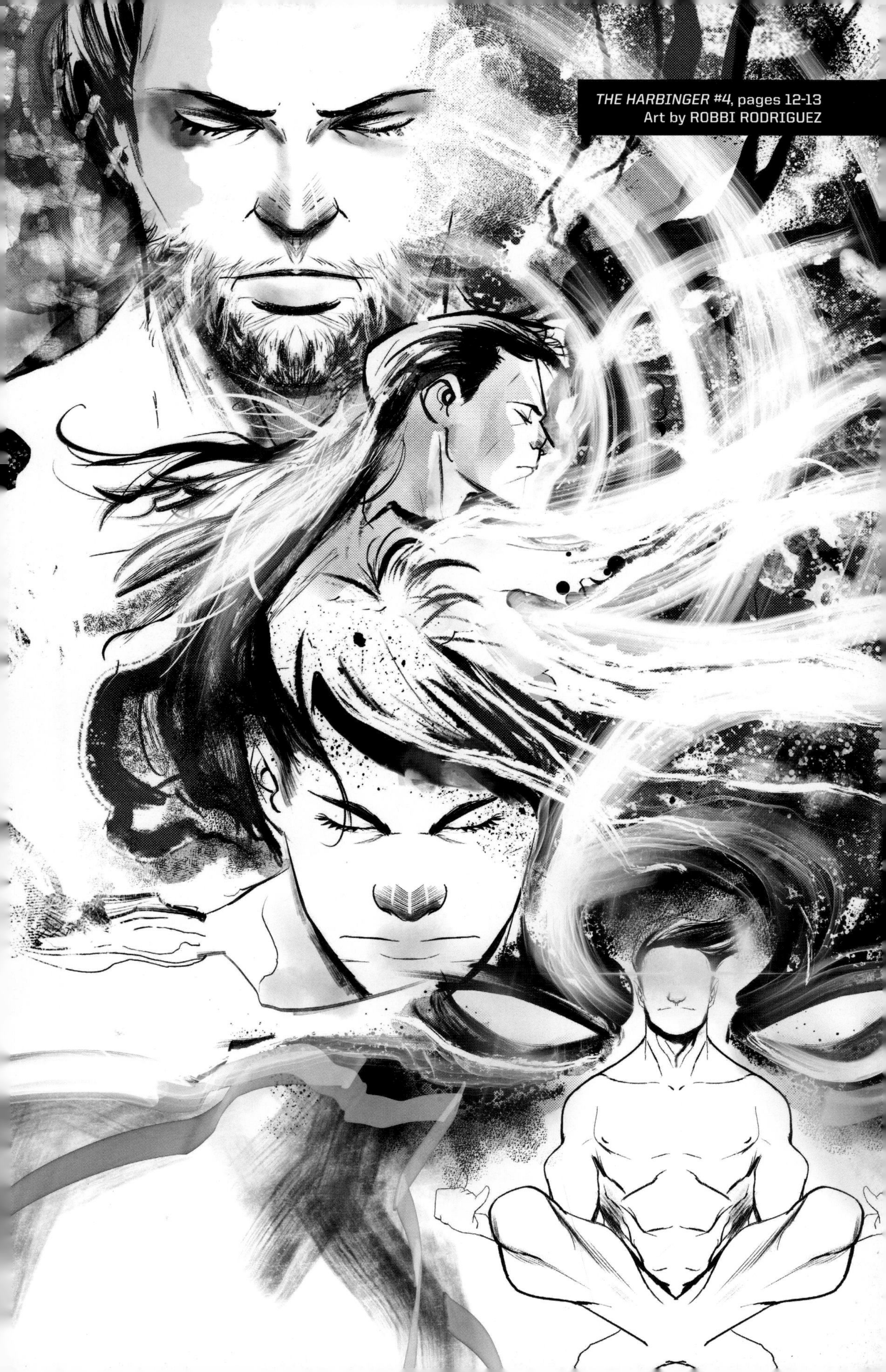

THE HARBINGER #4, pages 12-13
Art by ROBBI RODRIGUEZ

EXPLORE THE VALIANT U

ACTION & ADVENTURE

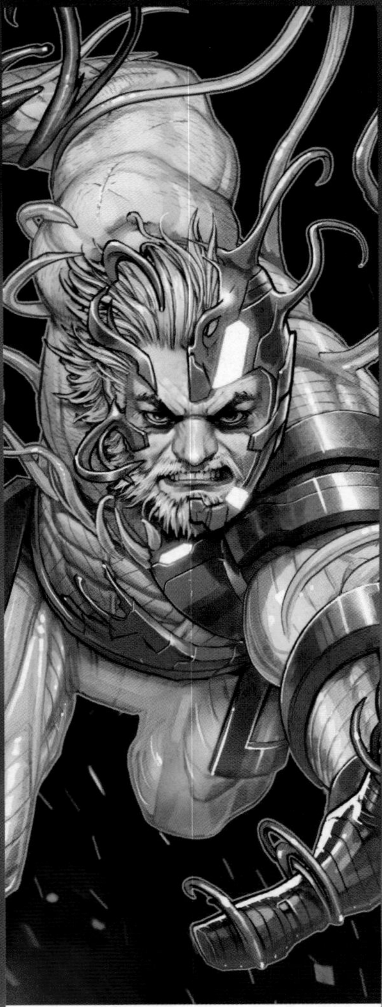

BLOODSHOT BOOK ONE
ISBN: 978-1-68215-255-3
NINJAK BOOK ONE
ISBN: 978-168215-410-6
SAVAGE
ISBN: 978-1-68215-189-1
WRATH OF THE ETERNAL WARRIOR VOL. 1: RISEN
ISBN: 978-1-68215-123-5
X-O MANOWAR (2019) BOOK ONE
ISBN: 978-1-68215-368-0

BLOCKBUSTER ADVENTURE

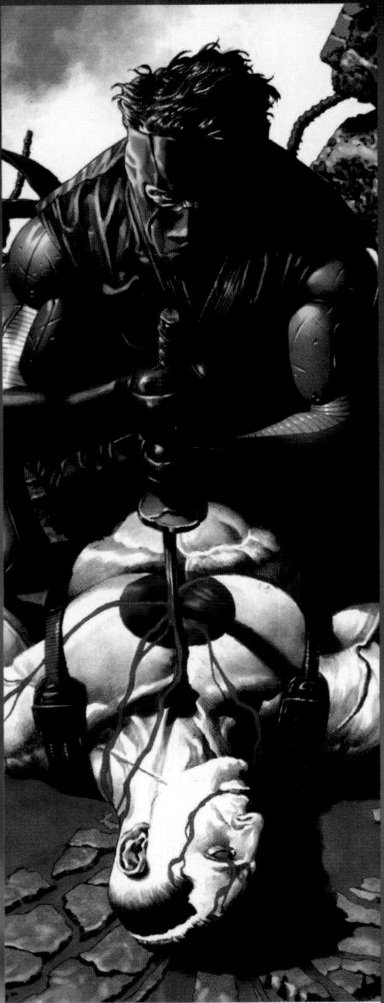

4001 A.D.
ISBN: 978-1-68215-143-3
ARMOR HUNTERS
ISBN: 978-1-939346-45-2
BOOK OF DEATH
ISBN: 978-1-939346-97-1
FALLEN WORLD
ISBN: 978-1-68215-331-4
HARBINGER WARS
ISBN: 978-1-939346-09-4
HARBINGER WARS 2
ISBN: 978-1-68215-289-8
INCURSION
ISBN: 978-1-68215-303-1
THE VALIANT
ISBN: 978-168215-364-2

COMEDY

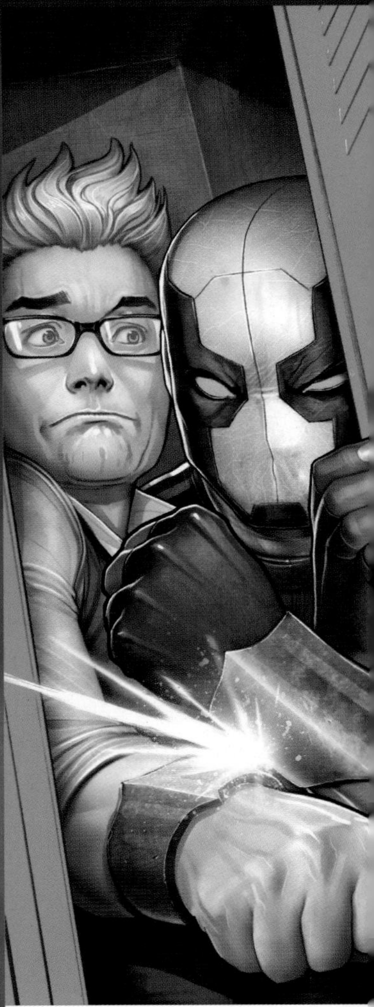

A&A: THE ADVENTURES OF ARCHER & ARMSTRONG VOL. 1: IN THE BAG
ISBN: 978-1-68215-149-5
THE DELINQUENTS
ISBN: 978-1-939346-51-3
QUANTUM AND WOODY! (2020): EARTH'S LAST CHOICE
ISBN: 978-1-68215-362-8

VERSE STARTING AT $9.99

HORROR & MYSTERY

SCIENCE FICTION & FANTASY

TEEN ADVENTURE

BRITANNIA
ISBN: 978-1-68215-185-3

DOCTOR MIRAGE
ISBN: 978-1-68215-346-8

PUNK MAMBO
ISBN: 978-1-68215-330-7

RAPTURE
ISBN: 978-1-68215-225-6

SHADOWMAN (2018) VOL. 1:
FEAR OF THE DARK
ISBN: 978-1-68215-239-3

THE VISITOR
ISBN: 978-168215-364-2

DIVINITY
ISBN: 978-1-939346-76-6

THE FORGOTTEN QUEEN
ISBN: 978-1-68215-324-6

IMPERIUM VOL. 1: COLLECTING MONSTERS
ISBN: 978-1-939346-75-9

IVAR, TIMEWALKER VOL. 1: MAKING HISTORY
ISBN: 978-1-939346-63-6

RAI BOOK ONE
ISBN: 978-1-682153-60-4

WAR MOTHER
ISBN: 978-1-68215-237-9

DOCTOR TOMORROW
ISBN: 978-1-68215-370-3

FAITH VOL. 1: HOLLYWOOD AND VINE
ISBN: 978-1-68215-121-1

GENERATION ZERO VOL. 1:
WE ARE THE FUTURE
ISBN: 978-1-68215-175-4

THE HARBINGER BOOK ONE
ISBN: 978-1-68215-424-3

LIVEWIRE VOL. 1: FUGITIVE
ISBN: 978-1-68215-301-7

SECRET WEAPONS
ISBN: 978-1-68215-229-4

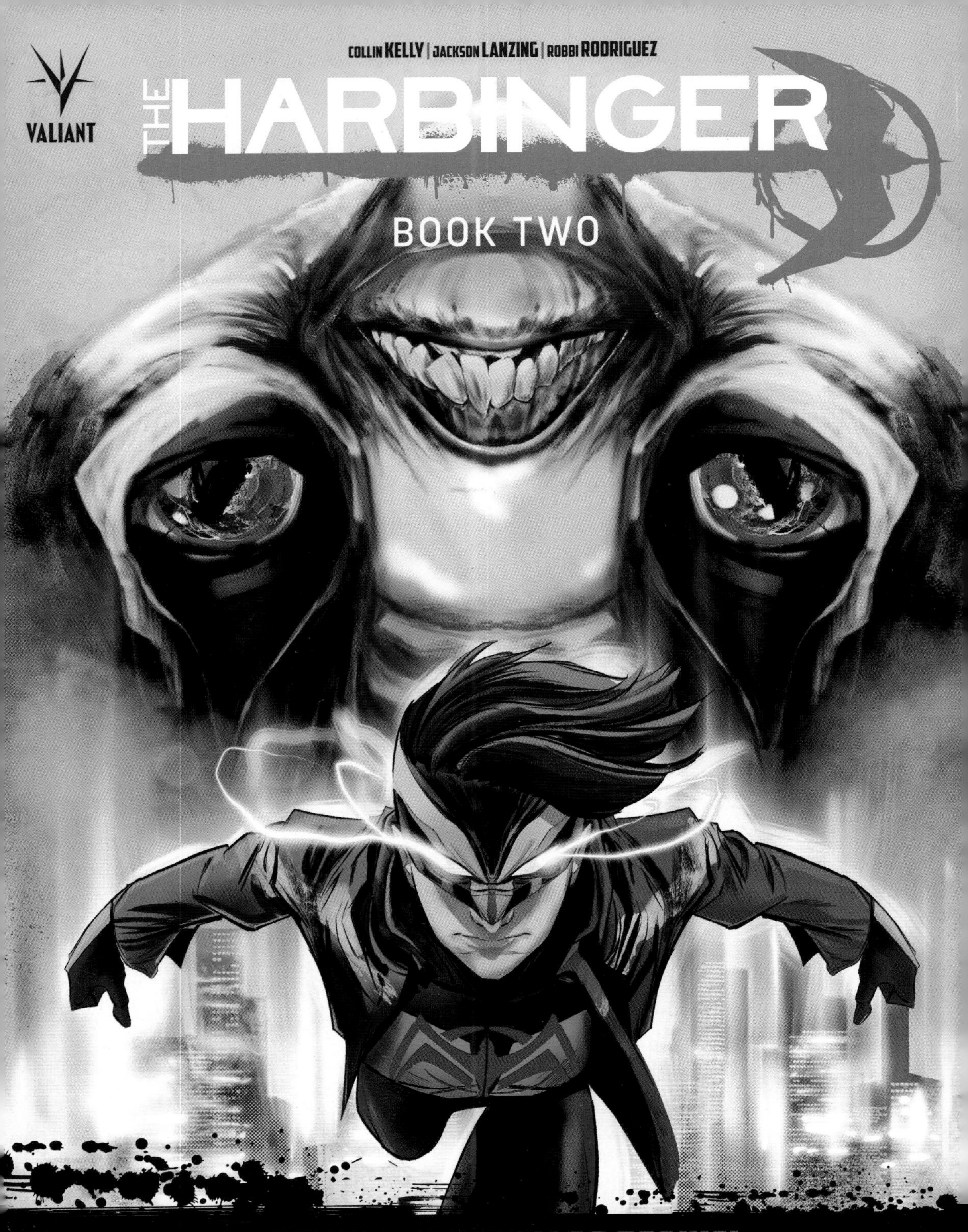

COLLIN **KELLY** | JACKSON **LANZING** | ROBBI **RODRIGUEZ**

THE **HARBINGER**

BOOK TWO

THE WAR FOR CHICAGO BEGINS!

It's Psiot City vs. the Renegade and Faith vs. the Harbinger. Peter Stanchek's one-time teammate and friend, the high-flying Faith Herbert, dives into the fray! Can Peter Stanchek save a city when everyone he knows has their knives at his neck?

Jump on board here with *New York Times* bestselling

Conqueror) and visionary artist Robbi Rodriguez (*Batgirl*) to find out why this is the series CBR calls "an urgent and beautiful reintroduction to Harbinger's exciting world."

Collecting THE HARBINGER #5-8.

TRADE PAPERBACK
ISBN: 978-1-68215-428-1